The Telling of the World

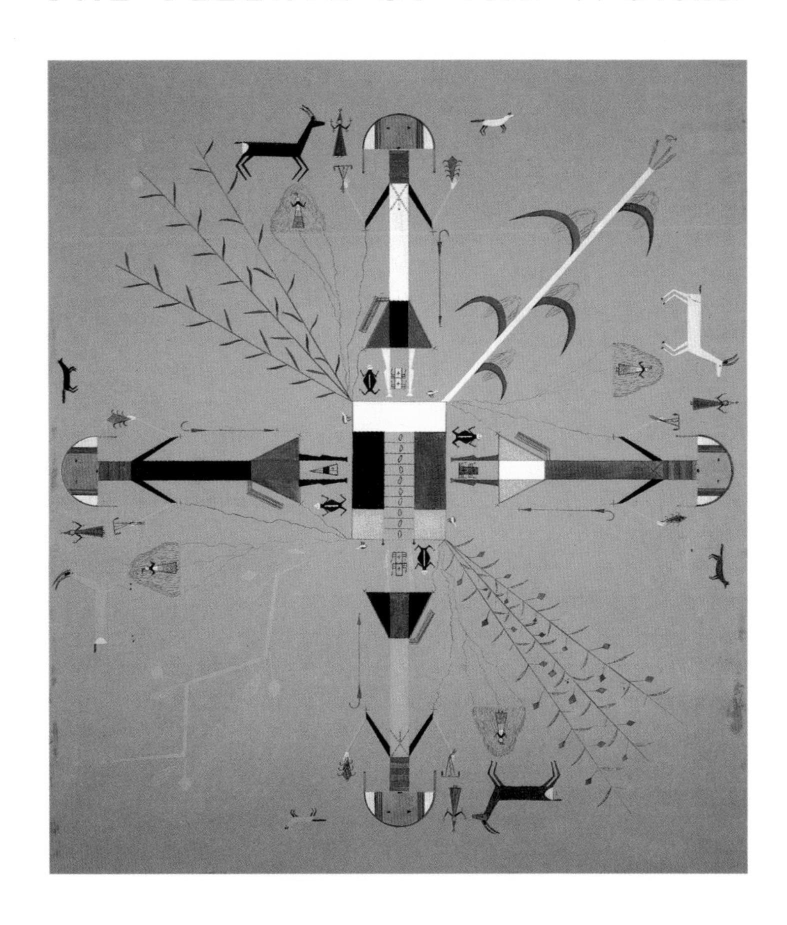

FOR whatever
Happens to THE PLANTS and Animals
Also HAPPENS To the HUMANS
CS 1854

THE TELLING OF THE WORLD

NATIVE AMERICAN STORIES AND ART

EDITED BY W. S. PENN

A FAIR STREET/WELCOME BOOK

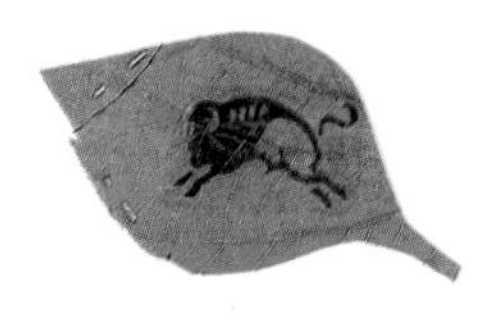

STEWART, TABORI & CHANG
NEW YORK

Contents

❖ ❖ ❖ ❖ ❖

PAGE 1: *Upward Reachingway, Emergence Sandpainting* (Navajo). Courtesy of the Wheelwright Museum of the American Indian, Santa Fe, NM.

PAGE 2: *Rainbow*, Jaune Quick-to-See Smith (Flathead/Shoshone/Cree), 1990. Courtesy of Steinbaum Krauss Gallery, New York, NY.

Preface

❖ ❖ ❖ ❖ ❖

Stories make our world. Stories are never memorized but always remembered, and they are the means by which we explore the world of things, beliefs, and ideas. Stories educate, entertain, and sometimes explain. Native American legends and stories combine over time, for the listener who hears them again and again, into a kind of epic of his community, her tribe, their family, and the relationship among them all. In that relationship the people find meaning; in maintaining that relationship, they find their value or worth as human beings. Storytelling for Indians is not something that happens in the past, though stories may tell about the past; it is a process that continues—its meaning and importance are present and even future. Above all, then, stories integrate; they put the "I" into the context of the "We," connect one person to another—whether that other be animal, mineral, or vegetable. Where an analytical mind like Samuel Taylor Coleridge's might theorize about a "willing suspension of disbelief," we give our stories a willing belief and participation, and figure Coleridge was sad. Our stories give us humor—not always the ha-ha humor of jokes, but the good humor of understanding that allows us to survive.

For though I am Nez Perce and Osage and Anglo, though I have looked into this business of telling stories, though I hope that I may be able to say things that other Indian people would agree are accurate or truthful or honorable, I cannot do more than say what I think and hope that the community of readers, regardless of background, understand or appreciate what I am saying.

When I was asked to engage in the process of selecting and editing eighty stories for this book, I was deeply involved in completing *All My Sins Are Relatives*. That endeavor influenced two of the conditions I set for this anthology. The first was that the word "myth" not appear in the title or subtitles, not because some of these stories are not mythic, but because so many people use the word "myth" to mean false, untrue, or not having a real effect on readers and listeners. But if a story strikes a communal chord and is told and re-told hundreds and thousands of times, it does become a "legend," a story about human or animal characters who represent the life-ways and values of the community. Such stories tie the individual into the active, imagined life of his or her community. Of course, legends may have redolent traits of "unreality": Flaubert's "The Legend of St. Julian the Hospitaller," for example, transforms Julian from a young, murderous terror into someone who succors the sick and scabrous. The legends in *The Telling of the World* present all sorts of transformations and changes—if you come from animal people then you may return to animal people; buffalo can turn into women who marry and whose husbands, seasonally or in certain circumstances, transform into buffalo. But while these stories have unrealistic elements, they are not unreal—at least in their effect, or in the truths they transmit.

Even though "myth" is avoided here, a "legend" becomes myth when it has been told so many times and over so much time that it is accepted by the community as an almost codified description of origins or beginnings of the world, the stars, the animals, plants, and human beings. So I confess freely that the first condition I imposed was purely rhetorical—to try to get the people who enjoy this book to understand that for me, for my Creek or Laguna or Choctaw or Cherokee or Osage friends, these stories continue to be important, continue to be vital and alive. We are not afraid to change them—as our grandmothers and grandfathers were not afraid—any more than we are afraid to add to them.

And that was my second condition, that this collection include some contemporary stories by contemporary mixblood people, in addition to the traditional tales narrated by well-known tellers such as Mari Watters, Sam Batwi, or Lawrence Aripa. So we have included "new" stories told or retold by wonderful storytellers, like Peter Blue Cloud, Lee Francis, and others, to underscore the continuing vitality of Native storytelling traditions. Because of that vitality, I decided to group the stories loosely into the seven stages of life: stories of creation, origins, beginnings, and renewal; stories of adolescence, including relationships between adolescents, human or animal, and the dream visions that guide or instruct them; stories of family, band, or tribe, including negotiations and relationships with outsiders—foreigners, as well as animals and Nature; stories of marriage, about husbands or wives, husbands and wives, and relationships between adult humans or adult animals; stories of children and community, including the recognition and preservation of community and connection; stories of old age and elder wisdom, often told around the fire at night to illustrate the knowledge gained by long life and experience; and, finally, stories about death and the afterworld. The groupings are not precise simply because of the various ways different stories can be read, and because the stories often cross from one division to another; storytelling traditions are flexible.

I added only one more condition in the process, to include stories that were not contemporary, but were made contemporary by the hard work of re-translating and re-evaluating them in light of Native American languages, structures, and legends. These new retranslators and transcribers of Native stories check and recheck their translations with Native tellers. They include aspects of the performance of the stories (laughter, nodding, pauses, changes in tone) in their transcriptions, or they ask that the whole of a story, such as "The Sun's Myth," be printed in books so that the reader can become familiar with the patterning and structure of some Native stories. These fresh translations give us the chance to "hear" the stories we have not grown up with and to imagine something of the contexts from which they come. This is not to denigrate all anthropological attempts at recording stories in the late-nineteenth and early-twentieth centuries; without some of those attempts, we might not have the privilege of retranslations. It is only to praise the work being done with respect by ethno-poets, linguists, and translators such as Dell Hymes, Dennis Tedlock, Rodney Frey, Brian Swann, Arnold Krupat, Jarold Ramsey, William Bright, John Bierhorst, Bill Vaudrin; and to thank people like Ella Clark, John R. Swanton, Richard Erdoes, Alfonso Ortiz, Dee Brown, Barry Lopez, and many others. It is also to commend the talent of storytellers like Mari Watters, Nettie Reuben, Lawrence Aripa, Sam Batwi, Peter Blue Cloud, Apinam Ashini, Leonard Crow Dog, Jim James, Jenny Leading Cloud, Henry Crow Dog, Young Crane, Harry Wheeler, Charles Cultee, John Rush Buffalo, Delos B. Kittle, Victoria Howard, Yellow Wolfe, Lee Francis, Timothy Benally, Sr., Harry Mad Bear, Dan Hanna, and Simon Ortiz.

To include some of these new translations seemed to me an added privilege for the reader, and enough to ask this anthology to do. No anthology—"a bunch of flowers," as Brian Swann reminds us—can do everything. Presenting these stories and art as alive and current, and making the claim that storytelling and retelling are alive and well out there among my friends and even my enemies, seemed sufficient.

Finally, a word about the art. The editors and I decided to put together a book that intended, not to erase differences and diversity, but to represent as many of the tribes and traditions as possible. Thus, this is *not* an illustrated collection of stories. Nor is it a verbally enhanced book of art and image. There is often no direct tribal linkage between the story and the image, except that a Coyote story may be accompanied by an image of Coyote from a different tribe or people. In my mind, this book is two books that go together, side by side, if only because for me all things really are connected like dandelions.

W. S. P.

The Telling of the World

❖ ❖ ❖ ❖ ❖

This book recognizes the continued existence and vitality of storytelling and artistic traditions of the mixed blood population that gets called Native America—traditional or nontraditional, urban or rural, in cities or on reservations. For several millions of North American people of Indian descent who grew up with Indian ideas, beliefs, or customs, their stories, like their art, are just as alive and meaningful as any other people's. We have our own flood stories—stories that have existed since long before the Judeo-Christian legend of Noah and his ark—that have been handed down orally for thousands of years. We have stories of death and resurrection with Raven and Rabbit. And we have the nearly ubiquitous stories of Coyote who, like an incorrigible novelist, is always tinkering with the world to make it a more agreeable place in which to live. Like a novelist stringing himself up on the difficulties of his structures or sentences, Coyote frequently tricks himself into a moral or psychological corner. Sometimes, he even gets himself killed. Just as a novelist often requires a good editor to bring the writing to life, Coyote's resurrection requires that Fox comes along. After deliberating over whether the world would be better or worse without Coyote, Fox decides in Coyote's favor and steps over his corpse a ritual number of times to resurrect him. The number differs from language group to language group or tribe to tribe. Often Fox steps across Coyote's corpse three, four, or five times—examples of the importance of trinitarian, quadrilinear, or pentangularian numerology. Almost as often as he is resurrected, Coyote denies that he has been dead—claiming that he's only been sleeping. When Fox exclaims in frustration or annoyance, "You were dead, man!" Coyote ignores him. He ignores his own responsibility, and off he trots on another journey, to another task, or into another story that explains less the creation of the world than the description of it, less the *what* of the world than the *how* of living in it, whether one is an animal or a human being.

Whether the stories are about Coyote, Rabbit, or Raven, the "Couple Befriended by the Moon" or the "Woman [who] Chooses Death," the way in which Bridal Veil Falls in Yosemite Park received its name, or "The Farewell Song," they are all about *process*. It is difficult to generalize—though less difficult than the false generalizations that group a variety of people under the heading of "Native American"—but *process* de-emphasizes moral, if by moral we mean a preachy and pointed conclusion to stories that are often as unimaginative as bumper-sticker bromides. Such stories are disconnected from a meaningful past, and are un-re-membered, if not unmemorable. They present conclusions that say to the listener, "From my podium of age and economics, parental, political, or religious position, I know better than you, and you will therefore conform to my way of seeing things or else."

For imagined stories that are memorable, *process* emphasizes guidance and instruction, but by entertaining, not by lecturing. Tribal parents and elders learned five thousand years ago that you do not guide by telling people what to do, but by involving them in how to do what they must do. One of the ways Indian people involve others is by humor. And one of the great teachers is Coyote himself, the trickster figure that occurs in abundance throughout the tribal legends. Other animals and Nature are also teachers; human beings interact with them on fairly equal terms, not to dominate or subdue—as the book of Genesis in the Christian *Bible* says—but to live within a respectful relationship giving back as well as getting. Some of the stories are seasonal, to be told only in December or in winter months when the people have the time to relax and reflect, and some are sacred.* All mean.

The meaning may at times escape the overtly analytical mind, especially the mind that, because of its habits of analysis, does not believe in ritual or in storytelling. To the analytical mind, some of these stories will seem to have no deductive conclusion, ending only with the oral teller saying something like "That's the end of the story," or "That's how it was (is)." Or in a story like "The Sun's Myth," the reader-listener will have to pay close attention to certain nuances: that the young man wants something his grandmother-in-law—who offered him buffalo skins, mountain goat blankets, and other gifts to take home to his people—does not want to give him; that he persists in insisting she give him "that old blanket of hers;" that she warns him it is he who chooses, who is responsible for what will happen; and that the burden of his choice, joined with his stubborn persistence, destroys his "reason." Once the young man has made his choice, he cannot so easily "shake it off," and his lack of wisdom and foresight (or vision) causes the death of his people.

Process also involves entertainment, and to entertain, storytellers adjust their language, pace, and details to the age and experience of their audience, as well as to the exigencies of the moment of telling—sacred or casual, instructive or plainly entertaining, perhaps to pass the long winter nights. Indeed, it is said that some Indian storytellers told false stories to the anthropologists who came to study the tribes as objects and artifacts; this explains why the task of ethno-poetic translators is even more difficult than we originally imagined.

In the "real" stories, however, a large part of this adjustment to audience is the way in which the storyteller creates the context for the performance of telling the story. Context—like the entered world of the novelist—allows the story to mean in its appropriate way. This is nothing new to the world at large: the story of Jesus Christ means one thing in the context of Christianity; to a Jew or a Buddhist, it may mean something different. The mythologizing legends about Martin Luther or Reverend Martin Luther King, Jr. take on meaning in relation to and in the context of the Reformation of Catholicism or the re-formation of the civil rights of human beings. The patience and helpfulness of Frog, the goodness and badness of Coyote, all depend on the context created at the moment that the story gets told. Thus context creates meaning, as well as allows it. But it also controls meaning. Without the ritual, without the investment and belief and activity of the community, a sacred story is something more than simple words, perhaps, but something less than the sacred story of a particular people.

Context is the past and present and the vital connection to the past that creates the potential of future. Context is the world: the world outside as well as the worlds inside—inside the community or tribe, inside the family or band, and even inside the identified self. "All men owe honor to the poets," Greek Homer proclaims. Even today, when there is so little respect and so little value put on being respectable, Native American storytellers are honored and respected. Beyond that respect, however, the storyteller could almost be anonymous. His or her first person "I" is not what is important; the story is. His or her ego is not what is important, the underpinning essence of the story in its renewed or changing and re-created context is. Even if the storyteller tells about remembering himself, creates an identity for himself in the process of telling, he creates or makes himself not as an ego, not as a romantic individualist, but as a voice, an organ of memory and transmission, an "I" speaking in the midst of many "I's" that make up the "We" of the audience. In re-creating himself—and without going too far into it, all identity, as well as all remembrance, is a re-creation—the storyteller does what everyone listening to him does and must do to be a self: remember as accurately and truly, with as much respect for words and with as much humor and understanding as possible. Humor and understanding both require a description of context, an explanation of the situation or location in which the self is "like this" or acts "like that." We can imagine an enemy who is so respectable that he not only merits but endures revenge. We can equally imagine with humor Fox telling Coyote not to seek revenge because Fox knows that Coyote's attempts at revenge might easily end up once again with Coyote dead and in need of Fox's help.

In re-creating history, the Nez Perce storyteller, whose memory and accuracy astonished early-contact whites, tells his history in the active presence of three, four, or five other storytellers who were also there at the event—the signing or refusing to sign away the Wallowa Valley, the battles, the logistics, the weariness, the sorrow, the determination. At any time, one of these other storyteller-historians not only may but will interrupt to corroborate, correct, or modify. In other words, the Nez Perce storyteller-historian does something similar to what writer-historians do, but the Nez Perce does it actively in the presence of other historians as well as his audience—a true test of the value he places on words and a true testament to the purpose of his words. They are not meant to aggrandize the storyteller, but to tell the story of his people. In some sense, this desire for active corroboration is one of the aspects of the potlatch ceremonies in the Northwest where the family gives gifts to people who witness the naming of a son or daughter. By giving gifts, they are obligating the witnesses to the future corroboration, "Yes, this is so-and-so, the son or daughter of so-and-so, whose place in our community was such."

With active corroboration and the investment of words with sacred value, the storytelling self loses his own "self" while the listening selves participate in the words of the story and create selves of their own, selves in relation to the selves listening, the selves telling, and all the selves who have come before—the grandmothers and grandfathers, great aunts and great uncles, sisters, brothers, and cousins. With all that connecting going on, the visceral connection to the future is obvious.

Participating in these connections is not always done quietly. While different people will do different things, many generally indicate their participation by audibly joining in with "uh-huh's" or laughter or "ummm's." This is not unlike, I suppose, the "Amens" shouted out by the old people in the Southern Baptist Church in which I was raised. Though I have looked out at a roomful of students with inexpressive faces and felt like a storyteller who is failing, more than once I have heard noises grow—"Ummm," (laughter), "Yes," "Uh-uh"—and where another person might hear interruption or even rudeness, I hear honor, respect, and best of all, participation. Some of the new ethno-poetic translators, in fact, insert parentheticals around the audience's laughter or the storyteller's change of tone or emphasis, to re-create for those unfamiliar with the process the fact of the pleasure—if not the pleasure itself—of hearing again the story, the legend, the tale.

And a good story may be heard again and again, with greater pleasure in the processes, added understanding, and guidance. There are no surprise endings and no attempts in the stories to surprise or shock or ironically twist. These are not "new" stories, even when they are contemporary. Indeed, long before literary theorists came along to act as though they had just "discovered" the idea (much the same way a European explorer, who was eight thousand miles off his mark, "discovered" North America), Native storytellers understood this. There are no new stories, if by story we mean elements like plot and character. Plots remain the same—Coyote meets a White Man and tricks himself into being taken advantage of by that White Man. Characters do not change; they only reveal themselves—Coyote will always be Coyote, and when the audience laughs or groans, it is in the recognition not only of this truth but also of the truth that in essence they, themselves, are undergoing a journey of revelation, not development.

So we can tell "Frog and Brook" over and over again—indeed, I have, to my seven-year-old daughter, just the same as we can tell the Sia story "Men and Women Try Living Apart" or the Blackfoot "Woman Chooses Death." The pleasure in hearing stories over again continues to be one that Native American children learn early. My seven year old never tires of hearing the same stories. Indeed, she not only takes great pleasure in hearing them again, but she often demands it, as her three-year-old brother is beginning to do, with an inflection that reminds me how my elder sisters always used to laugh at me because I began so many remembrances with the phrase, "When I was three." Of course, all my stories did not happen when I was three. But now I wonder if, like my son, I was three when I learned the power of stories, the need for context, and the demand for participation. And I wonder if the phrase, "When I was three" is not the same my grandfather used—a linguistic connection of grandson to great-grandfather, a sign that stories are, indeed, in the blood.

Native storytellers, then, want audience participation in a reciprocal relationship that merges the "I" with the "We" of the community. The details can change according to the teller, time of day or year, or age and experience of the audience. Details depend on whether one grows up hearing Mari Watters's story of "Coyote and the Swallowing Monster" or my grandfather's story of "Coyote and Ilpswetsichs." Regardless of whether the monster's name is *Its-welks* (Watters) or *Ilpswetsichs*, the *Nu-mi-pu*, or Human Beings, are created out of the blood of the monster's heart. The youngster raised on the story knows how important "heart" is, how you can know with the heart despite the splits and dualities of a mad Western philosopher named Descartes. Indeed, it is when Coyote's "head" loses touch with his "heart" that he tricks himself and gets taken advantage of or killed—too much head is simply not a good thing. Too little heart is downright deadly—or maybe, just very sad.

To the Native person who believes his head and his heart are connected, to the person who believes he came from animal people or from the blood of a monster's heart, concepts such as *real* and *unreal* lose their meaning. When I was three, I began to notice things. I could talk to my grandfather at a distance without a telephone. Some of my *Chicana* and *Chicano* friends would go to the local graveyard and sit leaning against the markers of close relatives, to whom they could speak and from whom they could still learn. Southern Baptists spoke with their God and His Son, often asking one or both for help to buy a double-wide trailer or pay a medical bill, and they believed that they could feel the Holy Ghost around them all the time. When I was three, I began to learn that all these ways of looking and understanding were not necessarily wrong or right, they just were; to understand a Southern Baptist, I had to be without prejudice. To understand my friends—well, that did not take much effort and sometimes I went with them to the graveyards to speak with their *viejos*.

None of this meant that the sciences were untrue. Physics continues to tell us a good deal in its description of the particular world, and the language of Mathematics allows the physicist to do his describing. But in order to know or to understand, we tell our stories in the contexts the stories themselves ask for. We do not tell some stories out of the context of the appropriate season. We do not tell stories of History as though they were the same as sacred stories of Religion, and we take great care when we select stories for anthologies and call them "Native American." Like the interplay of predestination and free will, the story's essence or fate is already known. The details change as the free will of the storyteller adjusts them to his time, her place. And in the interplay of this plotted fate and flexible free will, it is often humor that allows the teller and the audience to survive and go on.

For me stories are everything. Like the Navajo, the reality in which I live is created and transmitted by speaking, by the articulation of words. I remember a heated discussion I had three years ago about Judaism, Catholicism, and the Dreamer practices of the Nez Perce. In frustration, my father-in-law finally asked, "Then what do you believe in?" The answer came to my lips without thinking. "Stories," I said. So saying, I knew it was true; and saying so, I made it and made it true. If there is a difference between Christian stories and Native American stories, perhaps it is not in the reality of them but in the orality of them, in the way stories get told and retold, made up anew or changed to fit different contexts.

*In an effort to respect traditions that are not my own, I have tried not to include legends that are clearly sacred and to check with people from whatever tribes I could about the availability of stories to the general public. No doubt I have made mistakes. If I have included a story—and this may be inevitable in such a collection—or have edited stories that should not have been edited, I ask for the reader's patience. I also suggest that at best these stories come most alive in the oral telling of them, and that sacred stories become sacred in the context of people, place, song, dance, and ceremony.

from SPEARFISH SEQUENCE

TOLD BY DELL HYMES

But now it's really time—
Coyote,
Don of tricksters,
a generation is near now,
it needs to see the river
rush cold below the rimrock,

a generation is near now,
it needs the salmon,
the berries in the burnt brush . . .

so you set straight
this world before the world
this world should be . . . .

OPPOSITE: *Lifting the Sky, My Great Grandfather's Story*, Ron Hilbert Coy (Tulalip), 1993. Courtesy of the artist.

Creation

❖ ❖ ❖ ❖ ❖

Native American legends and stories tell the world. By speaking the stories, a Native storyteller not only brings the processes of creation alive, but also brings them into existence at the moment of telling in a way that assures the listener's participation. And, while telling the world into being, the storyteller also gives the listener an understanding of the processes of origin, as well as its purpose. He tells, "This is how you came to be," as well as "This is *how* you must continue to be." So Native American legends explain how the earth was brought into existence, how the animal people (who often came first) and human beings came to be upon the earth, and how people and animals keep their balance in relation to nature, maintain their sense of respect and care, and remain thankful for the gifts the earth and sky gave to them.

Here, then, are some of the ways differing tribes tell their world through stories that are both serious and humorous. We begin with Peter Blue Cloud's "The Cry," in which Creation is fertilized by a dream that came to be because of the cry. The story is a wonderful expression of how Creation interrelates the dream, the creation, and the cry—and avoids deciding which came first. The voice of the poem decides the cry is called Coyote, the trickster-maker of much of the world, who "In the Beginning of the Skagit World" joins with those other trickster-creators, Raven and Mink, to help Creator "plan the world."

A question that seems to come up when we talk about our stories is "Do you really believe that Coyote made the world?" Well, some of us believe that Coyote let himself be swallowed by the figure Mari Watters calls "Swallowing Monster," or *Its–welks*, though with difficuty, to keep the monster from suspecting Coyote's restorative, re-creative plans for the animal people that the monster had already consumed. And Jaime de Angulo attempts to answer this same question by setting up "How Coyote Made the World" as a dialogue between himself and the storyteller he is recording.

Many of the stories, in their most complete versions, also include instructions in the proper ways of being a member of a particular tribe or nation, and they explain why things are done the way they are. For example, the Cherokee story about the origin of medicine and the use of plants to cure and heal reminds us that "aspirin" was discovered by Indians centuries ago as a plant by-product that cured headaches and pains.

Towards the end of the section, Jim James's "Sweat Lodge" offers a partial justification for our reading and hearing all of these stories, if we are willing to set aside our assumptions about the people who get called "Indians"—assumptions that assume Christian stories about the flood "influenced" Indian stories and not the other way around, for example. Sweat Lodge creates the animals and birds and names them. Names are more important to many Native Americans than they were to the first inhabitants of Eden, whose tasks included naming. Sweat Lodge instructs the animals to tell the people and their children what to do when they grow up, how to be good hunters, fishermen, gamblers, and so on. Sweat Lodge says, "Whoever desires to construct me will have the right to do so." As long as the people pray, as long as they treat Sweat Lodge with respect and propriety, he will help them have good looks, be healed, or see into the next world.

These stories of origin and creation, then, are offered in that vein: that treated with respect and propriety, they may teach and entertain us all.

OPPOSITE: ***Creation Legend*, Tom Dorsey (Onondaga), 1946. The Philbrook Museum of Art, Tulsa, OK.**

THE CRY

❖ *Mohawk* ❖

TOLD BY PETER BLUE CLOUD

It was all darkness and always had been.
There was nothing there forever.
Creation was a tiny seed
awaiting a dream.

The dream came to be
because of the cry.
A howling cry which was
an echo in the emptiness of nothing.
The cry was very lonely and
caused the dream to
turn over in its sleep.
The dream did not want to awaken,
but the crying would not stop.

Well, thought the dream, opening its mind,
so now I am awake and there is something.
The dream floated above itself
and looked into its mind.
It wanted to see what the cry was.

What it saw was a dream
within its own dreaming.
And that other dream was Creation.
And Creation was the cry
seeking to begin something,
but it didn't know what,
and that is why it cried.

So the original dream lifted
the Creation dream from its mind
and set it free.
Then it went to the other end of nothing
and let itself go back
to dreamless sleep.

Creation floated all over the nothing,
dreaming of all the things it would do.
Its dreaming was interrupted
often by crying.

So, it wasn't me crying after all,
Creation thought.
Then it thought again,
but it is me because I dreamed it.
So, I have begun Creation with a cry.

When I begin to create the universe,
I must remember to give the cry
a very special place.

Perhaps
I'll call the cry
Coyote.

OPPOSITE: ***Ceramic Figurine*** **(Cochiti). Courtesy of the School of American Research, Santa Fe, NM.**

THE BEGINNING OF THE SKAGIT WORLD

❖ *Skagit* ❖

TOLD BY ANDREW JOE, RECORDED BY ELLA CLARK

In the beginning, Raven and Mink and Coyote helped the Creator plan the world. They were in on all the arguments. They helped the Creator decide to have all the rivers flow only one way; they first thought that the water should flow up one side of the river and down on the other. They decided that there should be bends in the rivers, so that there would be eddies where the fish could stop and rest. They decided that beasts should be placed in the forests. Human beings would have to keep out of their way.

Human beings will not live on this earth forever, agreed Raven and Mink, Coyote, and Old Creator. They will stay only for a short time. Then the body will go back to the earth and the spirit back to the spirit world. All living things, they said, will be male and female—animals and plants, fish and birds. And everything will get its food from the earth, the soil.

The Creator gave four names for the earth. He said that only a few people should know the names; those few should have special preparation for that knowledge, to receive that special spirit power. If many people should know the names, the world would change too soon and too suddenly. One of the names is for the sun, which rises in the east and brings warmth and light. Another is for the rivers, streams, and salt water. The third is for the soil; our bodies go back to it. The fourth is for the forest; the forest is older than human beings, and is for everyone on the earth.

After the world had been created for a while, everyone learned the four names for the earth. Everyone and everything spoke the Skagit language. When the people began to talk to the trees, then the change came. The change was a flood. Water covered everything but two high mountains—Kobah and Takobah. Those two mountains—Mount Baker and Mount Rainier—did not go under.

When the people saw the flood coming, they made a great big canoe. They loaded it with two of everything living on earth, with the male and female of every animal and plant. When the flood was over, the canoe landed on the prairie in the Skagit country. Five people were in the canoe. After the flood, when the land was dry again, they made their way back here.

A child was born to the man and his wife who had been in the canoe. He became Doquebuth, the new Creator. He created after the flood, after the world changed.

When he was old enough, Doquebuth was told to go to the lake—Lake Campbell it is called now—to swim and fast and get his spirit power. But the boy played around and did not obey orders. Coyote fed him, and the boy did not try to get his spirit power. So his family deserted him. When he came home, no one was there. His family had gone and had taken everything with them except what belonged to the boy. They left his dog behind and

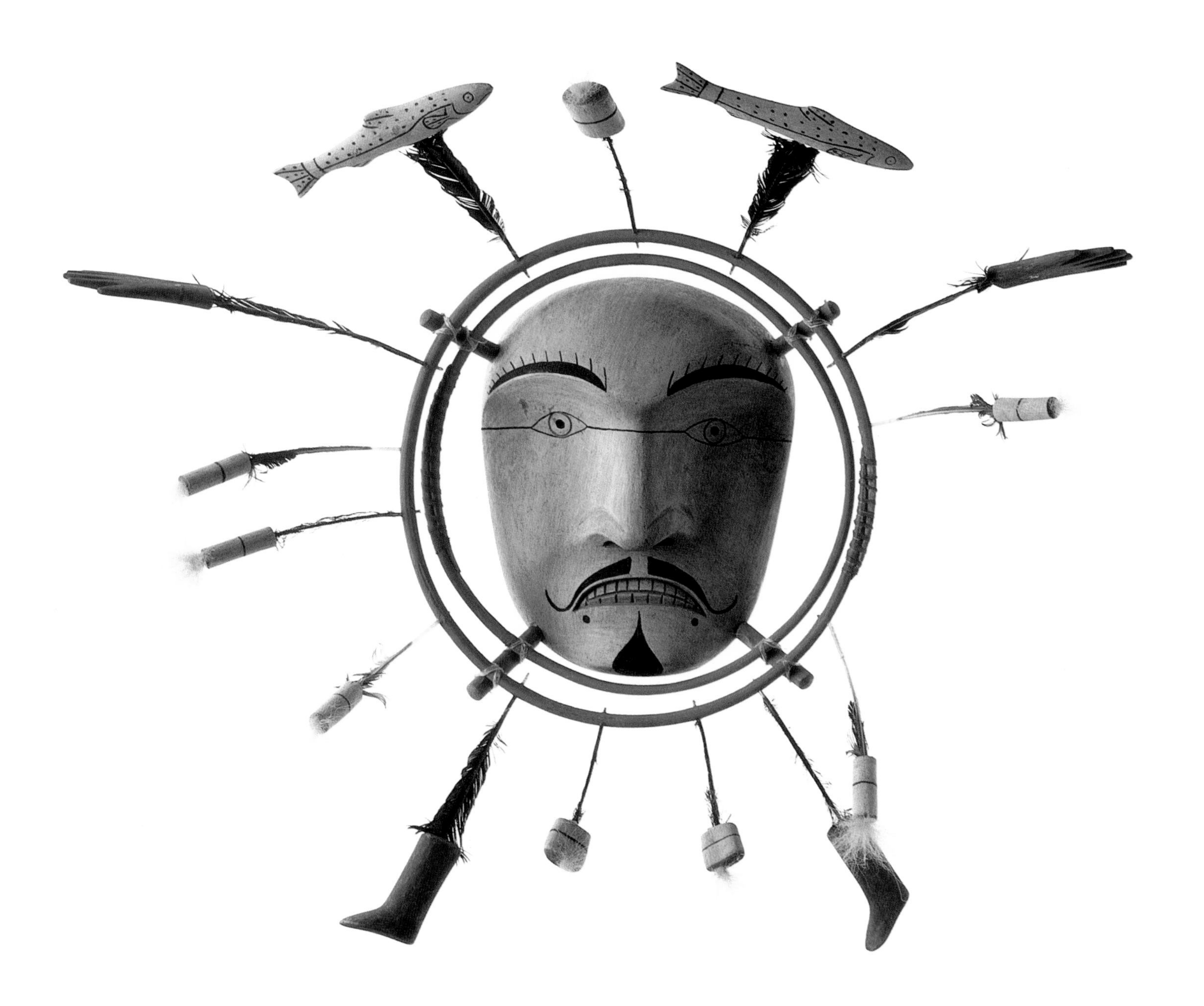

Face Mask **(Eskimo). San Diego Museum of Man, San Diego, CA.**

the hides of the chipmunks and squirrels the boy had shot when hunting. His grandmother left fire for him in a clamshell. From the skins which he had dried, the boy made a blanket.

When he found that his family had deserted him, he realized that he had done wrong. So he began to swim and to fast. For many, many days he swam and fasted. No one can get spirit power unless he is clean and unless his stomach is empty.

One day the boy dreamed that Old Creator came.

"Take my blanket," said Old Creator. "It is the blanket of the whole earth. Wave it over the waters, and name the four names of the earth. Then there will be food for everyone."

That is how the boy got his spirit power from Old Creator. He waved the blanket over the water and over the forest. Then there was food for everyone. But there were no people yet. The boy swam some more and kept on fasting.

Old Creator came to him again in a dream.

"Gather together all the bones of the people who lived here before the flood. Gather the bones and pile them into a big pile. Then wave my blanket over them, and name the four names of the earth."

Ancient Song III, **Dan Lomahaftewa (Hopi/Choctaw), 1992. Courtesy of Jan Cicero Gallery, Chicago, IL.**

The young man did as he was told in his dream, and people were created from the bones. But they could not talk. They moved about but were not quite completed.

The young Creator swam some more. A third time Old Creator came to him in a dream. This time he told the young man that he should make brains for the new people. So he waved the blanket over the earth and named the four names of the earth. That is how brains were made—from the soil of the earth.

Then the people could talk. They spoke many different languages. But where they should live the young Creator did not know. So he swam some more. In his dream, Old Creator told him to step over the big island, from ocean to ocean, and blow the people back where they belonged. So Doquebuth blew the people back to the place where they had lived before the flood. Some he placed in the buffalo country, some by the salt water, some by fresh water, some in the forests. That is why the people in the different places speak different languages.

The people created after the flood prophesied that a new language would be introduced into our country. It will be the only language spoken, when the next change comes. When we can understand animals, we will know that the change is halfway. When we can talk to the forest, we will know that the change has come.

The flood was one change. Another is yet to come. The world will change again. When it will change, we do not know.

HOW COYOTE MADE THE WORLD

❖ *Pit River* ❖

TOLD BY JAIME DE ANGULO

"Listen, Bill, tell me . . . Do the Indians think, really think, that Coyote made the world? I mean, do they really think so? Do you really think so?"

"Why, of course I do. . . . Why not? . . . Anyway . . . that's what the old people always said . . . only they don't all tell the same story. Here is one way I heard it: It seems like there was nothing everywhere but a kind of fog. Fog and water mixed, they say, no land anywhere, and this here Silver Fox. . . ."

"You mean Coyote?"

"No, no, I mean Silver Fox. Coyote comes later. You'll see, but right now, somewhere in the fog, they say, Silver Fox was wandering and feeling lonely. *Tsikuellaaduwi maandza tsikualaasa.* He was feeling lonely, the Silver Fox. I wish I would meet someone, he said to himself, the Silver Fox did. He was walking along in the fog. He met Coyote. 'I thought I was going to meet someone,' he said. The Coyote looked at him, but he didn't say anything. 'Where are you traveling?' says Fox. 'But where are YOU traveling? Why do you travel like that?' 'Because I am worried.' 'I also am wandering,' said the Coyote; I also am worrying and traveling.' 'I thought I would meet someone, I thought I would meet someone. Let's you and I travel together. It's better for two people to be traveling together, that's what they always say. . . .'"

"Wait a minute, Bill . . . Who said that?"

"The Fox said that. I don't know who he meant when he said: *That's what they always say.* It's funny, isn't it? How could he talk about *other* people since there had never been anybody before? I don't know. . . . I wonder about that sometimes, myself. I have asked some of the old people and they say: *That's what I have been wondering myself, but that's the way we have always heard it told.* And then you hear the Paiutes tell it different! And our own people down the river, they also tell it a little bit different from us. Doc, maybe the whole thing just never happened. . . . And maybe it did happen but everybody tells it different. People often do that, you know. . . ."

"Well, go on with the story. You said that Fox had met Coyote. . . ."

"Oh, yah. . . . Well, this Coyote he says, 'What are we going to do now?' 'What do you think?' says Fox. 'I don't know,' says Coyote. 'Well then,' says Fox, 'I'll tell you: LET'S MAKE THE WORLD.' 'And how are we going to do that?' 'WE WILL SING,' says the Fox.

"So, there they were singing up there in the sky. They were singing and stomping and dancing around each other in a circle. Then the Fox he thought in his mind: CLUMP OF SOD, come! ! That's the way he made it come: *by thinking.* Pretty soon he had it in his hands. And he was singing, all

***Untitled*, Fred Kabotie (Hopi), 1922. Courtesy of the School of American Research, Santa Fe, NM.**

the while he had it in his hands. They were both singing and stomping. All of a sudden the Fox threw that clump of sod, that *tsapettia,* he threw it down into the clouds. 'Don't look down!' he said to the Coyote. 'Keep on singing! Shut your eyes, and keep them shut until I tell you.' So they kept on singing and stomping around each other in a circle for quite a while. Then the Fox said to the Coyote: 'Now, look down there. What do you see?' 'I see something . . . I see something . . . but I don't know what it is.' 'All right. Shut your eyes again!' Now they started singing and stomping again, and the Fox thought and wished: Stretch! Stretch! 'Now look down again. What do you see?' 'Oh! It's getting bigger!' 'Shut your eyes again and don't look down!' And they went on singing and stomping up there in the sky. 'Now look down again!' 'Oooh! Now it's big enough!' said the Coyote.

"That's the way they made the world, Doc. Then they both jumped down on it and they stretched it some more. Then they made mountains and valleys; they made trees and rocks and everything. It took them a long time to do all that!"

"Didn't they make people, too?"

"No. Not people. Not Indians. The Indians came much later, after the world was spoiled by a crazy woman, Loon. But that's a long story. . . . I'll tell you someday."

Coyote and Swallowing Monster

❖ *Nez Perce* ❖

Told by Mari Watters, adapted by Rodney Frey

Coyote . . . was going upstream.
Coyote is a-a-lways going upstream.
and . . he's going upstream,
and he's going along the Clearwater
and he noticed . . . that Salmon . . .were
having some difficulty
there,
so, "*I'll* build a fish ladder so that the
Salmon can go upriver
and feed my people."

And so he's busy working along there,
and . . a Magpie flew over
and says
"*Wha-at's you doin', Coyote?*"
And Coyote looked up and says
"*I-'m-m* building a fish ladder for the fish to
go up, you know,
to feed my people."
And . . . Magpie looked at him
"*Ah-h-h-h,* there's no *reason* for the fish to go
up there.
The Monster, Its-welks, ate them all up.
He's up in the valley,
near Kamiah."

And Coyote says,
"Oh-h-h-h, *that's* what happened to them.
Oh, no wonder *nobody's* been around
to help me."

So . . he starts up that way
and he stops along the way
and he takes a sweat bath.
He *cleans* himself up *re-e-al* nice, you know,
and he says,
"Well, I'd better sweat real good to get
my *power,*
and also to clean myself in case
the Monster, . . .
if he should *eat me* he won't
find me repulsive!"
And so he takes a sweat bath.

And along the way he's going up over . . the
Camas Prairie,
and he stops
and he gets some flint
and makes some knives,
flint knives,
and makes something to start fire
and he grabs some . . dry moss
and things.

As he goes along,
he gets some . . camas
and some . . elderberries
and other . . serviceberries
and things like this
and he puts them . . all in his . . . pack

And . . . he gets himself and he's on his way,
and he's making these *ropes* out of hemp.
And he *goes* along,
ah-h he's thinking of a plan.

He said,
"Oh-h-h, I miss all my friends.
I was wondering where Fox went, you know,
Oh-h-h"

So he . . gets up to the top of the prairie,
"Well, . . . I'd better tie this rope around
Mason Butte." . . .
And he goes and ties it around there
And he goes up and ties one rope around Seven
Devil Mountains,
and the other around . . . *Cottonwood* Butte . . .
And he ties them around his waist

And Coyote gets up to the Breaks and looking
into Kamiah,
and, "Ah-h-h, I don't want him to see me right away."
So he *covers* himself . . with clay
and he's sort of . . . hard to see
And he *pe-e-eks* over the side there, you know,
and spreads the weeds . . .
and grass and what not
and *lo-o-oks* over
and sees the Monster.
Monster has just eaten a whole bunch,
and he's sort of laying there . . . sleeping,
with his head on his hands, you know,
sleeping away,
"Ah-ah-ah-ah." (whispering voice)

Coyote yells out, (whispering voice)
"*Its-we-e-lks, Its-we-e-lks!*" . . (loud voice)

The Monster looks around,
"*Who's* that? you know,
who's that calling me?"
He looks around . . over . . the Breaks,
and he can't see anybody.
Coyote is well-camouflaged . . .
And . . he says,
"*Who is* that?"
And Coyote says,
"*It's me!*" . . (louder)
Monster looks,
"'It's me?'
Who's 'It's me'
I don't know anybody named, 'It's me'!" . .
And Coyote *stood* up
and he said
"It's me, Coyote." (loud voice)
"*Oh-h-h, there you are.*
What are you doing up there?" . .
"*Well,* I'm coming down
and we're . . going to test our powers out.
We're going to . . . see who's going to *draw* each
other in." . . .
And the Monster,
"Haugh, haugh,
okay, alright, you go first.
We'll do it *three* times." . .

So Coyote gets up there
and he checks his ropes, you know,
and he's all tied up nice.
And he goes
"Ooh-ooh-ooh-ooh!"
And the only thing that happens is that maybe a hair on
Monster's ear . . .
wiggles around.
"Haugh, haugh, haugh."

***Emerging Earth Diver*, George C. Longfish (Seneca/Tuscarora), 1989. Courtesy of the artist.**

Coyote yells down at him
"*It's your turn*, Its-welks,
you try to suck me in."
So Its-welks opens his mouth and,
"Ooh-ooh-ooh-ooh!"
And the Coyote starts going down
but the ropes hold him back. . . .
And Its-welks looks
"*He-e-e-y!*
He's got a lot more power than I thought,
you know!"

"Okay, it's your turn."
And Coyote gets up there,
"Ooh-ooh-ooh-ooh!"
A-a-a-nd nothing happens, you know
Monster goes
"Hey-hey-hey-hey, haugh haugh haugh.
I knew he couldn't do anything, you know.
He thinks he's got power.
I-'ve got more power."

And Coyote says
"*Ok-a-ay, it's* your turn."
So . . Its-welks, he opens his mouth
and drives in the *biggest* air.
"Ooh-ooh-ooh-ooh-ooh-ooh."

And with that Coyote cuts some of the ropes
and starts sli-i-ding down the hill, you know.
And the Monster's just about got him,
maybe the next time . . .

Your turn Coyote."
And Coyote,
"Ooh-ooh-ooh-ooh."
And no-o-thing happened
and Monster's sitting there,
"*Hey-hey-hey,* haugh-haugh-haugh."

"*Ok-a-ay* get ready now!"
And he opens his mouth,
"Ooh-ooh-ooh-ooh-ooh"
And Coyote goes *flying* through the air,
he reaches into his backpack,
and throws out the roots and berries he brought with him.
And says,
"Soon, the human beings will be coming,
and they will find these
and be happy!"

And Coyote went *scootching* into his mouth, you know
"Aam-aam-aam-ay-ay-ay."
Its-welks lies down, . . .
and he's content there.

And Coyote is inside,
he gets his flint
and makes a little torch
And he goes along,
and . . sees all these animals,
all these friends . . . and what not
and, "*Hello hello.*"
And they're glad to see him,
some of them are jumping up and down.

And Old Grizzly Bear comes up,
Bear comes up
"*Gra-ah, r-a-a-ah!*
What are you doing here?
I was going to save the people.
You didn't have to come down."

And Coyote looks at him,
"What are you getting so worked up for?
You are so *ferocious* to *m-e-e,*
why are you doing that?"
And pushed him in the nose, you know,
pushed him back out of the way.
And that's why the Grizzly Bear has a different kind of nose than the Black
Bear! . .

And . . . he's going along with his light, you know,
and Fox ran up to him.
"*Fox,* how are you?"
"I'm doing just fine!
I was wondering when you were going to come and save us."
"Well, . . I need some help.
You go and get all the boys together,
and you have them gather all the bones of all the dead people,
and put them by all the openings,
and then have them gather a-a-ll
the wood
and bring it to the heart.
But you have to show me where the heart is,
you know."
And so Coyote goes on.

Fox runs on,
and tells all the boys,
and they gather the bones of the dead people
and they put them by *a-a-ll* the openings,
you know.

They gather wood,
and they show him where the *heart is* . .

But on the way there . . . they run into Rattlesnake,
and Rattlesnake is just *mad* . . and *rattling,*
"Chish, chish, chish, . . . wish, chish, chish. . . .
What are you doing here?
I was going to save the people.
I'm the one who has the *power,*
you know."
And Coyote says,
"*Oh,* you are so ferocious to everybody else,
and to me! you know.
Ah, you are nothing but a *pest!*"
And *stepped* on his . . . head,
and that's why a Rattlesnake has a flat head.
And he says,
"From now on,
you're just going to be a *pest.*
And you'll really be . . *scared* of people
and you'll *run away* when they come by.
But . . . sometimes you'll be brave
and they'll *kill* you."
And that's what happens to rattlesnakes today! . .

But he found the heart.
Coyote takes pitch from his backpack,
and starts a fire with the gathered wood under the Monster's heart.
He jumped on the heart.
and he starts cutting away at the heart.
Smoke begins to come out the Monster's eyes,
ears,
nose
and back end.

And as he cuts into the heart
Its-welks, Monster,
"O-o-oh, I'm getting heartburn.
O-o-oh, I knew I shouldn't have eaten that Coyote,
O-o-oh."
And he opens his mouth and some of his openings
and . . . *a-a-ll* the boys throw out the bones,
as many as possible.
And he keeps cutting,
and every time he'd do that
the Monster, Its-welks,
"*O-o-o-oh, o-o-oh.*"
And Coyote keeps cutting,
and everything he does,
that Monster,
"*O-o-o-oh,*"
and everything opens up
and the boys throw out more bones.
Coyote breaks one knife,
and then another,
and finally he is down to his *last* knife, and what not.
Coyote keeps cutting away at the heart.
And he says to the people,
"As soon . . as he opens up again,
you all *run out*
and I'll *run* out too, . .
and he'll be *dead.*"
So he cuts it and cuts it and cuts it,
and finally the *last* knife breaks
and the heart falls off.
And the Monster goes,
"*O-o-o-o-o-oh!*"
And with that . . *everybody* runs out, . . .
out of his *nose,*
out of his *eyes,*
out of his *ears,*
out his *mouth,*
out of the *back end* . . .

And . . *Muskrat* . . was the last one to run out of the back end.
But he was *slo-o-ow* . .
And as the Monster died he closed his back end . . . .
over the Muskrat's furry tail,
beautiful furry tail.
And Muskrat,
"*Oh, no!*"
And he's sitting there, pulling his tail,
and he's pulled all his hair off.
And Coyote looked at him,
"*And* now what will you do?
We're *always* being the last one out.
You'll be just a scavenger the rest of
your life!"
That's why Muskrat doesn't have any hair on his tail! . .

And at this point . . the . . . animals all are standing around
and . . . he starts . . . cutting the Monster up.
And gets some blood,
and . . . sprinkles it on the bones, . . .
and *a-a-ll* those . . dead people come to life.
And *everybody's* going,
"*Yeah, yeah, yeah,*" you know.

Monster's all dead,
and . . . with the help of his friends,
they cut up the Monster,
and they throw different parts into different areas.
The feet landed over toward Montana
and that's where the *Blackfeet* came from.
Part of the head he threw over to another part
of Montana,
and the *Flatheads,* you know, came over from there.
And . . . part of the tail,
they threw over to . . . the *Umatillas.*

And they threw some south,
the *Navajos,* . . .
and the *Shoshone,*
and every place . . else.
They threw part of the belly over into Montana
and that's the *Assiniboine* . . the "*big bellies!*"
And . . . ah, he was busy just *throwing* meat every which way,
parts of the Monster

And Fox comes up to him and says, . . .
"*What about* the *people here?* . . .
You forgot all about them."
The only thing left was the heart,
the kidney,
and a breast.
I guess the Monster was a woman.
Anyway,
and he says,
"*Oh, I* forgot *a-a-ll* about that. . . .
Go get some water from this clear . . . river,
the Clearwater."
And he got him water.
"Now *pour* it over my hands."
And Coyote washed his blood off, you know,
and it dripped down.
He said,
"Where this blood . . . lands
and with this heart will grow a people . . .
They'll be *strong.*
They'll be *brave.*
They'll have *good* hearts.
They will lead good lives.
And these will be the Nez Perce." . .
And that's where the Nez Perce came from . . .

OPPOSITE: *Double Heart Turtle II,* G. Peter Jemison (Cattaraugus/Seneca), 1982. Courtesy of the artist.

CREATION OF THE ANIMAL PEOPLE

❖ *Okanogan* ❖

RECORDED BY ELLA CLARK, ADAPTED BY RICHARD ERDOES

The earth was once a human being: Old One made her out of a woman. "You will be the mother of all people," he said.

Earth is alive yet, but she has been changed. The soil is her flesh, the rocks are her bones, the wind is her breath, trees and grass are her hair. She lives spread out, and we live on her. When she moves, we have an earthquake.

After taking the woman and changing her to earth, Old One gathered some of her flesh and rolled it into balls, as people do with mud or clay. He made the first group of these balls into the ancients, the beings of the early world.

The ancients were people, yet also animals. In form some looked human while some walked on all fours like animals. Some could fly like birds; others could swim like fishes. All had the gift of speech, as well as greater powers and cunning than either animals or people. But deer were never among the ancients; they were always animals, even as they are today.

Besides the ancients, real people and real animals lived on the earth at that time. Old One made the people out of the last balls of mud he took from the earth. He rolled them over and over, shaped them like Indians, and blew on them to bring them alive. They were so ignorant that they were the most helpless of all the creatures Old One had made.

Old One made people and animals into males and females so that they might breed and multiply. Thus all living things came from the earth. When we look around, we see part of our mother everywhere.

The difficulty with the early world was that most of the ancients were selfish and some were monsters, and there was much trouble among them. They were also very stupid in some ways. Though they knew they had to hunt in order to live, they did not know which creatures were deer and which were people, and sometimes they ate people by mistake.

At last Old One said, "There will soon be no people if I let things go on like this." So he sent Coyote to kill all the monsters and other evil beings among the ancients and teach the Indians how to do things.

And Coyote began to travel on the earth, teaching the Indians, making life easier and better for them, and performing many wonderful deeds.

ABOVE: *Spiro Mound, Deerman Mask* (Caddo). National Museum of the American Indian, Smithsonian Institution, New York, NY.

OPPOSITE: *Brush Poppers*, Jaune Quick-to-See Smith (Flathead/Shoshone/Cree), 1984.

REMAKING THE WORLD

❖ *Brule Sioux* ❖

TOLD BY LEONARD CROW DOG, RECORDED BY RICHARD ERDOES

There was a world before this world, but the people in it did not know how to behave themselves or how to act human. The creating power was not pleased with that earlier world. He said to himself: "I will make a new world." He had the pipe bag and the chief pipe, which he put on the pipe rack that he had made in the sacred manner. He took four dry buffalo chips, placed three of them under the three sticks, and saved the fourth one to light the pipe.

The Creating Power said to himself: "I will sing three songs, which will bring a heavy rain. Then I'll sing a fourth song and stamp four times on the earth, and the earth will crack wide open. Water will come out of the cracks and cover the land." When he sang the first song, it started to rain. When he sang the second, it poured. When he sang the third, the rain-swollen rivers overflowed their beds. But when he sang the fourth song and stamped on the earth, it split open in many places like a shattered gourd, and water flowed from the cracks until it covered everything.

The Creating Power floated on the sacred pipe and on his huge pipe bag. He let himself be carried by waves and wind this way and that, drifting for a long time. At last the rain stopped, and by then all the people and animals had drowned. Only Kangi, the crow, survived, though it had no place to rest and was very tired. Flying above the pipe, "Tunkashila, Grandfather, I must soon rest"; and three times the crow asked him to make a place for it to light.

The Creating Power thought: "It's time to unwrap the pipe and open the pipe bag." The wrapping and the bag contained all manner of animals and birds, from which he selected four animals known for their ability to stay under water for a long time. First he sang a song and took the loon out of the bag. He commanded the loon to dive and bring up a lump of mud. The loon did dive, but it brought up nothing. "I dived and dived but couldn't reach bottom," the loon said. "I almost died. The water is too deep."

The Creating Power sang a second song and took the otter out of the bag. He ordered the otter to dive and bring up some mud. The sleek otter at once dived into the water, using its strong webbed feet to go

***Turtle Umbilical Amulets, Girl's Love Charm* (Lakota). Courtesy of America Hurrah Archive, New York, NY.**

down, down, down. It was submerged for a long time, but when it finally came to the surface, it brought nothing.

Taking the beaver out of the pipe's wrapping, the Creating Power sang a third song. He commanded the beaver to go down deep below the water and bring some mud. The beaver thrust itself into the water, using its great flat tail to propel itself downward. It stayed under water longer than the others, but when it finally came up again, it too brought nothing.

At last the Creating Power sang the fourth song and took the turtle out of the bag. The turtle is very strong. Among our people it stands for long life and endurance and the power to survive. A turtle heart is great medicine, for it keeps on beating a long time after the turtle is dead. "You must bring the mud," the Creating Power told the turtle. It dove into the water and stayed below so long that the other three animals shouted: "The turtle is dead; it will never come up again!"

All the time, the crow was flying around and begging for a place to light.

After what seemed to be eons, the turtle broke the surface of the water and paddled to the Creating Power. "I got to the bottom!" the turtle cried. "I brought some earth!" And sure enough, its feet and claws—even the space in the cracks on its sides between its upper and lower shell—were filled with mud.

Scooping mud from the turtle's feet and sides, the Creating Power began to sing. He sang all the while that he shaped the mud in his hands and spread it on the water to make a spot of dry land for himself. When he had sung the fourth song, there was enough land for the Creating Power and for the crow.

"Come down and rest," said the Creating Power to the crow, and the bird was glad to.

Then the Creating Power took from his bag two long wing feathers of the eagle. He waved them over his plot of ground and commanded it to spread until it covered everything. Soon all the water was replaced by earth. "Water without earth is not good," thought the Creating Power, "but land without water is not good either." Feeling pity for the land, he wept for the earth and the creatures he would put upon it, and his tears became oceans, streams and lakes. "That's better," he thought.

Out of his pipe bag the Creating Power took all kinds of animals, birds, plants and scattered them over the land. When he stamped on the earth, they all came alive.

From the earth the Creating Power formed the shapes of men and women. He used red earth and white earth, black earth and yellow earth, and made as many as he thought would do for a start. He stamped on the earth and the shapes came alive, each taking the color of the earth out of which it was made. The Creating Power gave all of them understanding and speech and told them what tribes they belonged to.

The Creating Power said to them: "The first world I made was bad; the creatures on it were bad. So I burned it up. The second world I made was bad too, so I drowned it. This is the third world I have made. Look: I have created a rainbow for you as a sign that there will be no more Great Flood. Whenever you see a rainbow, you will know that it has stopped raining."

The Creating Power continued: "Now, if you have learned how to behave like human beings and how to live in peace with each other and with the other living things—the two-legged, the four-legged, the man-legged, the fliers, the no-legs, the green plants of this universe—then all will be well. But if you make this world bad and ugly, then I will destroy this world too. It's up to you."

The Creating Power gave the people the pipe. "Live by it," he said. He named this land the Turtle Continent because it was there that the turtle came up with the mud out of which the third world was made.

"Someday there might be a fourth world," the Creating Power thought. Then he rested.

***Thunderknives*, Pablita Velarde (Santa Clara Pueblo), 1957. Museum of Indian Arts & Culture/Laboratory of Anthropology, Santa Fe, NM.**

Sweat Lodge

❖ *Sanpoil* ❖

Told by Jim James, adapted by Rodney Frey

Sweat Lodge was chief long,
long ago.
But he wasn't called Sweat Lodge then.
He was just called chief.

He decided to create all the animals and all the birds.
So he created them.
and *named* them all.
He *named* each animal and each bird.

Then he *told* each one of them,
"In times to come,
when people have been created,
and they send their children out,
during the day or during the night,
you *talk* with them,
and *tell* them what they will be able to do when they grow up.
You will *tell* the boys that they are to get things easily,
are to be good hunters,
good fishermen,
good gamblers,
and so on.
You will *tell* the girls that they will be able to get things easily.
All that time I will be Sweat Lodge, myself."

Then he *spoke* to them again,
"I'll have no body,
no head,
nor will I be able to see.
Whoever desires to construct me will have the right to do so.
The one that builds me may pray to me for good looks,
or whatever he may wish,
the one that made me.
I'll take pity on him,

***Rattle* (Tlingit).**
Courtesy of Thomas Burke Memorial Washington State Museum, Seattle, WA.

and I'll give him what he requests,
the one that made me.
Thus people may approach me,
if anyone is injured,
or if he is sick,
or if he is poisoned,
he may come to me for help,
and I'll give it to him.
Also, when anyone is dying,
he may come to me,
and I'll help him then also.
I'll help him see the next world.
So in this world I am Sweat Lodge,
for the help of human beings."

THE ORIGIN OF MEDICINE

❖ *Cherokee* ❖

RECORDED BY LEWIS SPENCE, ADAPTED BY ELLA CLARK, EDITED BY W. S. PENN

t one time, animals and people lived together peaceably and talked with each other. But when mankind began to multiply, the animals were crowded into forests and deserts.

Man began to destroy animals wholesale for their skins and furs, not just for food. The animals became angry at such treatment by their former friends and resolved to punish mankind.

The bear tribe met in council, presided over by Old White Bear. After several bears had spoken against mankind for their bloodthirsty ways, they decided to go to war. But what kinds of weapons would they use?

Chief Old White Bear said man's weapon, the bow and arrow, should be turned against him. The council agreed. The bears worked and made bows and arrows, but they were without bowstrings, so one of them sacrificed himself to provide the strings. When they tried the first bow, their claws could not release the strings to shoot the arrow. So, one bear offered to cut his claws. Chief Old White Bear would not let him to do that. Without claws he could not climb trees for food and safety and might starve.

The deer tribe called together its council led by Chief Little Deer. They decided that any Indian hunters who killed deer without asking pardon in a suitable manner would be afflicted with rheumatism.

Chief Little Deer sent a messenger to their neighbors, the Cherokee.

"From now on, your hunters must first offer a prayer to the deer before killing him," said the messenger. "You must ask his pardon, stating you are forced only by hunger to kill the deer. Otherwise, a terrible disease will come to the hunter."

So when a deer is slain by a hunter, Chief Little Deer runs to the spot and asks the slain deer's spirit, "Did you hear the hunter's prayer for pardon?"

If the reply is yes, all is well and Chief Little Deer returns to his cave. If the answer is no, the Chief tracks the hunter to his lodge and strikes him with rheumatism, making him a helpless cripple unable to hunt again.

All the fishes and reptiles then held a council and decided they would haunt those Cherokee who tormented them by telling them hideous dreams of serpents coiling around them and eating them alive. These dreams began to occur often among the Cherokee. To get relief, they no longer torment the snakes and fish.

Now when the friendly plants heard

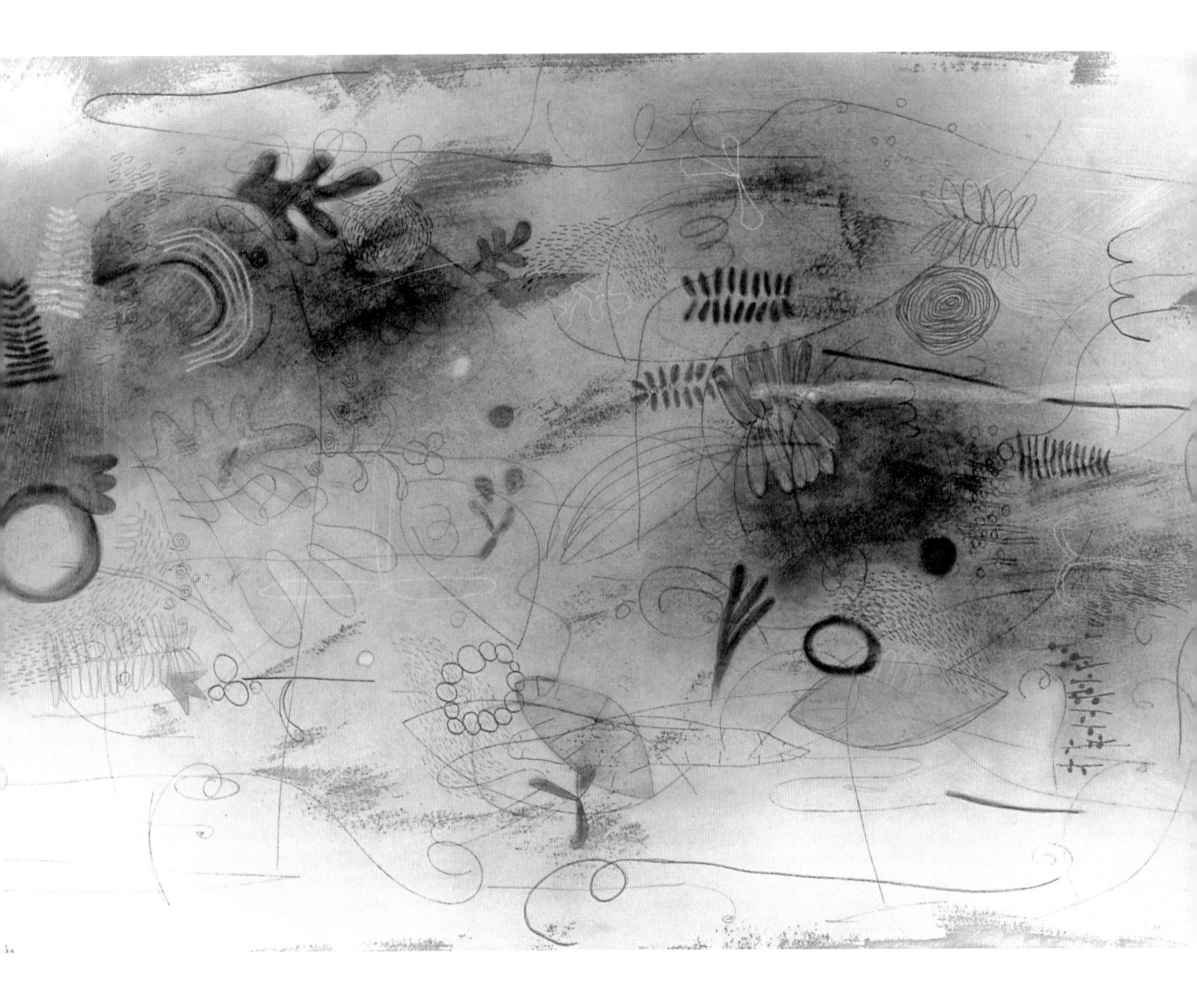

Verdant II, **Emmi Whitehorse (Navajo), 1995. Courtesy of the artist.**

what the animals had decided, they decided to help the people. Each tree, shrub, herb, grass, and moss agreed to furnish a cure for one of the diseases named by the animals and insects. After that when the Cherokee were wounded or they contracted diseases or had bad dreams, their medicine men consulted the plants and always found a cure.

That was the beginning of medicine from plants among the Cherokee tribe a long, long time ago.

Adolescence

❖ ❖ ❖ ❖ ❖

Adolescence is as difficult for Native American children as for any other. However, because they have been reared hearing the "lessons for life" told through stories, American Indian adolescents have actually been given the instructions necessary for negotiating this stage of life—if the children understand and heed the stories that grandparents, uncles and aunts, and elders have told and retold during long winter nights, or while hiking across meadows and valleys or over the endless plains of shopping malls.

In an oral tradition, stories offer young people the teachings that tell them how to be—in the family, tribe, or world at large—but they do it in a palatable way, entertaining while they teach. Sometimes, the entertainment is so great that the teaching seems small by comparison; told over and over again, however, as small as the teachings may seem, the lessons become clear and are clearly remembered. In general, the narratives of the stories gathered in this section move from those that offer lessons, through those that are about achieving identity—name, position, and status—to stories that deal with the late adolescent forces of lust and love.

Note, for instance, that in the Dena'ina "Second Beaver Story," it is not the parents but the extensions of family, two mean and cranky uncles, who take their lazy nephew beaver hunting. Notice, too, that while teaching about the need for hard work and industry, the story considers the points of view of both participants—the uncles and the child entering adolescence. From the child's viewpoint, the uncles *are* mean and cranky—and any child listening to the story would laugh in empathy at this opening statement which probably reflects his or her own thoughts about those older folks who teach, modify behavior, praise, or reprimand. Are adults just mean and cranky in general? Or are they mean and cranky because the child is lazy? For the adult storyteller, this legend contains an element of self-awareness and learning, too: if you try to teach children properly, you may well appear to be "mean and cranky." Whatever the motivations, this legend does not record "perfect" adults lecturing "imperfect" children, but human beings recognizing the importance of what the story teaches.

Elsewhere in these stories for adolescence, children learn the propriety of keeping promises, or the belief that when you give you should give forever without expecting something in return. They learn to respect the tiniest of animals, and to avoid cruelty, even if you begin life as a spoiled "Rich Man's Son." They also learn about friendship, about being a true friend and valuing friendship at all times; they learn that not to understand those responsibilities may cause you to lose your voice—in an oral world, to lose your voice is to lose yourself. Or, in a story like "Buffalo and Eagle Wing" which seems as powerful now as when it was first told, children learn that when they discover their power—their talent in life—it will have one and only one source. Drinking from that power means to take care of it, but if you try to do too many things or seek refreshment and nourishment from other pools, you risk the loss of the power itself; once lost, it is gone forever.

Power comes with identity, in part, and so this section moves on to stories about how an adolescent earns his or her name and gains identity through deeds. In "Home Boy," respect and honor are not given and not granted easily. Rather than learning, "I am somebody," the child learns that without deeds, one is nobody; he or she is not merely without value or importance, but is without a center, without a self that lives in active

relation to the world from which he or she derives meaning. A Makah woodcarver once said that you have to honor and keep the name you are given, polish it, and keep it bright and shiny so that in the generations to come, when the name is given to someone else, it will be a good name to have. In "Wolf Story," Wolf tries to change his name, to hide from himself; as a result, he consumes himself and needs Fox to bring him back to wholeness or life.

Finally, the stories in this section move to one of the great concerns of all adolescents, lust and love. Lust is a normal aspect of life, and though few are represented here, many Native American story traditions contain a number of what non-Natives might call gratuitously salacious stories. But lust and love carry recognition combined with taboo: if, like the boy in "A Youth's Double," one half of you abuses your sister incestuously and treats her with disrespect, the balance of life will be lost and both halves will die. The shyness of love, the process of wooing, and the power of music may end in love; and yet, as in "Teeth in the Wrong Places," one still needs to be cautious and wary to achieve a lasting, good relationship. And finally, we learn about the value of loyalty in a sweetheart, if only because a "Loyal Sweetheart" will become a loyal wife. Steadfastness is an aspect of character that reveals a strong and vital identity and sense of self in relation to others.

***I Can Not Speak (Cherokee) #1*, Phil Young (Cherokee), 1991. Courtesy of the artist.**

SECOND BEAVER STORY

❖ *Tanaina (Dena'ina)* ❖

ADAPTED BY BILL VAUDRIN

long time ago two mean, cranky uncles took their lazy nephew beaver-hunting in the old style. They chopped a hole in the top of the beaver house and put him down in it to watch for beavers coming up. Then they went and waited at the two doors. The sound of the chopping had scared the beavers away, but they would come back to the house sooner or later.

However, after they had watched a long while and nothing had happened, the two uncles decided to leave. So they went back to the hole in the roof where they found their lazy nephew asleep.

One of the uncles said, "Such a nephew is not worth having."

The other agreed, so together they patched the top back over and left the boy in it to die.

Late that night when he woke up cold and hungry the nephew knew what had happened and he was afraid.

Just then two big beavers came up out of the water into the house. They started talking to each other:

"There's a lost man. He's cold and hungry."

One of the beavers came up to the nephew and began talking to him.

"They left you here to die because you're lazy and asleep all the time," the beaver told him. "But now you'll be better than them."

They started a fire. Then they killed and cooked up one of their slaves and fed him to the abandoned nephew.

They put another slave to work cutting a hole in the roof.

When it was finished he thanked them and started to leave.

"You will be a mighty hunter now," they told him.

But he promised them he would never hunt beavers again. Then he got out and went home.

When he arrived back at the village, he really scared the people—especially the cranky old uncles—because he wouldn't tell them how he got out of the beaver house.

As time went by people discovered that he was not a lazy nephew any longer either. He was a hard worker and a mighty hunter.

But no one ever knew why it was that he refused to hunt beavers again until the day he died.

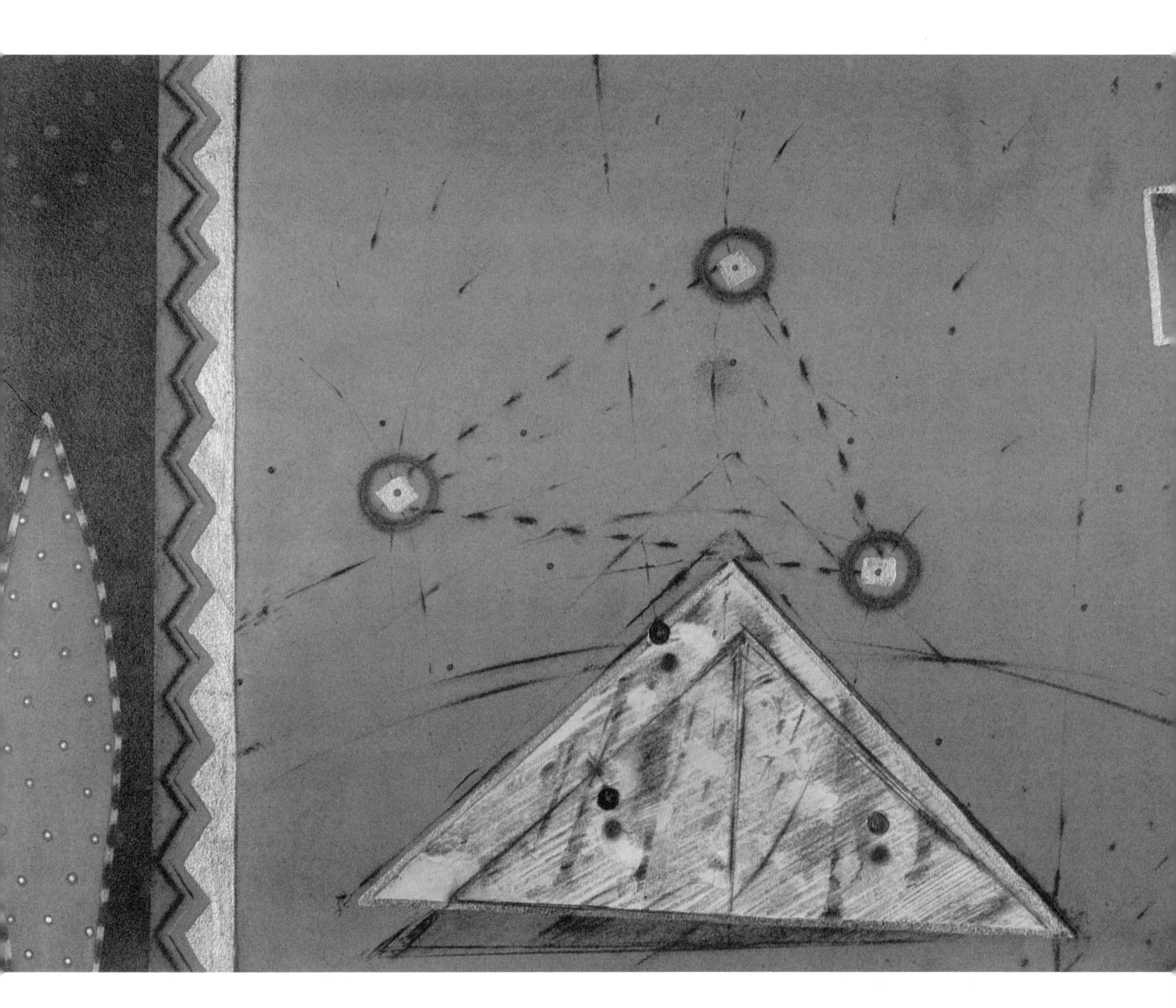

Calvario Series #181, **Marty Avrett (Coushatta/Choctaw/Cherokee), 1994. Courtesy of the artist.**

BUFFALO AND EAGLE WING

❖ *Great Plains* ❖

TOLD BY A STUDENT AT HASKELL INDIAN INSTITUTE, RECORDED BY ELLA CLARK, EDITED BY W. S. PENN

A long time ago there were no stones on the earth. The mountains, hills, and valleys were not rough, and it was easy to walk on the ground. There were no small trees at that time either. All the bushes and trees were tall and straight and were at equal distances. So a man could travel through a forest without having to make a path.

At that time, a large buffalo roamed over the land. He had obtained the power to change anything into some other form from a certain pool of water. He would have that power as long as he drank only from that pool.

Beaded Bag with Two Buffaloes and Arrows **(Yakima). Courtesy of America Hurrah Archive, New York, NY.**

Buffalo often traveled across a high mountain. He liked this mountain and one day he asked it, "Would you like to be changed into something else?"

"Yes," said the mountain. "I would like to be changed into something nobody would want to climb over."

"All right," said Buffalo. "I will change you into something hard that I will call 'stone.' You will be so hard that no one will want to break you, and so smooth that no one will want to climb you."

So Buffalo changed the mountain into a large stone. "I give you the power to change yourself into anything else as long as you do not break yourself."

Only buffaloes lived in this part of the land. No people lived here. On the other side of the mountain lived cruel men who killed animals. The buffaloes knew about them and stayed away from them. But one day Buffalo thought he would like to see these men. He hoped to make friends with them and persuade them not to kill buffaloes.

So he went over the mountain and traveled along a stream until he came to a lodge. There lived an old woman and her grandson. The little boy liked Buffalo, and Buffalo liked the little boy and his grandmother. He said to them, "I have the power to change you into any form you wish. What would you like most to be?"

"I want always to be with my grandson. I want to be anything that will let me be with him always."

"I will take you to the home of the buffaloes," said their guest. "I will ask them to teach the boy to become a swift runner. I will ask the water to change you into something, so you two can always be together."

So Buffalo, the grandmother, and the little boy went over the mountain to the land of the buffaloes.

"We will teach you to run swiftly," they told the boy, "if you will promise to keep your people from hunting and killing buffaloes."

"I promise," said the boy.

The buffaloes taught him to run so fast that not one of them could keep up with him. The grandmother was changed into Wind and followed him everywhere.

The boy stayed with the buffaloes until he became a man. Then they sent him back to his people, reminding him of his promise. Because he was such a swift runner, he became a leader of the hunters. They called him Eagle Wing.

One day the chief called Eagle Wing to him and said to him, "My son, I want you to take the hunters to the buffalo country. We have never been able to kill buffaloes because they run so very fast. But you too can run fast. If you will kill some buffaloes and bring home the meat and the skins, I will adopt you as my son. And when I die, you will become chief of the tribe."

Eagle Wing wanted so much to become chief that he forgot his promise to the buffaloes. He started out with the hunters, but he climbed the mountain so fast that they were soon left far behind. On the other side of the mountain, he saw a herd of buffaloes. They started to run in fright, but Eagle Wing followed them and killed most of them.

Buffalo, the great one, was away from home at the time of the hunt. On his way back he grew so thirsty that he drank water on the other side of the mountain and not from his special pool. When he reached home, he saw what the hunter had done, and he became angry. He tried to turn the men into grass, but he could not. He had lost his power to transform.

Buffalo went to the big stone that had once been a mountain.

"What can you do to punish the hunter for what he has done?" he asked Stone.

"I will ask the trees to tangle themselves so that it will be difficult for men to travel through them," answered Stone. "I will break myself into many pieces and scatter myself all over the land. Then the swift runner and his followers cannot run over me without hurting their feet."

"That will punish them," agreed Buffalo.

So Stone broke itself into many pieces and scattered itself all over the land. Whenever the swift runner, Eagle Wing, and his followers tried to run over the mountain, stones cut their feet. Bushes scratched and bruised their bodies.

That is how Eagle Wing was punished for not keeping his promise to Buffalo.

FROG AND BROOK

❖ *Nez Perce/Osage* ❖

TOLD BY W. S. PENN

Once there was Brook. He was thin and clear and lived high in the Wallowa Mountains with Elk and Bear and the Human Beings. He loved to sing. He sang as he twisted and turned slowly through the forest over stones and under the hooves of Elk. He sang because he liked to sing and he liked the Human Beings who came to cup their hands and drink up his pure singing. One day Brook was humming along when he came to a rock that was not there before. The rock was large, a boulder. It blocked his way. Brook felt himself starting to pool so he pushed and pushed at Rock and Rock refused to move. Brook was afraid. He saw Frog. Frog was asleep in a shaft of sun on a fallen branch sticking out from the bank. Frog loved Brook. Frog said Brook was his best friend. Frog, Brook sang, help me. Help me move this rock. After, I will let you swim with me. Frog, he thought, Brook is my friend. I will help him for his letting me swim in him yesterday and the many days before. So Frog, he hopped over and helped brook push and push at Rock. Rock barely budged but Brook felt Rock's budging and he thought, Now I will have to let Frog swim in my clear waters. I will be stuck with him all day. Try lower down, Brook said to Frog. I'll push up here and together we will move Rock. Frog dove beneath the clear water and pushed at Rock's feet. He pushed and pushed, and at last Rock tumbled over once. Out of breath from so much pushing he kicked to the surface. Brook, he said, whew. But Brook was nowhere to be seen. You know that Brook, he had rushed on and hidden himself in Stream. Oh well, Frog thinks, he probably forgot his words, and feeling hungry from his work, he swam off to hunt for flies. The sun ended that day and the next and Frog forgot Brook's broken words. On the third day, Frog was floating along, minding his own business and keeping his eye out for Water Walkers and flies. He heard a strange singing. He went to see. The strange singing was coming from Stream. Stream, said Frog, what is wrong with your voice? And Stream said, It is my cousin Brook. You hear how he sings? He's been staying with me for three days. Brook looked out and saw Frog. Hey-uh, Brook said. I thought you had become lost. What happened? When I came up you were. . . , Frog began. He wanted to explain. He did not know yet if it was necessary. I saved you these, Brook interrupted. He gave Frog flies, still living, caught in a floating spider's web. Frog was happy. He was very happy that his friend brought him such gifts. Thank you, Frog said, ashamed that he ever thought that Brook had sneaked off on purpose. Frog accepted Brook's gift. He ate the flies, and fell asleep to the strange harmony of Brook and Stream singing together. When he woke, the singing was stopped and Stream was sad. Stream, Frog

OPPOSITE: ***Untitled*****, Joe Herrera (Cochiti), 1951. Collection of Jonson Gallery, University of New Mexico Art Museum, Albuquerque, NM.**

Shell Frog **(Hohokam). Museum of Indian Arts & Culture/Laboratory of Anthropology, Santa Fe, NM.**

said, why are you silent? Brook left, Stream said. In the middle of a spirit song. The sun ended that day and the next. On the third day, Frog was hopping along the floor of the valley. He came to Pool where he heard singing. Low and soft, the singing was, as though the singer sang beneath his blanket. It was Brook. Brook was singing softly. His pure voice was muted by the still deep waters in Pool. It was sad singing that made Frog's heart heavy. He sat on the edge of the pool. He waited for night to come to the mountains. He saw Brook in the moon's light. Why are you sad? Frog asked Brook. You who used to sing a happy song. I am stuck in this Pool, Brook whispered. It is dark and warm. Help me, Brook told Frog in the darkness. I gave you those flies. You are my best friend, Frog said. I will help you because I love your singing. But I thank you for the generous gift flies, too. What do I do? Frog asked. Pool has me caught, Brook answered. But if there were a hole in Beaver's dam I could seep through it. Can you make a hole like that? Yes, Frog said. I will do it. Frog dove beneath the still water. He turned his back to Beaver's dam and kicked. He kicked and he kicked. It hurt his feet to kick and yet Frog rose to the air, swallowed, and returned to his kicking. The wall of Beaver's dam grew thin. Are you ready? he asked Brook. I am ready, Brook said, and before Frog dived for the kicks that would break Beaver's dam, he made a promise that Frog forgot. He understood now that Brook would not keep it. The hole in the dam was frogkick small, but it was enough for Brook to slip through. Brook widened the hole as he went, taking twigs and the stones with him as he rushed faster and faster to the other side. The next day Frog waited by the shores of River. He heard no singing. He missed it. The day after was the same. He missed Brook's singing even more. All Frog heard was the rush and roar of the falls where River tumbled at the salty water below. On the third day, Frog reached the ocean and looked and listened for his best friend Brook. But Brook was gone forever. His singing mingled in the waves and he was lost. Frog felt very lonely, then. From that day, Frog pretends he has no words. When the waters sing to him, he flicks his tongue and answers, Rivet.

COYOTE, IKTOME, AND THE ROCK

❖ *White River Sioux* ❖

TOLD BY JENNY LEADING CLOUD, RECORDED BY RICHARD ERDOES

Coyote was walking with his friend Iktome. Along their path stood Iya, the rock. This was not just any rock; it was special. It had those spidery lines of green moss all over it, the kind that tell a story. Iya had power.

Coyote said: "Why, this is a nice-looking rock. I think it has power." Coyote took off the thick blanket he was wearing and put it on the rock. "Here, Iya, take this as a present. Take this blanket, friend rock, to keep you from freezing. You must feel cold."

"Wow, a giveaway!" said Iktome. "You sure are in a giving mood today, friend."

"Ah, it's nothing. I'm always giving things away. Iya looks real nice in my blanket."

"His blanket, now," said Iktome.

The two friends went on. Pretty soon a cold rain started. The rain turned to hail. The hail turned to slush. Coyote and Iktome took refuge in a cave, which was cold and wet. Iktome was all right; he had his thick buffalo robe. Coyote had only his shirt, and he was shivering. He was freezing. His teeth were chattering.

"*Kola,* friend of mine," Coyote said to Iktome, "go back and get me my fine blanket. I need it, and that rock has no use for it. He's been getting along without a blanket for ages. Hurry; I'm freezing!"

Iktome went back to Iya, saying: "Can I have that blanket back please?"

The rock said: "No, I like it. What is given is given."

Iktome returned and told Coyote: "He won't give it back."

"That no-good, ungrateful rock!" said Coyote. "Has he paid for the blanket? Has he worked for it? I'll go get it myself."

"Friend," said Iktome, "Tunka, Iya, the rock—there's a lot of power there! Maybe you should let him keep it."

"Are you crazy? This is an expensive blanket of many colors and great thickness. I'll go talk to him."

Coyote went back and told Iya: "Hey, rock! What's the meaning of this? What do you need a blanket for? Let me have it back right now!"

"No," said the rock, "what is given is given."

"You're a bad rock! Don't you care that I'm freezing to death? That I'll catch a cold?" Coyote jerked the blanket away from Iya and put it on. "So there; that's the end of it."

"By no means the end," said the rock.

Coyote went back to the cave. The rain and hail stopped and the sun came out again, so Coyote and Iktome sat before the cave, sunning themselves, eating pemmican and fry-bread and *wojapi,* berry soup. After eating, they took out their pipes and had a smoke.

***Untitled*, Fred Kabotie (Hopi), 1922. Courtesy of the School of American Research, Santa Fe, NM.**

All of a sudden Iktome said: "What's that noise?"

"What noise? I don't hear anything."

"A crashing, a rumble far off."

"Yes, friend, I hear it now."

"Friend Coyote, it's getting stronger and nearer, like thunder or an earthquake."

"It is rather strong and loud. I wonder what it can be."

"I have a pretty good idea, friend," said Iktome.

Then they saw the great rock. It was Iya, rolling, thundering, crashing upon them.

"Friend, let's run for it!" cried Iktome; "Iya means to kill us!"

The two ran as fast as they could while the rock rolled after them, coming closer and closer.

"Friend, let's swim the river. The rock is so heavy, he sure can't swim!" cried Iktome. So they swam the river, but Iya, the great rock, also swam over the river as if he had been made of wood.

"Friend, into the timber, among the big trees," cried Coyote. "That big rock surely can't get through this thick forest." They ran among the trees, but the huge Iya came rolling along after them, shivering and splintering the big pines to pieces, left and right.

The two came out onto the flats. "Oh! Oh!" cried Iktome, Spider Man.

"Friend Coyote, this is really not my quarrel. I just remembered, I have pressing business to attend to. So long!" Iktome rolled himself into a tiny ball and became a spider. He disappeared into a mousehole.

Coyote ran on and on, the big rock thundering close at his heels. Then Iya, the big rock, rolled right over Coyote, flattening him out altogether.

Iya took the blanket and rolled back to his own place, saying: "So there!"

A *wasichu* rancher riding along saw Coyote lying there all flattened out. "What a nice rug!" said the rancher, picking Coyote up, and he took the rug home.

The rancher put Coyote right in front of his fireplace. Whenever Coyote is killed, he can make himself come to life again, but it took him the whole night to puff himself up into his usual shape. In the morning the rancher's wife told her husband: "I just saw your rug running away."

Friends, hear this: always be generous in heart. If you have something to give, give it forever.

THE MOUSE STORY (THE RICH MAN'S SON)

❖ *Tanaina (Dena'ina)* ❖

ADAPTED BY BILL VAUDRIN

Once there was a rich man's son who was unbelievably lazy. This *cushkaveah* never did any more than he was forced to do. He just refused to work. In falltime, when all the villagers pitched in to put up fish for the winter, he wouldn't lift a finger. He was spoiled because his father was the rich man, or chief, of the village, and had slaves captured from other tribes to do most of the work around their house.

One time when his mother absolutely forced him to work a little, he got his whole village in trouble. She'd been boiling fish inside their *nichithl* and had told him to keep spooning the foam off as it formed on the surface of the water. (Even if salmon are scrubbed down before cooking, as they boil a sudsy scum which must be scraped off forms on top of the water. It is gurry from the outside of the fish and is sometimes poisonous.)

As he was spooning off the foam, the rich man's son saw a mouse running across the floor. So he scooped up a large spoonful of the boiling water and threw it at the tiny animal, who squeaked with pain and ran out the door badly burned.

The rich man's son didn't think much about what he'd done, so he never mentioned it to any of the other villagers, and it was lucky for him that he didn't. For the people were very superstitious about certain things in those days. For instance, they would never brag about how much

Male Doll **(Eskimo). Courtesy of America Hurrah Archive, New York, NY.**

food they had or how easy life was. And they were careful not to injure little animals. They had more respect for mice, mountain squirrels, shrews, etc., than we do today, because they figured the little animals were people to one another. The old-timers believed that mice look at other mice just as we look at other people, and that these little folk have certain power over the lives of humans. The people were afraid that if they broke any of these taboos, hard times would come and game would get scarce. But the young man paid no attention to these things—or to the older people—and nothing was said.

***Bowl with Caribou* (Eskimo). Courtesy of W. E. Channing & Co., Santa Fe, NM.**

Leaves began dropping from the trees as the nights turned colder, and the slaves hurried to put up the last of the fish before freeze-up. Fall passed and winter came on hard. With the first snows the village hunters were out day and night looking for signs of game, but there weren't any to be found. They drove far back into the mountains with their mixed-breed dog teams to places beyond their usual hunting grounds, but there wasn't any game.

Things were getting desperate at the village as the people started using up the last of the fish. Many were forced to kill off their dogs, for they couldn't afford to feed them any longer. They were having to eat the dog's flesh themselves.

When they got down to nothing, it began to storm. It was snowing and drifting and blowing for days on end, and then it turned bitter cold. By this time the people were starving. They had been on strict rations for some time, but now the last of everything was gone. No one had the strength to go out and cut wood. They were so weak they couldn't get out of their beds.

Even the rich man's son was getting weak—although he wasn't so bad off as the rest, because he'd been sneaking a little above his ration at nights. But, as the end came in sight, he thought of what he'd done that summer, and he knew that the famine was his fault.

With the little strength he had left, he slipped on his clothes and went off into the woods packing his bow and arrows. He walked and walked and walked through the timbers until he found a *kon,* or colony of mice. Even through the storm he could see all the little mouse holes in the frozen moss and trails in the snow.

Then he heard a woman's voice.

"Shut your eyes," it said. "Put your sleeve over your face, and walk around the colony three times in the same direction that the sun moves. Then put your head down against the ground."

The rich man's son was afraid, but he did as he was told, and when he laid his head against the ground . . . BANG! . . . he fell right into a house. When he opened his eyes he was on the floor of a small room, and there was a woman close to him sitting in a chair. She looked just like any other woman, and a fire was burning softly in the center of the room. She offered him a chair.

"I know your village is starving," the woman said. "I'm the one who made you come here." She had a kind voice. "Do you remember doing anything this past summer that you shouldn't have done?" she asked him.

The rich man's son thought for a moment. Then he remembered the mouse. He felt very bad about it, but he admitted to her that he'd poured boiling water on a little mouse.

"Yes," she said. "That's right. You burned my little baby pretty badly." The woman stood up and he followed her over to a small room set apart by a blanket. She drew the cover aside and there was her little baby. He was crusted with scars and blisters.

"That's why you people are starving," she said. "I've always told the little ones never to run away from home, but this one wouldn't mind, and ran down to your village."

For the first time in his life the rich man's son felt really bad. He was ashamed of what he'd done, and he honestly told her how sorry he was.

The woman could see that he was being truthful, so she invited him to sit up and have supper with her. Afterward, she spoke to him again.

"You can go back to the village now," she said, "and things will be all right. Just be sure you never harm any little ones again."

She told him to leave the same way he'd come. "Close your eyes and put your sleeve over your face, then put your head against the door."

He did, and when he opened his eyes, he was outside again—standing in the same place as before. When he looked around there was no house in sight—only the mouse holes.

So he picked up his bow and arrows and started walking back toward the village, feeling stronger after that good meal. Not far from home he heard sounds ahead of him on the trail. So he sneaked along through the timber until he spotted what made the noise—a herd of caribou! He got right in close, then jumped up and started shooting with his bow and arrow. He killed about a dozen.

He cut one open and carried the heart and liver back to his people. They were still too weak to help themselves, so he cut wood and cooked for them. For the first time in his life he really worked—and he found that he didn't mind it at all.

When the meat was done, he gave each a spoonful. He knew they shouldn't eat too much all at once after being starved for so long. Gradually, then, as time passed, he increased their ration, until a few of the men were strong enough to go help him pack the rest of the meat in.

So life returned to normal in the village, and from then on the rich man's son was the hardest worker of them all. And never again was he to injure one of the little people. He'd learned his lesson.

HOME BOY

❖ *Hidatsa* ❖

RECORDED BY EDWARD CURTIS

In the days of Tattooed Face and Good Fur Robe, there lived in one of the villages near Heart River the son of Black Coyote. He was a handsome, well-formed young man, with long brown hair, and his beauty and elegant dress won the admiration of all the women; for his soft thick buffalo robe was decorated with eagle feathers, and at the shoulders dangled pure white weasel skins. From his lance, too, fluttered many eagle feathers. While he was in appearance the ideal warrior youth, he had never been on the war path. He would stroll through the village singing, or perhaps climb to the top of his father's lodge to gaze upon the young women as they passed. His actions were so peculiar as to bring upon him the ridicule of the men, for it seemed to them that he should desire to win honors in strife, and on account of his reluctance to join the warriors he was derisively called Home Boy.

On the south side of Heart River, where it emerges from the hills and flows across the valley, rises a high butte. Men would often go there to fast, but never stayed more than a day or two, for something in that place seemed to frighten them. One day Black Coyote called his son to him and said:

"You have no deeds; you are nothing. It is time you distinguished yourself in some manner, for you are a strong young man. Go up on that hill and fast for a time; perhaps the spirits will help you."

So Home Boy went to the hill and stood upon its summit, crying to the spirits. During the night he heard sounds as though the enemy were coming. He could almost feel the ground tremble under their horses' hoofs, and terrified he fled back to the village. In the morning the people went to the hill to verify his story, but they saw no broken ground or trampled grass.

His father said, "You are a coward! What do you suppose people will think of you if you always remain in the village, doing nothing? Tonight you must go to the hill again and stay there no matter what happens."

So Home Boy went again to the hill and cried. Again he heard the enemy coming, and turning, seemed to see a party of mounted warriors charging upon him. The one in advance discharged an arrow, which pierced him, and as he fell the others swept by and struck him with their coupsticks. Then the spirits promised Home Boy that he should kill many enemies and count many coups. He returned to the village in the morning.

Shortly afterward the village was attacked by the Sioux, but Home Boy took no part in the battle; at night, however, after the enemy had withdrawn, he went out and dragged the bodies of their slain into a row. Taking the eagle feathers from his lance, he laid one on the dead body of each warrior, and said, "Here is something for you to take on your long

OPPOSITE: ***Coming Home Bernice*, George C. Longfish (Seneca/Tuscarora), 1988. Courtesy of the artist.**

journey." Then he lay down in the middle of the row. In a vision as he slept there, the spirits of the dead came and told him to arise and to be not afraid, for they were to make great medicine for him. One of the warriors then took his bow and shot his arrows through Home Boy. This made him invulnerable.

But when war parties formed, Home Boy still remained behind, and the finger of scorn was ever pointed at him. One day he and his friend were sitting on the housetop watching the people assemble for the Dahpiké. Suddenly Home Boy leaped up and said with determination, "Today I will dance in the lodge of the sun!" His friend looked at him in wonder, for only warriors of note participated in that ceremony. But he went with Home Boy to the sun lodge, and watched his sober face as he marched in carrying his lance.

The people were at first astonished at his temerity, then they began to laugh and to nudge each other, saying, "Look, Home Boy is going to dance; he must be growing foolish!" He boldly stepped up to the bowl of white clay with which the warriors painted themselves, and with which they smeared stripes across their arms to represent the coups they had struck. Home Boy painted himself, and placed a wisp of grass in his hair, a symbol worn only by scout leaders, to represent the hills from which they had viewed the enemy's country.

His mother and sisters drew their blankets over their faces and went out. His father said, "I have tried to rear my son from childhood according to our traditions and customs, and to make him a brave warrior, but now before all my people he has disgraced me." And drawing his blanket over his head, he too went out.

The warriors sat in four rows according to the rank their deeds gave them. Home Boy, with a wolf skin thrown over his shoulders and lance in hand, stepped into the front line, as though he had a perfect right to be there. As the warriors danced out of the lodge, making a circle and reentering, Home Boy danced with them. He stepped on the black stone at the foot of the sun pole, thus swearing that he spoke only the truth; and though he had performed no deeds in war, he told of his visions, while the people all laughed at him.

A short time after the dance a war party was about to start, and as they marched around the village singing, Home Boy joined them and sang with them. The chief said, "Young man, you always sing with these war parties, but you never go out to fight. You are making us ashamed."

His friend, who was one of the party, drew him aside and said, "You must go with us, or you can never hold up your head in this village again."

Home Boy replied, "My friend, I am going. I shall not join you now, but I shall be with this party when it reaches the enemy. Four days from now you will hear from me. Procure some buffalo meat for me, the muscles of the foreleg, the shoulder blade, the tongue, and an intestine stuffed with chopped meat. When you camp the fourth night, watch which way the wind blows and listen carefully and you will hear me howl like a wolf. Then bring out the four pieces of meat and throw them to the big white wolf you will see outside, but do not come too near it. Say, 'Here is some food for you, wolf.' Early in the morning join the scouting party and you will meet a lone wolf coming toward you. Say to those with you, 'There is Home Boy. He has seen the enemy, and I have seen them second.' They will laugh at you, but do not heed them. Remember what I say, and do these things."

The second day after the war party had left, Home Boy told his mother to make him some moccasins, for he wished to go on the war path. His mother begged him not to go. "You have never been away from the village since you were born," she said, "and you will surely be lost." But his determination was firm, and he went out of the lodge, leaving his mother to begin work on the moccasins. When Black Coyote came in, his wife told him of their son's intention, and the father replied, "Let him go. I have done everything I could to rear him well, but he has brought shame on our household. Perhaps he will die somewhere. It is well."

The morning of the fourth day the son went to his mother and said, "Are my moccasins ready?" She gave them to him, and Home Boy said, "Mother, come with me until I ford the river; then you may return home." She went with him, and when they reached the stream, he leaped into the water and disappeared, and a moment later a white wolf emerged, dripping, at the other side. She waited long for a glimpse of Home Boy, but in vain; and she was puzzled, but remembering all the queer actions of her son, she came to the conclusion that he had done something wonderful. The wolf looked back once, and then trotted away.

Home Boy's friend sat that night in the brush shelter, feasting with the others on the buffalo they had killed, and he laid aside certain portions of the meat, saying, "This is for Home Boy."

The others laughed, and said ironically, "Yes, that is for Home Boy!"

Soon they heard the wolf-howl outside, and the friend jumped up, saying, "Home Boy has come!" and, picking up the meat, ran out.

The chief, who had brought his beautiful young wife with him, in the belief that she and Home Boy were lovers, now turned to her and said sneeringly, "There is your sweetheart howling outside." And they all laughed.

When the young man came back into the lodge, the people asked, "Did you see your friend?"

"Yes," he replied, "Home Boy was out there"; but they laughed at him derisively.

The next morning, when the scouting party went out, Home Boy's friend accompanied them. The sun was halfway to the zenith when they saw a wolf running toward them along a ridge, now and again looking backward across his shoulder. The young man with the scouts said, "There is Home Boy. Whatever he sees, I claim second honor." The others smiled, and cheerfully assented. They saw the wolf run into a little coulee, and suddenly on the rim appeared Home Boy, dressed in a beautiful war shirt and fringed leggings. His face was painted and his hair tied with strips of wolf skin.

The scouts were filled with astonishment and wonder. In answer to their questions, he said, "Nearby is a large war party camped in a circle. They are so close you had better return to the main body." When the scouts were some distance from the camp, they began to run zigzag as a signal that they had seen the enemy. The warriors came out and piled up buffalo chips, and, forming in a half circle behind the heap, stood singing and awaiting the return of the scouts. Home Boy ran at their head, his long brown hair flowing in the wind, and the tail of his wolf skin streaming behind him. When he

Nickwich, Rick Bartow (Yurok), 1994. Courtesy of Froelick Adelhart Gallery, Portand, OR.

Shirt **(Hidatsa). Courtesy of W. E. Channing & Co., Santa Fe, NM.**

BELOW AND OPPOSITE: **Details of *Shirt*.**

reached the buffalo chips, he kicked the pile over, signifying that he would count coup on the enemy in the battle. The warriors were amazed, and murmured in awe-stricken tones, "Home Boy is here!"

He told them that a great number of the enemy were encamped but a short distance away, and that they had better prepare at once for a battle. His report caused great excitement, and the chief spread a buffalo robe on the ground and invited Home Boy to speak with him privately. "There are timber and water here," the youth told him, "and it is a good place to fight. My plan is to take warriors who are swift runners and strong. I will leave a number of these men at three points between here and the enemy. With the fourth party we will make the attack and surprise our foe; then we will retreat to the third body, and they will cover our retreat to the second, and so on to this camp, where we will make a stand together." The chief called a number of the older men and told them of the plan; they approved it.

To Home Boy was given the command, and he started out with the best warriors, leaving the inexperienced men and the old fighters in camp. At selected points he left reserve forces, and at the last stop he told the chief that from there to the enemy's camp the distance was great. "I shall take only my friend with me," said Home Boy, "for the way is long and some of you might tire and be unable to retreat." So the two set out alone and reached the enemy's camp after dark. "Whatever I do," said Home Boy, "follow right behind me and you shall have second honor."

They lay in the brush all night. Early in the morning one of the women of the village came out to work on a hide while the air was cool. Home Boy stole upon her through the grass and, rising beside her, pierced her with his lance, and his friend counted second coup. The death cry of the woman roused the village, and Home Boy said, "Start back as fast as you can, and after I have scalped the woman I shall follow you." Waving the bloody scalp and picking up the bone hide-scraper which the woman had dropped, he started after his friend, while the warriors of the village followed in hot pursuit. Soon his friend began to tire, and Home Boy said, "Swing your head from side to side, and blow like a wolf." When he did so the young man began to feel refreshed. But his feet grew heavy again, and Home Boy said, "Put your hands in front of you, and lope like a wolf." That again brought renewed strength, and when for the third time he became exhausted, Home Boy said, "Pretend you have a tail, and put it between your legs as a wolf does when he is pursued." This gave the young man strength enough to reach the third party of warriors, where a sharp fight took place. Home Boy fought bravely, and went forward with his lance, and his friend close behind counted second coup.

Then they retreated to the spot where the second party waited, and another engagement occurred; again Home Boy killed an enemy, and his friend counted second coup. And so it was until they reached the main camp on the river, where, in the sight of all, Home Boy killed one of the bravest warriors of the enemy. Here the fighting was very severe, and the enemy were soon driven back.

After the battle was over, Home Boy gave the scalp of the woman he had killed to the chief and the hide-scraper to his wife. The chief was ashamed when he remembered what he had said of Home Boy the evening before, and invited him to

sit beside him, while his wife brought food to Home Boy and held a horn of water to his lips.

When the war party started homeward, the hero told his friend that he himself would go alone. He watched the others out of sight, then started off and reached the village on the night of the next day, coming in while all were asleep. He hung his lance and robe where he usually kept them, over the headrest of his bed, and lay down to sleep. When the father awoke in the morning and saw his son lying there, he said to himself, "I suppose he was lost in the hills, and came home after wandering about." But his mother, as always, was glad to see him, and prepared food for him, and when he had eaten he lay down to sleep again. Soon the returning war party was heard across the river. The people gathered at the bank, and some paddled across in bull boats to welcome them. They told of their triumphs, but above all praised the bravery and leadership of Home Boy. His parents heard, but, thinking the people were still ridiculing their son, covered their heads and went back into their lodge. As was the custom, the clansmen of the father came to the lodge and sang the praises of Home Boy, but instead of bringing out gifts as was usual when a young man had returned from his first war party with deeds of valor to his credit, Black Coyote sat inside in deep humiliation.

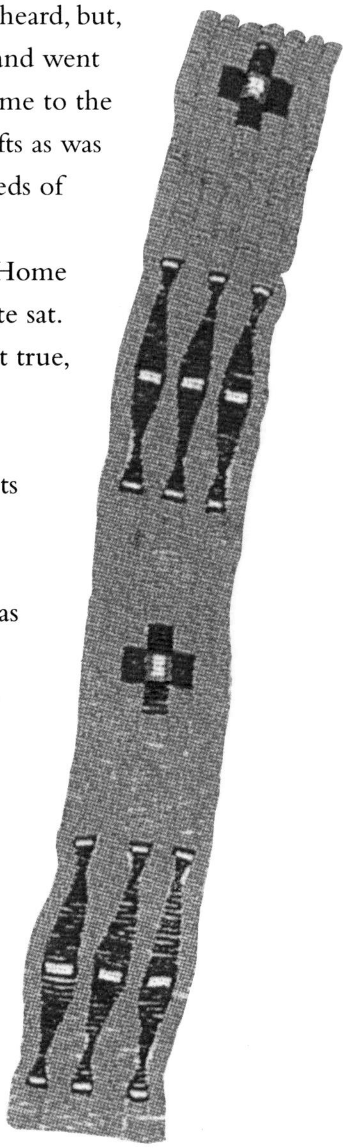

Soon an old woman entered and pulled a blanket from the bed of Home Boy's mother; another took a robe from the pile on which Black Coyote sat. When he saw these signs, he called in Home Boy's friend and said, "Is it true, my child, what these people are saying?"

"Yes," he answered, "it is all true."

Black Coyote's eyes were filled with tears, and he pulled the blankets from his son and said, "My son, tell me truly, did you do these things?"

"Father, look at my lance," said Home Boy. When Black Coyote beheld the lance covered with blood, he was convinced, and knew it was all true.

A few days later, when quiet was restored, the chief told his wife to clean the lodge well and to make it smell sweet with incense. Then he sent her to invite the young man, as he wished to speak to him. When Home Boy entered, the chief said:

"Young Wolf, you have brought great honor to me. You scalped the enemy in the village and brought the scalp to me. All your brave deeds are good. I said that you were foolish when you danced in the sun lodge, but I did not know your medicine then. My wife is handsome and good. She looks with favor upon you; whenever you come near she is pleased. Take her for your own."

Home Boy replied, "Old Man Wolf, your speech is good. I fought that day to prove to you that what you had said was wrong. I killed the enemy in the village that your name might be in the mouths of all. As for this young woman, I admire her only with my eyes. I will come and eat with you and talk with you, but she must throw away any affection she may have for me. I will be a warrior under your leadership and help you in many battles. You shall be known as a great chief among us."

Home Boy fought and lived for many years. He continued to bear the name of Home Boy, and it became a good name, for he won his eagle feathers many times over.

WOLF STORY

❖ *Nez Perce/Osage* ❖

TOLD BY W. S. PENN

ne time, Wolf come through the forest looking to hide. Bear helped him capture Elk and Wolf tricked him and stole the carcass. He cut himself skinning the Elk he stole from Bear and he licked where he was cut and this Wolf liked the taste of his blood so much that he began to eat himself. He was hungry, you know. It was winter and he couldn't stop eating himself, so he was going through the woods looking for ways to hide because if he didn't stop eating himself soon he would eat himself all up. Then he would need Coyote to help him bring himself back to life. Wolf didn't like Coyote much, you see, 'cause Coyote was so much like him that at a little ways you can hardly tell Coyote from Wolf. So Wolf, he runs through the forest. He tries to hide beneath the fir trees, but Snowbird sees him. 'Wolf,' Snowbird says, 'What are you doing there beneath the fir trees?' and Wolf, he says to Snowbird, 'I'm not Wolf,' and he takes a bite out of himself and as he is chewing, Snowbird laughs at him and says, 'Sure you are Wolf and you are eating yourself all up.' Well, with that, Wolf runs away. He goes down to the river and Badger sees him and calls to him, 'Wolf, why are you eating yourself behind those rocks there?' and Wolf says, 'I'm not Wolf,' and Badger laughs at him, 'Sure you are Wolf.' Well, that Wolf he doesn't know what to do, so he decides to change his name. Wolf decides to add an extra letter to his name, two *effs*, he decides, then I will stop eating Wolf and I will be eating Wolff instead. Well, Ollokot (Frog) put his head up and he sees Wolf-Two-Effs eating and eating himself and he knows Wolf cannot stop so he swims to the river to get Coyote. 'Wolf is eating himself up again,' Ollokot told to Coyote. Coyote, he doesn't forget, but he doesn't remember until Wolf tricked him with the Elk. 'I asked Wolf for help,' Coyote said. 'He's greedy and eats himself all up and I helped him and helped him and I asked him to help me. Remember?' Coyote was sick and asked Wolf to help him and Wolf, he said he was busy. He would save his help for Badger or Fox, not waste it with Coyote. But Coyote knew how much they were alike, him and Wolf, even though Wolf grew fat eating himself all the time. So when Ollokot said 'come,' Coyote just said to him, 'why should I?' 'Hurry,' said Ollokot. 'He has changed his name to Wolff.' So Coyote went with Frog to the place beside Badger's river and found Wolf's jaws which were all that was left of Wolf. He took the jaws and buried them. The he stepped over them five times the way Fox taught him and he brought Wolf back to the world. Even if Wolf sewed on three *effs* to his name, Coyote would always bring him back to the world, 'cause Coyote knew they were brothers.

"That made Wolf real angry and afraid that Coyote should know their likeness, but it only made Coyote laugh. He didn't want to be like Wolf either. But without Wolf, who would know?"

OPPOSITE: ***Dance Mask, St. Michael Alaska*** **(Yup'ik). Courtesy of Donald Ellis Gallery, Ontario.**

Untitled, **Fred Kabotie, (Hopi), 1922. Courtesy of the American School of Research, Santa Fe, NM.**

COYOTE AND THE MALLARD DUCKS

❖ *Nez Perce* ❖

TOLD BY BARRY LOPEZ TO ALFONSO ORTIZ AND RICHARD ERDOES

Coyote was traveling up the river when he saw five mallard duck girls swimming on the other side. He hid himself in the bushes and became aroused right away. Then he thought out a plan to satisfy himself.

Coyote lengthened his penis and let it fall into the river. It floated on top of the water. Coyote didn't like this, so he pulled it back in and tied a rock to it to keep it below the surface of the water. He threw his penis back in and tied a smaller rock to it. This was just right. It floated just below the surface of the water, where no one could see it. He sent it across to where the girls were swimming. He began copulating with the oldest girl.

Now, these girls did not know what was wrong with their older sister, the way she was moving around in the water and making strange sounds. Then they saw what was happening and they grabbed the penis and tried to pull it out. When they couldn't, they got out on the bank and held down their older sister and tried to pull it out that way, but they couldn't and they began laughing about it.

When Coyote had satisfied himself, he called over to the girls and said, "My sisters, what is the problem over there?" They told him. He said, "Cut the thing off with some wire grass." They did, and Coyote cut the other end off where he was and the middle section of the penis fell in the river and became a ledge.

The eldest girl became ill then. Coyote went down the river a short distance, swam across and then came upstream to the girls' camp where the oldest girl was almost dead.

The girls recognized Coyote and said, "Coyote, the medicine man, has come." They asked him to cure the sick girl. He told them that he would do it, but they had to close up all the chinks in the lodge so no one could see in and steal his medicine by watching. He told them to leave him alone with the girl for a while.

He got the sisters together around the lodge and told them to sing a song and keep time on a log with sticks. "Keep time on the log very carefully, for now I am going to take it out."

Coyote began singing, "I will stick it back on, I will stick it back on." He went into the lodge and copulated again with the mallard duck girl and recovered the end of his penis. The girl was cured.

After that everyone said the medicine of Coyote was very powerful.

A Youth's Double Abuses His Sister

❖ *Seneca* ❖

Told by Delos B. Kittle to Arthur Parker

There was a lodge in the forest where very few people ever came, and there dwelt a young man and his sister. The youth was unlike other persons for one half of his head had hair of a reddish cast, while the other side was black.

He used to leave his sister in the lodge and go away on long hunting trips. On one occasion the young woman, his sister, saw, so she thought, her brother coming down the path to the lodge. "I thought you just went away to hunt," said the sister. "Oh, I thought I would come back," said he.

Then he sat down on the bed with the sister and embraced her and acted as a lover. The sister reproached him and said that she was very angry. But again he endeavored to fondle her in a familiar way, but again was repulsed. This time he went away.

The next day the brother returned and found his sister very angry. She would scarcely speak to him, though hitherto she had talked a great deal.

"My sister," said he. "I am at loss to know why you treat me thus. It is not your custom."

"Oh you ought to know that you have abused me," said the girl.

"I never abused you. What are you talking about?" he said.

"Oh you know that you embraced me in an improper way yesterday," said the sister.

"I was not here yesterday," asserted the youth. "I believe that my friend who resembles me in every respect has been here."

"You have given a poor excuse," replied his sister. "I hope your actions will not continue."

Soon the brother went away again, stating that he would be absent three days. In a short time the sister saw, as she thought, a figure looking like her brother skulking in the underbrush. His shirt and leggings were the same as her brother's and his hair was the same. So then she knew that her brother had returned for mischief. Soon he entered the lodge and embraced her, and this time in anger she tore his cheeks with her nails and sent him away.

In three days the brother returned with a deer, but his sister would not speak to him. Said he, "My sister, I perceive that you are angry at me. Has my friend been here?"

Beaded Bag with Two Horses and Riders **(Lakota). Courtesy of America Hurrah Archive, New York, NY.**

It was some time before the sister replied, and then she wept, saying, "My brother, you have abused me and I scratched your face. I perceive that it is still torn by my finger nails."

"Oh, my face," laughed the brother. "My face was torn by thorns as I hunted deer. If you scratched my friend that is the reason I am scratched. Whatever happens to either one of us happens to the other." But the sister would not believe this.

Again the brother went on a hunting trip, and again the familiar figure returned. This time the sister tore his hunting shirt from the throat down to the waist line. Moreover she threw a ladle of hot bear grease on the shirt. This caused his quick departure.

***Moisture Bringers I*, Dan Lomahaftewa (Hopi/Choctaw), 1991. Courtesy of Jan Cicero Gallery, Chicago, IL.**

Returning in due time the brother brought in his game and threw it down. Again the sister was angry and finally accused him. Pointing to his grease-smeared torn shirt she said that this was evidence enough.

"Oh my sister," explained the brother. "I tore my shirt on a broken limb as I climbed a tree after a raccoon. In making soup from bear meat I spilled it on my shirt." Still the sister refused to believe him.

"Oh my sister," said the brother, in distressed tones. "I am greatly saddened to think you will not believe me. My friend looks exactly as I do, and whatever happens to him happens to me. I shall now be compelled to find my friend and bring him to you and when I do I shall be compelled to kill him before you for his evil designs upon you. If you would believe me nothing evil would befall us, but I now think I myself shall die.

The sister said nothing for she would not believe her brother.

The brother now began to pile up dried meat and to repair the lodge. He then went out into the forest without his bow and arrows, and in a short time returned with another man exactly resembling him, and whose clothing was spotted and torn in a similar way. Leading him to the lodge fire he began to scold him in an angry manner. "You have betrayed me and abused my sister," he said. "Now is the time for you to die." Taking out an arrow from a quiver he cast it into the heart of his double and killed him. The sister saw her assailant fall to the floor, and then looked up as she heard her brother give a war cry and fall as dead with blood streaming from a wound in his chest over his heart.

THE LEGEND OF THE FLUTE

❖ *Brule Sioux* ❖

TOLD BY HENRY CROW DOG, RECORDED BY RICHARD ERDOES

Well, you know our flutes; you've heard their sound and seen how beautifully they are made. That flute of ours, the *siyotanka,* is for only one kind of music—love music. In the old days the men would sit by themselves, maybe lean hidden, unseen, against a tree in the dark of night. They would make up their own special tunes, their courting songs.

We Indians are shy. Even if he was a warrior who had already counted coup on an enemy, a young man might hardly screw up courage enough to talk to a nice-looking *winchinchala*—a girl he was in love with. Also, there was no place where a young man and a girl could be alone inside the village. The family tipi was always crowded with people. And naturally, you couldn't just walk out of the village hand in hand with your girl, even if hand holding had been one of our customs, which it wasn't. Out there in the tall grass and sagebrush you could be gored by a buffalo, clawed by a grizzly, or tomahawked by a Pawnee, or you could run into the Mila Hanska, the Long Knives, namely the U.S. Cavalry.

The only chance you had to meet your *winchinchala* was to wait for her at daybreak when the women went to the river or brook with their skin bags to get water. When that girl you had your eye on finally came down the water trail, you popped up from behind some bush and stood so she could see you. And that was about all you could do to show her that you were interested—standing there grinning, looking at your moccasins, scratching your ear, maybe.

The *winchinchala* didn't do much either, except get red in the face, giggle, maybe throw a wild turnip at you. If she liked you, the only way she would let you know was to take her time filling her water bag and peek at you a few times over her shoulder.

So the flutes did all the talking. At night, lying on her buffalo robe in her parents' tipi, the girl would hear the moaning, crying sound of the *siyotanka.* By the way it was played, she would know that it was her lover who was out there someplace. And if the elk medicine was very strong in him and her, maybe she would sneak out to follow that sound and meet him without anybody noticing it.

The flute is always made of cedarwood. In shape it describes the long neck and head of a bird with an open beak. The sound comes out of the beak, and that's where the legend comes in, the legend of how the Lakota people acquired the flute.

Once many generations ago, the people had drums, gourd rattles, and bull-roarers, but no flutes. At that long-ago time a young man went out to hunt. Meat was scarce, and the people in his camp were hungry. He found the tracks of an elk and followed them for a long time. The elk, wise and swift, is the one who owns the love charm. If a man possesses

OPPOSITE: ***Charlo Series,*** **Jaune Quick-to-See Smith (Flathead/Shoshone/Cree), 1985. Courtesy of the artist.**

elk medicine, the girl he likes can't help sleeping with him. He will also be a lucky hunter. This young man I'm talking about had no elk medicine.

After many hours he finally sighted his game. He was skilled with bow and arrows, and had a fine new bow and a quiver full of straight, well-feathered, flint-tipped arrows. Yet the elk always managed to stay just out of range, leading him on and on. The young man was so intent on following his prey that he hardly noticed where he went.

When night came, he found himself deep inside a thick forest. The tracks had disappeared and so had the elk, and there was no moon. He realized that he was lost and that it was too dark to find his way out. Luckily he came upon a stream with cool, clear water. And he had been careful enough to bring a hide bag of *wasna*—dried meat pounded with berries and kidney fat—strong food that will keep a man going for a few days. After he had drunk and eaten, he rolled himself into his fur robe, propped his back against a tree, and tried to rest. But he couldn't sleep; the forest was full of strange noises, the cries of night animals, the hooting of owls, the groaning of trees in the wind. It was as if he heard these sounds for the first time.

Suddenly there was an entirely new sound, of a kind neither he nor anyone else had ever heard before. It was mournful and ghost-like. It made him afraid, so that he drew his robe tightly about himself and reached for his bow to make sure that it was properly strung. On the other hand, the sound was like a song, sad but beautiful, full of love, hope, and yearning. Then before he knew it, he was asleep. He dreamed that the bird called *wagnuka,* the redheaded woodpecker, appeared singing the strangely beautiful song and telling him: "Follow me and I will teach you."

When the hunter awoke, the sun was already high. On a branch of the tree against which he was leaning, he saw a redheaded woodpecker. The bird flew away to another tree, and another, but never very far, looking back all the time at the young man as if to say: "Come on!" Then once more he heard that wonderful song, and his heart yearned to find the singer. Flying toward the sound, leading the hunter, the bird flitted through the leaves, while its bright red top made it easy to follow. At last it lighted on a cedar tree and began hammering on a branch, making a noise like the fast beating of a small drum. Suddenly there was a gust of wind, and again the hunter heard that beautiful sound right above him.

Then he discovered that the song came from the dead branch that the woodpecker was tapping with his beak. He realized also that it was the wind which made the sound as it whistled through the holes the bird had drilled.

"*Kola,* friend," said the hunter, "let me take this branch home. You can make yourself another."

He took the branch, a hollow piece of wood full of woodpecker holes that was about the length of his forearm. He walked back to his village bringing no meat, but happy all the same.

In his tipi the young man tried to make the branch sing for him. He blew on it, he waved it around; no sound came. It made him sad, he wanted so much to hear that wonderful new sound. He purified himself in the sweat lodge and climbed to the top of a lonely hill. There, resting with his back against a large rock, he fasted, going without food or water for four days and nights, crying for a vision which would tell him how to make the branch sing. In the middle of the fourth night, *wagnuka,* the bird with the bright-red top, appeared, saying, "Watch me," turning himself into a man, showing the hunter how to make the branch sing, saying again and again: "Watch this, now." And in his dream the young man watched and observed very carefully.

When he awoke, he found a cedar tree. He broke off a branch and, working many hours, hollowed it out with a bowstring drill, just as he had seen the woodpecker do it in his dream. He whittled the branch into the shape of a bird with a long neck and an open beak. He painted the top of the bird's head with *washasha,* the sacred red color. He prayed. He smoked the branch up with incense of burning sage, cedar, and sweet grass. He fingered the holes as he had seen the man-bird do in his vision, meanwhile blowing softly into the mouthpiece. All at once there was the song, ghost-like and beautiful beyond words drifting all the way to the village, where the people were astounded and joyful to hear it. With the help of the wind and the woodpecker, the young man had brought them the first flute.

In the village lived an *itanchan*—a big chief. This *itanchan* had a daughter who was beautiful but also very proud, and convinced that there was no young man good enough for her. Many had come courting, but she had sent them all away. Now, the hunter who had made the flute decided that she was just the woman for him. Thinking of her he composed a special song, and one night, standing behind a tall tree, he played it on his *siyotanka* in hopes that it might have a charm to make her love him.

All at once the *winchinchala* heard it. She was sitting in her father's tipi, eating buffalo-hump meat and tongue, feeling good. She wanted to stay there, in the tipi by the fire, but her feet wanted to go outside. She pulled back, but the feet pulled forward, and the feet won. Her head said, "Go slow, go slow!" but the feet said, "Faster, faster!" She saw the young man standing in the moonlight; she heard the flute. Her head said, "Don't go to him; he's poor." Her feet said, "Go; run!" and again the feet prevailed.

So they stood face to face. The girl's head told her to be silent, but the feet told her to speak, and speak she did, saying: *"Koshkalaka,* young man, I am yours altogether." So they lay down together, the young man and the *winchinchala,* under one blanket.

Later she told him: *"Koshkalaka,* warrior, I like you. Let your parents send a gift to my father, the chief. No matter how small, it will be accepted. Let your father speak for you to my father. Do it soon! Do it now!"

And so the two fathers quickly agreed to the wishes of their children. The proud *winchinchala* became the hunter's wife, and he himself became a great chief. All the other young men had heard and seen. Soon they too began to whittle cedar branches into the shape of birds' heads with long necks and open beaks. The beautiful love music traveled from tribe to tribe, and made young girls' feet go where they shouldn't. And that's how the flute was brought to the people, thanks to the cedar, the woodpecker, and this young man, who shot no elk, but knew how to listen.

TEETH IN THE WRONG PLACES

❖ *Ponca-Otoe* ❖

TOLD BY AN ANONYMOUS WOMAN, RECORDED BY RICHARD ERDOES

When Coyote was roaming around for adventures, looking for great deeds to do, someone told him of an evil sorceress, an old woman who lived with her two wicked daughters. Many young men went there to sleep with the daughters, who were very handsome, but none was ever seen alive again.

Coyote said, "That's just the place I want to go."

"Be careful," said the person who had told him about it. "Whatever you do, don't sleep with these girls. It would kill you, or so I've been told."

"How could sleeping with two pretty women kill a man?" thought Coyote, and off he went.

BELOW AND OPPOSITE: *Male and Female Beaded Indian Dolls* **(Lakota). Courtesy of America Hurrah Archive, New York, NY.**

The old woman was very nice to him when he arrived, her two daughters were very beautiful. "Come in, come in," the mother said. "You're a good-looking young man, just the kind of person I'd like to have for a son-in-law."

Coyote went into the tipi with his bow and quiver. "Sit down, sit down," the old woman said. "You'll get something good to eat. My daughters will serve you."

The girls brought Coyote many good dishes—buffalo hump, tongues, all kinds of meat. One of the daughters, the older one, said: "You sure are handsome." Coyote thought to himself: "My informant was wrong; these are good people."

By nightfall, Coyote was full of good food and getting drowsy. "You must be tired after your journey," the old woman said. "And it's cold outside. Lie down to sleep between my two daughters—they'll keep you warm."

Coyote snuggled between the two girls. He felt amorous, but he wondered. In the dark the face of the younger girl brushed his; she was whispering in his ear: "Pretty soon my sister will ask you to sleep with her. I'm supposed to ask you too, but you mustn't do it."

"Why not?" asked Coyote.

"The old woman is a witch," said the girl. "She's not really my mother; I'm her prisoner, though the other girl is her daughter. This witch has put teeth into both our vaginas, and when a man comes to visit she gets him to copulate with us. Then these teeth take hold of his penis and chew it to bits. Once he puts it in, he can't pull it out no matter how hard he tries. You should hear those poor young men cry; they cry until they die."

"Why do you tell me this?"

"I like you and I hate doing the old woman's dirty work. After the poor young men are dead, she takes all their things. She likes robbing them, but she likes hearing them die even better."

"I don't believe you."

"Then listen. Do you hear the noise?"

"Yes, I do hear it, a strange noise."

"It's the grinding of the sharp teeth inside our vaginas."

Coyote heard the grinding. He believed what the girl said.

Coyote and the girl pretended to sleep. After a while the older girl, the old woman's daughter, pulled at his sleeve. "Strong young man," she whispered, "you must be hot for us. Let me make you happy. Get on top of me. Quick, get into me;" Coyote could hear the teeth gnashing furiously inside her vagina.

"I've been thinking of nothing else since I first saw you, pretty one," said Coyote, "but let me get my clothes off."

"Hurry up," said the impatient girl. "Don't dawdle. Put it in!"

Coyote took hold of a thick, long stick still warm from the fire, and stuck it deep into that wicked girl's vagina.

"Oh, a real man at last," said the girl, "how good it feels. A real big one for a change!" The teeth inside her were chewing, and wood splinters were flying out of her all over Coyote. "Whew!" he thought. "This is really something!" Quickly he grabbed an arrow from his quiver and thrust it deep into the girl before the teeth could snap shut. The teeth closed upon the shaft near the feathers, but it was too late: the arrowhead had already reached the evil girl's heart, and she died.

Then Coyote went over to the old woman and killed her with his knife. He told the younger girl: "You've saved my life, so come with me and I'll marry you."

"How can you?" said the girl. "I'd like to be your wife, but I have these teeth in the wrong place."

"I'll take care of that," Coyote told her, "so come on."

They started off for Coyote's house and walked all one day. When evening came, Coyote built a brush shelter for the two of them. He put sage into it for a bed. "Now I'm going to make love to you," he said.

"No, never!" said the girl. "It would kill you."

"Well, of course, first I have to knock your teeth out," said Coyote. "And not the ones in your head!"

So he knocked out the teeth in the girl's vagina—except for one blunt tooth that was very thrilling when making love. They were happy, Coyote and this girl.

THE LOYAL SWEETHEART

❖ *Passamaquoddy* ❖

RECORDED BY JOHN PRINCE, ADAPTED BY ELLA CLARK

Long ago, in a village beside a river, there lived a beautiful girl whom many a young man wished to marry. But she smiled on all alike and encouraged no one. Her name was Blue Flower.

Among her admirers was a young man who was especially skilled in hunting. For many moons he looked upon the girl with longing, but without any hope that he could win her favor.

At last, one autumn, she gave him reason to hope. And so he dared to consult the old woman of the village who carried proposals of marriage. He wanted to know his chances before he departed on the winter's hunt.

To the young man's great joy, the marriage-maker brought back a favorable reply from both the girl and her father. The message made him determined to win even greater fame as a hunter. He wanted to prove to the girl's father that he was indeed worthy of so beautiful a daughter.

"Will you wait for me until we return from the winter's hunt?" he asked her.

The girl gave her consent to his plan and her promise to remain true to him, whatever happened. She added the promise, "If you do not return, I will remain a maiden all my life. I will never marry any other man."

So the young man completed his plans to join the others of the village on the long winter's hunt. On the evening before their departure, he and the girl had a final canoe ride on the river. Then he sang his farewell in this love song of his people:

Often on a lonely day, my love,
You look on the beautiful river
And down the shining stream.

When last I looked upon you,
How beautiful was the stream,
How beautiful was the moon,
And how happy were we!
Since that night, my fair one,
I have thought of you always.

Often on a lonely day, my love,
You look on the beautiful river
And down the shining stream.

When we paddled the canoe together
On that beautiful water,
How fair the mountains looked,
How beautiful the red leaves
As the gentle wind whirled them!

***Birch Bark Basket* (Woodlands). Courtesy of San Diego Museum of Man, San Diego, CA.**

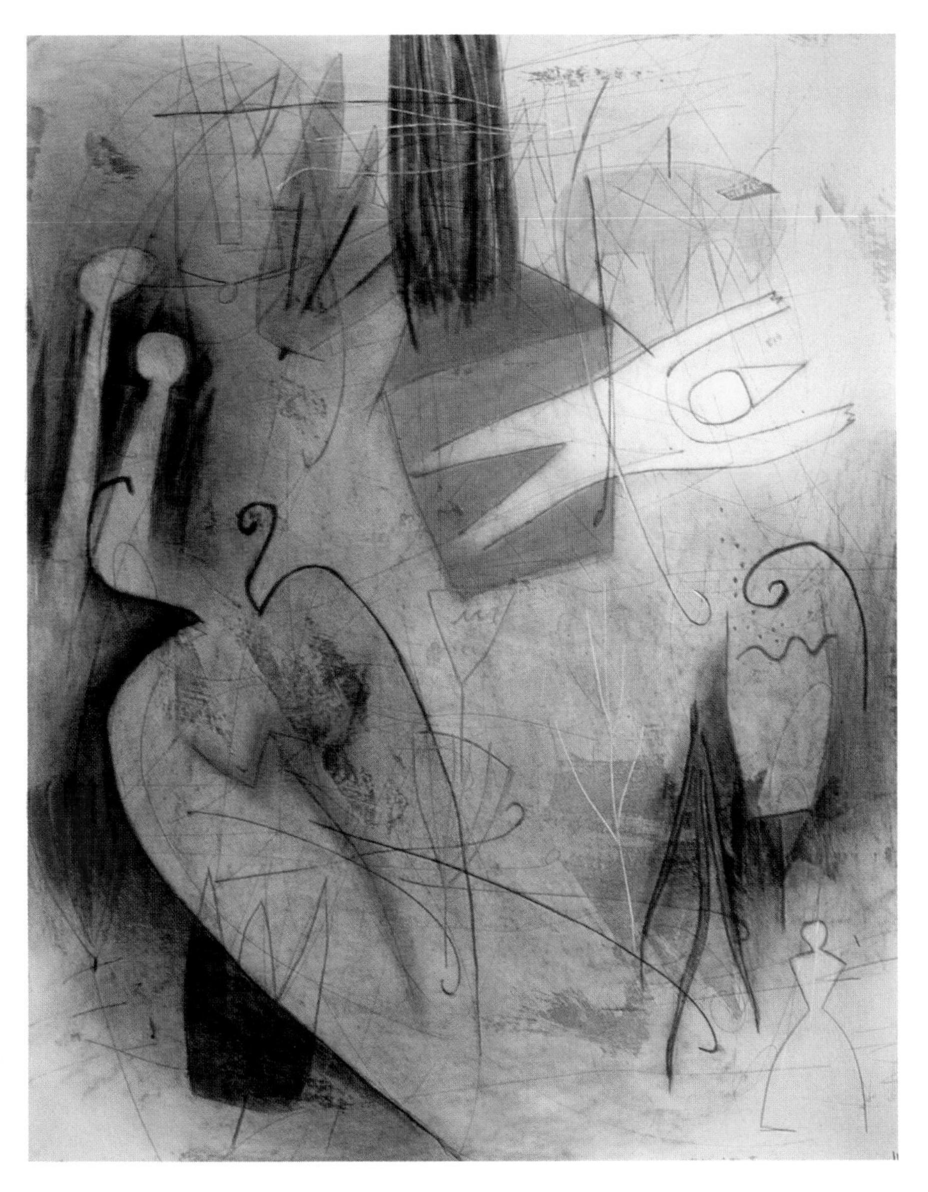

***White Shell Woman*, Emmi Whitehorse (Navajo), 1989. Courtesy of the artist.**

After the winter snows,
When spring has come once more,
We will paddle again together.
Then the leaves will be green,
The mountains fresh and fair.

Often on a lonely day, my love,
Look on the beautiful river,
Down the shining stream,
And know that spring will come.

Next day, the hunters departed. The old men, the women, and the children settled down to finish the autumn's work of preparing for the winter.

Not many days afterward, a war party attacked the village and destroyed it. They carried away as prisoners all the young girls. Among them was the promised bride of the hunter. When the warriors reached their home territory, they persuaded, or forced, many of the young women to become their wives. But Blue Flower refused to submit. The warriors threatened to burn her alive. Still she refused. She preferred death to breaking her promise to her sweetheart.

The warriors complained to their chief and asked that she be burned at the stake. But he would not listen to the cruel counsel of his men. Instead, he gave the girl a longer time in which to make up her mind. Her bravery greatly impressed him. He would save her life now, he thought, and marry her later to one of his best warriors, in order that their children might become a race of heroes.

Weeks passed, and the hunters returned. When they found their village in ashes, they knew which war party had struck. The young hunter, singing his vengeance song, gathered a host of warriors and started northward. They surprised the largest village of their enemy, killed many people, and took others as prisoners.

When the fighting was over, the victors and their friends who had been held captive by the enemy were reunited. There was great rejoicing. Perhaps happiest of all were the young hunter-warrior and Blue Flower, who had remained true to him in spite of threats and promises.

The young man, still thirsting for revenge, wanted to torture and burn the enemy that had been taken prisoners. But his sweetheart stopped him. She reminded him that they had not treated her cruelly.

She was a gentle and peace-loving girl, as well as a loyal sweetheart. In a short time, she became a loyal wife.

Family

❖ ❖ ❖ ❖ ❖

Family in the Native American world is often synonymous with "band" or even "tribe," and one of the important aspects of maintaining the tribe is the relationship among its members, with Nature, and with the world at large. "Couple Befriended by the Moon," which could have been included in "Adolescence," is placed here because it bridges the gap between the individual learning of young people and the communal learning of the group as a whole. The story teaches about respecting one's elders, even those who appear to be less fortunate; the final punishment levied—exclusion from the hunt, as well as the repetition of the phrase, "the people are camped there"—makes this story more about the people, the band, or the tribe. And in the context of "tribe," exclusion as a punishment for rudeness takes on its true severity.

In "The Man Who Loved Frog Songs," we learn the penalties for eco-nostalgia: that if we love some aspect of nature without understanding its complexities, our families, as well as ourselves, will endure the punishment. Larger infractions—the lack of humility, an abuse of power, or complete disrespect for the laws—result in greater retribution, as in "Montezuma and the Great Flood." (Readers should be aware that this Montezuma is a hero of the Southwest and not the Aztec emperor).

"The Sun's Myth" expresses a similar kind of penalty for greed, for wanting too much, for wanting what is not rightly one's own. Whether or not Dell Hymes is correct in suggesting that the story records the destruction of the tribe by a terrible plague or disease, it offers the participatory reader-listener a drama of reason destroyed by greed, desire, or false choices. It is imbalance that causes the death of the people; the idea that imbalance is not so easily shaken off emphasizes the need for careful choices, wise decisions, and personal responsibility. Thus, the story has allegorical extensions that are nearly limitless.

"Two Coyotes," one of my personal favorites, gives a particular example of how language creates the world, as well as how the perceptions of others, articulated in language, make us who we are. The story does it with the humor and quiet wit that seem so characteristic of many Native American stories. On the other hand, "Rabbit and the Old Man" warns us more seriously that while language makes us, it can also trick us. Tricky though language may be, it ultimately can save us, as it does in "Rabbit Deceives the Other Animals." Here, the mild joke about God destroying the world is possibly an amused, but particularly Indian, response to the threats invoked by Christian missionaries.

The section ends with a funny story about contact with the outside world, in the form of an anthropologist who has come to study the "mythology" of Indians. This Peter Blue Cloud story should delight its readers.

OPPOSITE: ***Grandmother Dilemma*, George C. Longfish (Seneca/Tuscarora), 1984. Courtesy of the artist.**

L. LOMAHAFTEWA · 1978

THE COUPLE BEFRIENDED BY THE MOON

❖ *Crow* ❖

TOLD BY YOUNG CRANE, ADAPTED BY RODNEY FREY

ver there,
the Crow people are coming.
They are walking towards the mountains.
It's a big camp.

A man,
who does not see well,
has a wife.

They have only one horse;
their lodge is small,
packed on one side of the horse;
they have little meat,
packed on one side of the horse.
With a root digger,
the woman gathers plant foods.
They are on one side of the camp;
a hunter kills plenty of game animals;
the couple takes some of it.

The people are camped there;
the couple are camped on the outside of the encampment.
They are very poor;
they follow the tracks of the people when they travel.
The woman lets her husband hold her horse;
she goes out digging roots.

The Moon comes,
from where the wife does not know.
The Moon befriends the wife.
This Moon is a woman;
she wears an elk-tooth dress.
From where the Moon comes the wife does not know;
the Moon has a big blue-handled knife.
From where the Moon comes the wife does not know.

OPPOSITE: *Cosmic Hands*, Linda Lomahaftewa (Hopi/Choctaw), 1978. Courtesy of the artist.

Then the wife comes there,
    to one side of the road.
Then Moon comes,
    to one side of the road.
"Daughter,
    look for someone to assist you;
        your husband is nearly blind," the Moon says.

The people are camped there;
    the couple are camped on the outside of the encampment.
There is plenty of meat;
    the people stay for some time.
"We are poor;
I have been told to look for someone to assist us;
    over there at the Musselshell River there are horses for you,"
    the wife says.
"A roan,
    a big-bellied mare are there," she says.

The Hidatsa are camped there.
Those who do not have guns, powder, tobacco, horses,
    they traded for these things.
Then they travel on,
    towards the mountains.

The wife has some powdered turnips.
"Make some pudding from the turnips," the husband says.
"Call to our lodge,
    four very brave young men," he says.
The wife calls in the four young men.
She gives them some pudding;
    they eat.

The husband is there,
    with the four young men.
"Have your moccasins made," he says.
"My horses are at the Musselshell River;
    let us go there," he says.
The wife smokes the pipe with the men.

The four young men go out from the lodge.
"When you have gone out,
    have moccasins made," the couple say.

These four young men go out from the lodge,
they meet,
they speak with one another.

Two of the young men are friends;
the other two are also friends.
"Well,
what are we going to do about this offer?" one young man says.
"If he really has good medicine,
he would not be a poor man," the first young men say.
"We will go with him," the other two young men say.

The wife cuts up her lodge cover;
she makes moccasins from it.
"When you go tonight,
your moccasins will be ready," she says.
The wife makes a padded saddle for her husband.
"When you bring in your horses,
ride on this saddle," she says.
The Moon had given the wife an hourglass-shaped medicine bag.
They tie the bag inside their lodge.

When it gets dark,
two young men come;
"We have come," they say.
The other two young men had doubted the man;
they do not come.
"We have come," they say.
"Wait for me outside the lodge;
I am getting ready," the husband says.
Then the husband comes outside.

Then the wife takes the medicine bag;
she goes outside with her husband.
The husband packs the padded saddle;
he is ready.
The wife sings a glad song.
A fine scouting song she sings.
"Go that way;
the roan is at the Musselshell River," she says.

When it gets dark,
then the three men go.
At the Yellowstone River,
the three men kill a very fat buffalo.

The three men build a fire;
the meat is cooked;
the three men pack the meat;
they will eat of this meat.
From now on,
the three men do not build a fire.

"Here is the Musselshell River," the three men say.
"Now,
go.
I will stay here," the husband says.
"In the mountain valley there is a herd of horses;
bring them to me," he says.

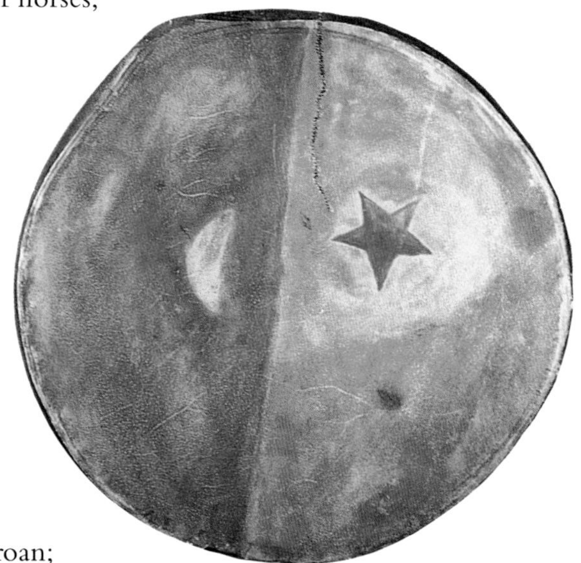

"Look for the roan," the husband says.
The young men search for the roan;
it is among the herd of horses.
They capture the roan;
they drive it back.
They take it to the poor man.

"Here is the roan,
take it," they say.
They give it to him.
The man puts the padded saddle on the roan;
he rides the roan.

"Look for the big-bellied mare," the husband says.
The young men search for the mare;
it is among the herd of horses.
They capture the mare;
they drive it back to the man.
The man puts a rope on the mare;
he leads the mare.

"Let the horses come," the husband says.
The young men drive the horses behind the man.
They come to Bull Hill;
there they swim with their horses across Pryor Creek.

"Those with medicine will find what they seek;
those without medicine will come last," they say.

***Drum* (Crow). Courtesy of W. E. Channing & Co., Santa Fe, NM.**

They bring in to the camp eighty horses;
the two young men have ten horses each;
this man has sixty horses.
"They have come with horses," the people say.
"That man really has medicine," they say.
All three men have geldings.

When they get to the edge of the camp,
this man cuts out his sixty horses he brought.
When he comes with horses,
they buy a very large lodge;
they furnish the lodge with the horses brought;
now they have something.
The young men are in the couple's lodge;
praise songs are sung;
in their own lodge,
praise songs are sung.
"With medicine I will find what I seek;
four times I will find what I seek," says one young man.
"With medicine I will find what I seek;
four times I will find what I seek," says the other young man.

"Look for someone to assist you,
that is what the Moon said," the wife says.
"These two young men who took pity on us,
they really have medicine," she says.
"Those two young men who insulted us,
they do not have medicine," she says.
"When you go on a horse raid,
send those two young men away,
send them home," she says.

The two young men who pitied the couple go on a horse raid;
they would bring many horses;
they would take many coups;
they are very good.
A group of young men go on a horse raid;
when those who insulted the couple go,
they would be sent away by themselves;
now they cry.

That is the end.

THE MAN WHO LOVED THE FROG SONGS

❖ *Menominee* ❖

RECORDED BY ALANSON SKINNER AND JOHN V. SATTERLEE

Button Blanket **(Tlingit). Courtesy of Thomas Burke Memorial Washington State Museum, Seattle, WA.**

nce an Indian had a revelation from the head of all the frogs and toads. In the early spring, when all the frogs and toads thaw out they sing and shout more noisily than at any other time of the year. This Indian made it a practice to listen to the frogs every spring when they first began, as he admired their songs, and wanted to learn something from them. He would stand near the puddles, marshes, and lakes to hear them better, and once when night came he lay right down to hear them.

In the morning, when he woke up, the frogs spoke to him, saying: "We are not all happy, but in very deep sadness. You seem to like our crying but this is our reason for weeping. In early spring, when we first thaw out and revive we wail for our dead, for lots of us don't wake up from our winter sleep. Now you will cry in your turn as we did."

Sure enough, the next spring the Indian's wife and children all died, and the Indian died likewise, to pay for his curiosity to hear the multitude of frogs. So this Indian was taught what has been known ever since by all Indians—that they must not go on purpose to listen to the cries of frogs in the early spring.

The Man Who Looked at an Owl

❖ *Menominee* ❖

Adapted by Alanson Skinner and John V. Satterlee

nce a sacred dreamer heard the t'otopa or screech owl. Although he was warned not to do so he went to the place whence the sound came, only to see this big-eyed tiny bird. The owl was concealed behind some trees and kept moving away until he got up close. The tiny owl was screeching behind a tree, but when the dreamer approached he showed himself, an awful object, terrible to behold, so that the man fell down on the ground in a faint. When he revived he went home and told all the others about it. It is known to this day that no Indian may ever approach this screech owl at night when he is about calling. . . .

***For Whom the Bell Tolls*, Jeffrey Chapman (Ojibwa), 1986. Courtesy of Jan Cicero Gallery, Chicago, IL.**

MONTEZUMA AND THE GREAT FLOOD

❖ *Papago (Tohono O'odham)* ❖

RETOLD BY ALFONSO ORTIZ AND RICHARD ERDOES

Before he made man, the Great Mystery Power made the earth and all things which lived upon it. The Great Mystery came down to earth, where he dug out some clay and formed it into a shape and ascended with it into the sky. Then he dropped it into the hole he had dug. At once out of that hole came the Great Montezuma, leading behind him all the Indian tribes. Last to come out of the hole were the wild, untameable Apaches, running off in all directions as fast as they were created.

The wise Montezuma taught the people all they needed to know: how to make baskets and pottery, how to plant corn with a digging stick, how to make a fire to cook the food. It was a happy time. The sun was much nearer the earth then, so that it was always pleasantly warm. There was no winter and no freezing cold. Men and animals lived as brothers, speaking a common language all could understand, so that a bug or a bird could talk to a human.

But then came the great flood. Long before it engulfed the earth, Montezuma's friend, Coyote, had foretold its coming. "You must make a big dugout canoe," Coyote told Montezuma, who could make anything. "You will need it soon," Coyote said.

Montezuma, following Coyote's advice, built the boat, keeping it ready on top of the high mountain that the whites call Monte Rosa. Coyote also made a strange vessel for himself, gnawing at a tree trunk until it fell down, then hollowing it out with his teeth. Coyote closed up the open end with piñon resin. When the great flood which Coyote had foretold finally swept over the land, Coyote crawled into the tree-trunk vessel he had made, while Montezuma climbed into his big dugout canoe. And so they floated upon the waters while all other living things perished. As the waters subsided, the top of Monte Rosa's peak rose a little above the flood. Both Montezuma and Coyote steered for this spot, the only piece of dry land far and wide. Thus the two friends met, glad to be alive.

Montezuma said to Coyote: "Friend, there must be other dry spots somewhere. You travel fast on four legs. Go west and do some scouting." Coyote went off and came back tired after four days, saying: "In that direction of the universe I found only water, nothing but water."

Montezuma told him: "Coyote, my friend, rest a while, and then go and see what you can find in the south." Coyote rested and then went southward. Again he came back after four days, saying: "Over there in the south, everything is also covered with water." He went east, and it was the same; water everywhere. Finally Montezuma sent Coyote toward the north,

OPPOSITE: *Apparition*, Norman Akers (Osage/Pawnee), 1989. Courtesy of Jan Cicero Gallery, Chicago, IL.

and this time Coyote came back saying: "In the north the waters are receding, and there is much dry land." Montezuma was well pleased to hear this. He told Coyote, "Friend, there in the north we must begin to make a new world."

The Great Mystery Power again was busy peopling the earth with men and animals. After life had been recreated, he put Montezuma in charge of everything. Montezuma divided tribes into nations again, giving them just laws to govern themselves, and once again taught humans how to live. And in these tasks Coyote was Montezuma's faithful helper. Soon the people were increasing together with animals, and all were happy.

But then Montezuma's power, which the Great Mystery had given him, went to his head. "We don't need a Creator," he said. "I am a Creator myself. My power is equal to the Great Mystery Power. I need nobody to command me; I myself am the Great Commander."

Coyote warned him to be more humble. "You know that there is a power above us greater than yours—the Power of the Universe. Obey its laws."

Montezuma answered: "I don't need your advice. Who are you to try to correct Great Montezuma? Am I not high above you? Am I not your master? Go; I don't need you anymore." Coyote left, shaking his head, wondering.

Now Montezuma called all the tribes together and said, "I am greater than anything that has ever been, greater than anything which exists now, and greater than anything that will ever be. Now, you people shall build me a tall house, floor upon floor upon floor, a house rising into the sky, rising far above this earth into the heavens, where I shall rule as Chief of all the Universe."

The Great Mystery Power descended from the sky to reason with Montezuma, telling him to stop challenging that which cannot be challenged, but Montezuma would not listen. He said: "I am almighty. Let no power stand in my way. I am the Great Rebel. I shall turn this world upside down to my own liking."

Then good changed to evil. Men began to hunt and kill animals. Disregarding the eternal laws by which humans had lived, they began to fight among themselves. The Great Mystery Power tried to warn Montezuma and the people by pushing the sun farther away from the earth and placing it where it is now. Winter, snow, ice, and hail appeared, but no one heeded this warning.

In the meantime Montezuma made the people labor to put up his many-storied house, whose rooms were of coral and jet, turquoise and mother-of-pearl. It rose higher and higher, but just as it began to soar above the clouds far into the sky, the Great Mystery Power made the earth tremble. Montezuma's many-storied house of precious stones collapsed into a heap of rubble.

When that happened, the people discovered that they could no longer understand the language of the animals, and the different tribes, even though they were all human beings, could no longer understand each other. Then Montezuma shook his fists toward the sky and called: "Great Mystery Power, I defy you. I shall fight you. I shall tell the people not to pray or make sacrifices of corn and fruit to the Creator. I, Montezuma, am taking your place!"

The Great Mystery Power sighed, and even wept, because the one he had chosen to lead mankind had rebelled against him. Then the Great Mystery resolved to vanquish those who rose against him. He sent the locust flying far across the eastern waters, to summon a people in an unknown

***The End of the Innocences*,**
George C. Longfish (Seneca/Tuscarora), 1992. Courtesy of the artist.

land, people whose faces and bodies were full of hair, who rode astride strange beasts, who were encased in iron, wielding iron weapons, who had magic hollow sticks spitting fire, thunder, and destruction. The Great Mystery Power allowed these bearded, pitiless people to come in ships across the great waters out of the east—permitted them to come to Montezuma's country, taking away Montezuma's power and destroying him utterly.

THE SUN'S MYTH

❖ *Kathlamet (Chinook)* ❖

TOLD BY CHARLES CULTEE, RECORDED BY FRANZ BOAS, RETRANSLATED BY DELL HYMES

They live there, those people of a town.
Five the towns of his relatives, that chief.

In the early light,
now he used to go out,
and outside,
now he used to stay;
now he used to see that sun:
she would nearly come out, that sun.
Now he told his wife,
"What would you think,
if I went to look for that sun?"
She told him, his wife,
"You think it is near?
And you will wish to go to that sun?"

Another day,
again in the early light,
he went out;
now again he saw that sun:
she did nearly come out there, that sun.
He told his wife,
"You shall make ten pairs of moccasins,
you shall make me leggings,
leggings for ten people."
Now she made them for him, his wife,
moccasins for ten people,
the leggings of as many.

Again it became dawn,
now he went,
far he went.
He used up his moccasins;
he used up his leggings;
he put on others of his moccasins and leggings.
Five months he went;
five of his moccasins he used up;
five of his leggings he used up.
Ten months he went—
now she would rise nearby, that sun—
he used up his moccasins.
Now he reached a house,
a large house,
he opened the door,
now some young girl is there;
he entered the house,
he stayed.

Now he saw there on the side of that house:
arrows are hanging on it,
quivers full of arrows are hanging on it,
armors of elk skin are hanging on it,
armors of wood are hanging on it,
shields are hanging on it,
axes are hanging on it,
war clubs are hanging on it,
feathered regalia are hanging on it—
all men's property there on the side of that house.

OPPOSITE: ***Red Chevrons*,**
Joe Feddersen (Colville),
1988. Courtesy of the artist.

There on the other side of that house:
mountain goat blankets are hanging on it,
painted elk-skin blankets are hanging on it,
buffalo skins are hanging on it,
dressed buckskins are hanging on it,
long dentalia are hanging on it,
shell beads are hanging on it,
short dentalia are hanging on it—
Now, near the door, some large thing hangs over there;
he did not recognize it.

Then he asked the young girl,
"Whose property are those quivers?"
"Her property, my father's mother,
she saves them for my maturity."
"Whose property are those elk-skin armors?"
"Our property, my father's mother [and I],
she saves them for my maturity."
"Whose property are those arrows?"
"Our property, my father's mother [and I],
she saves them for my maturity."

"Whose property are those wooden armors?"
"Our property, my father's mother [and I],
she saves them for my maturity."
"Whose property are those shields,
and those bone war clubs?"
"Our property, my father's mother [and I]."
"Whose property are those stone axes?"
"Our property, my father's mother [and I]."

Then again on the other side of that house:
"Whose property are those buffalo skins?"
"Our buffalo skins, my father's mother [and I],
she saves them for my maturity."
"Whose property are those mountain goat blankets?"
"Our property, my father's mother [and I],
she saves them for my maturity."
"Whose property are those dressed buckskins?"
"Our property, my father's mother [and I],
she saves them for my maturity."

"Whose property are those deerskin blankets?"
"Our property, my father's mother [and I],
she saves them for my maturity."
"Whose property are those shell beads?"
"Our property, my father's mother [and I],
she saves them for my maturity."
"Whose property are those long dentalia?
"Whose property are those short dentalia?"
"Her property, my father's mother,
she saves them for my maturity."

He asked her about all those things.
He thought,
"I will take her."

ABOVE AND OPPOSITE: Details of *Hide with Bundling Couples* (Southern Cheyenne). Courtesy of America Hurrah Archive, New York, NY.

At dark,
now that old woman came home.
Now again she hung up one [thing],
that which he wanted,
that thing shining all over.
He stayed there.

A long time he stayed there,
now he took that young girl.
They stayed there.

In the early light,
already that old woman was gone.
In the evening,
she would come home;
she would bring things,
she would bring arrows;
sometimes mountain goat blankets she would bring,
sometimes elk-skin armors she would bring.
Every day like this.

A long time he stayed.
Now he felt homesick.
Twice he slept,
he did not get up.
That old woman said to her grandchild,
"Did you scold him,
and he is angry?"
"No, I did not scold him,
he feels homesick."

Now she told her son-in-law,
"What will you carry when you go home?
Will you carry those buffalo skins?"
He told her,
"No."
"Will you carry those mountain goat blankets?"
He told her,
"No."
"Will you carry all those elk-skin armors?"
He told her,
"No."

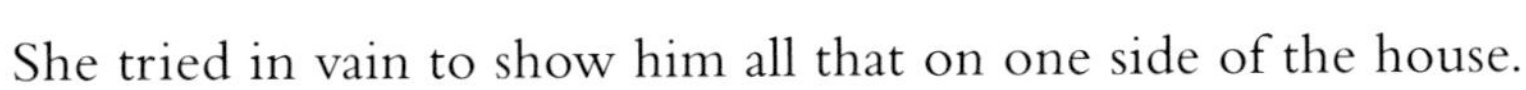
She tried in vain to show him all that on one side of the house.
Next all those [other] things.
She tried in vain to show him all, *every*thing.
He wants only that,
that thing that is large,
that [thing] put up away.
When it would sway,
that thing put up away,
it would become turned around,
at once his eyes would be extinguished;
that thing [is] shining all over,
now he wants only that thing there.

He told his wife,
"She shall give me one [thing],
that blanket of hers, that old woman."
His wife told him,
"She will never give it to you.
In vain people continue to try to trade from her;
she will never do it."
Now again he became angry.

Several times he slept.
Now again she would ask him,
"Will you carry that?"
she would tell him.
She would try in vain to show him all those things of hers;
she would try in vain to show him those men's things;
she would try in vain to show him all.
She would reach that [thing] put up away,
now she would become silent.
When she would reach that [thing] put away,
now her heart became tired.
Now she told him:
"You must carry it then!
Take care! if you carry it.
It is you who choose.
I try to love you,
indeed I do love you."

Sun Mask, Thunderbird Mask **(Kwajiulth). Courtesy of Donald Ellis Gallery, Ontario.**

She hung it on him,
she hung it all on him.
Now she gave him a stone ax.
She told him:
"Go home now!"

He went out,
now he went,
he went home;
he did not see a land;
he arrived near his father's brother's town.
Now that which he had taken throbbed,
now that which he had taken said,
"We two shall strike your town,
we two shall strike your town,"
said that which he had taken.
His reason became nothing,
he did it to his father's brother's town,
he crushed, crushed, crushed it,
he killed all the people.
He recovered—
all those houses are crushed,
his hands are full of blood.

He thought,
"O I am a fool!
See, that is what it is like, this thing!
Why was I made to love this?"
In vain he tried to begin shaking it off,
and his flesh would be pulled.

Now again he went,
and he went a little while—
Now again his reason became nothing—
he arrived near another father's brother's town.
Now again it said,
"We two shall strike your town,
we two shall strike your town."
In vain he would try to still it,
it was never still.
In vain he would try to throw it away,
always those fingers of his would cramp.

Now again his reason became nothing,
now again he did it to his father's brother's town,
he crushed it all.
He recovered:
his father's brother's town [is] nothing,
the people all are dead.
Now he cried.

In vain he tried in the fork of a tree,
there in vain he would try squeezing through it;
in vain he would try to shake it off,
it would not come off,
and his flesh would be pulled;
in vain he would keep beating what he had taken on rocks,
it would never be crushed.

Again he would go,
he would arrive near another father's brother's town.

Now again that which he had taken would shake:
"We two shall strike your town,
we two shall strike your town."

His reason would become nothing,
    he would do it to his father's brother's town,
        crush, crush, crush, crush;
    all his father's brother's town he would destroy,
        and he would destroy the people.
He would recover;
    he would cry out;
        he would grieve for his relatives.

In vain he would try diving into water;
    in vain he would try to shake it off,
        and his flesh would be pulled.
In vain he would try rolling in a thicket;
    in vain he would keep beating what he had taken on
            rocks;
        he would abandon hope.
Now he would cry out.

Again he would go.
Now again he would arrive at another town,
    a father's brother's town.
Now again what he had taken would shake:
    "We two shall strike your town,
    we two shall strike your town."

His reason would become nothing,
    he would do it to the town,
        crush, crush, crush, crush,
            and the people.
He would recover:
    all the people and the town [are] no more;
        his hands and arms [are] only blood.
He would become
    "Qa! qa! qa! qa!"
    he would cry out.

In vain he would try to beat it on the rocks,
    what he had taken would not be crushed.
In vain he would try to throw away what he had taken,
    always his fingers stick to it.

Again he would go.
Now his too, his town,
    he would be near his town.
In vain he would try to stand, that one;
    see, something would pull his feet.

His reason would become nothing,
    he would do it to his town,
    crush, crush, crush, crush;
    all his town he would destroy,
        and he would destroy his relatives.
He would recover:
    his town is nothing;
        the dead fill the ground.
He would become
    "Qa! qa! qa! qa!"
    he would cry out.

In vain he would try to bathe;
    in vain he would try to shake off what he wears,
        and his flesh would be pulled.
Sometimes he would roll about on rocks;
    he would think,
        "Perhaps it will break apart";
         he would abandon hope.
Now again he would cry out,
    and he wept.

He looked back.
Now she is standing near him, that old woman.
"You,"
she told him,
    "You.
In vain I try to love you,
    in vain I try to love your relatives.
Why do you weep?
    It is you who choose;
        now you carried that blanket of mine."
Now she took it,
        she lifted off what he had taken;
    now she left him,
        she went home.
He stayed there;
    he went a little distance
        there he built a house,
        a small house.

TWO COYOTES

❖ *Nez Perce* ❖

TOLD BY HARRY WHEELER, ADAPTED BY RODNEY FREY

ne more story which is wonderful,
true,
and funny.

Two coyotes went up the river
and they came to a big bench
and from there they saw people living below,
near the river.
And the two friends said to each other,
"You go ahead."
Then one said,
"No.
You go."
And the other said,
"No."
And for a long time they argued,
they contested.

***Untitled*, Fred Kabotie (Hopi), 1922. Courtesy of the School of American Research, Santa Fe, NM.**

Then one said,
"Then you go first.
They will see you soon
and they will say,
'That coyote is going on the trail.'"
"I am not a coyote." [the second coyote said]
"But you are the same as I am. [the first coyote said]
We are the same in every way
and we are both coyotes."
"No. [the second coyote said]
I am 'another one.'"
Thus they contested.

Then one said, [the second coyote]
"Now you go first."
There was a ridge on which the people from below could see everything.
When he walked on [the first coyote]

Coyote and the Gourd, **Duane Slick (Mesquakie/ Winnebago), 1992. Courtesy of the artist.**

he went on,
went over a small ridge,
the people below said to each other,
"That coyote is going upstream."
And they came out [the people]
and watched the coyote going.

"See," he said to his friend, [the first coyote]
"what did they say?
You are a coyote."
"Then you come too," he said, [the first coyote]
"and they are going to say the same to you.
You are a coyote."
"Alright, I'll go," [the second coyote said]
and he slowly started walking on the trail from there.
Then [the people said]
"Ah, another one again,
another one again."
Then he came, [the second coyote]
"See, I am not a coyote.
I am 'another one.'
See, the people said that I am 'another one.'"

That's all.

RABBIT AND THE OLD MAN

❖ *Hitchiti* ❖

RECORDED BY STITH THOMPSON, ADAPTED BY JOHN SWANTON

A man had two daughters whom Rabbit wanted. At that time the old man's many hogs were disappearing, and he did not know what caused it. Then Rabbit shouted from a place near the house and the old man started out. When he got there, Rabbit sat holding a hog's tail, and Rabbit said, "You have been saying 'My hogs are disappearing.' I found them going under the ground, seized this one by the tail, and sat here with it while I called you." "Well, I will hold it while you go and bring a grubbing hoe and shovel," he said to Rabbit. So Rabbit went to the house, and when he got there he said to the old man's two daughters whom he wanted, "I have come because your father told me to have intercourse with both of you and come back." When he told the girls this, they said, "You might lie." When they said this to Rabbit, he called out to that old man, "Did you say both?" Then he answered back, "Yes, I said both," and Rabbit said, "You hear what he says," so they agreed and he had intercourse with both of them.

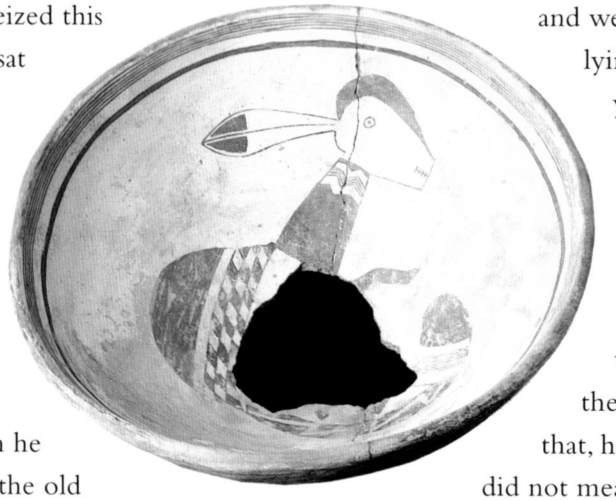

After he had gone off, that old man waited, holding the hog tail. After he had sat there for a while, he gave a hard pull and pulled it out, because it was only fastened to the ground. He threw it away and came back. When he got to the house, Rabbit had left and when he asked for him, they said, "He is gone. He said you told him to have intercourse with both of us, and we said, 'You may be lying.' He called out to you if you meant both and you answered. 'Yes.' So he had intercourse with both of us and went off." When they told the old man that, he was very angry. "I did not mean that. I told him to get the grubbing hoe and shovel, and he came for them, and I thought he meant those when I called back to him, 'I said both.' But when he did not come while I was waiting for him, I pulled hard and pulled out the hog tail, which was just stuck to the ground, and I threw it away and came back. If I see Rabbit I will knock him down and throw him away," the old man said, he was so angry.

That is how it is told.

***Rabbit Bowl* (Membrace Valley). From the Collection of the Dayton Museum of Natural History, Dayton, OH.**

RABBIT DECEIVES THE OTHER ANIMALS

❖ *Creek* ❖

ADAPTED BY JOHN R. SWANTON

The Rabbit was under arrest and, when brought before the assembled council of all the other animals, he said to them:

"I have a great message to deliver to all of you. God has appeared to me and he has told me that he intends to destroy the world, because you animals are so wicked. The only way for you to escape is to choose me to rule over you to guide you aright. God will destroy the world in a short time if you do not act better."

The animals greeted his speech with laughter. "You are such a great liar," said they, "that we know this is another trick."

***Sundown*, Jaune Quick-to-See Smith (Flathead/Shoshone/Cree), 1984. Courtesy of the artist.**

"Well, all you have to do is to wait and see," replied the Rabbit, with a solemn look.

"We are not afraid of your lies."

The following night, after the council had separated, the Rabbit sought out the king of the Partridges and said to him:

"I have a plan by which you can save me from this trouble and I can be of great service to you. If you will help me I will see that you and your subjects shall have the privilege of roving over the whole world and eating where you will instead of being restricted to one kind of food, as you now are."

"What can I do?" asked the king of the Partridges.

"This. Go and gather all the Partridges into one immense flock and to-morrow, when the council meets, station your subjects to the south of the council ground and, at a certain signal from me, let every Partridge fly into the air and flutter with all his might, and make as much noise as possible.

The king of the Partridges consented.

"On the second day," continued the Rabbit, "carry your subjects to the east of the council ground and act likewise when you see me stand before the council and give the signal. On the third day go to the north, and on the fourth day be in the west, but remember to keep out of sight all the time, and on each day make a louder noise than on the preceding day. Do this and the world shall be your feeding ground."

Then they separated.

The council assembled again and summoned the Rabbit, who came smiling and bowing and said: "I love all of you, and am sorry to know that your wickedness is leading you to destruction. God will not permit such wicked animals to live. To-day, I fear, you will hear a warning in the south. If you do not heed it and turn an innocent brother loose, then, to-morrow, the warning will become louder in the east. On the third day the sound of coming down will be heard in the north and, if you still persist in your persecution, a terrible rumbling in the west will precede the world's destruction, and then, on the fifth day, the world will be destroyed."

For this the animals jeered at him and cried, "Oh, what a lie. Tell us another."

Then the Rabbit turned to the south and gave the agreed signal when a strange low, rumbling sound came from that direction.

The animals looked at one another and whispered, "What is that?"

"God's warning," replied the Rabbit.

Some said: "Let's let him go. He may be innocent." Others said, "It's one of his tricks. He is a cunning little rascal."

The second day came, and the Rabbit said, "You are doomed. To-day another warning will come from the east." He gave the signal and there was a louder thundering than on the previous day.

Some of the animals became alarmed at this and said, "Perhaps he's speaking the truth this time. Maybe the world will be destroyed."

"It is one of his tricks," said others. "But how can he make such a noise? He is here and the noise is yonder."

The council separated without a decision. On the third day the Rabbit appeared with a solemn air and, when called on, said:

"You still refuse to do me justice. The warning will come to-day from the north." Hardly had he spoken, when there came a tremendous roar, shaking the air and ground, and the animals trembled in terror.

"Let him go, let him go," shouted many to their leaders.

It was decided to wait one day more and if no trick could be discovered the Rabbit should be let go.

On the fourth day the animals came slowly to the council ground and cast fearful looks to the west. The Rabbit, amid profound silence, was led out.

"Alas," said he, "what a fate—all the animals to be destroyed when one act of justice could save them," and suddenly from the west came such a fluttering, buzzing, quivering, shaking roar that all the animals cried aloud:

"Let him go, let him go. He is right. The world will be destroyed."

So they let him go, and away he hopped to the king of the Partridges. "The world is yours," said he. "Go where you will and eat your fill."

Ever since then partridges have roved over the whole world. . . .

OPPOSITE: ***Weaving with Black and White Horses and Chickens*** **(Navajo). Courtesy of America Hurrah Archive, New York, NY.**

COYOTE'S ANTHRO

❖ *Mohawk* ❖

TOLD BY PETER BLUE CLOUD

The anthropologist was very excited. He'd just received his doctorate after having delivered his paper, entitled: The Mythology of Coyote: Trickster, Thief, Fool and World-Maker's Helper. He was at this very moment in the process of gathering further data, working on a generous grant from a well-known Foundation. He'd just set up camp in the sagebrush not far from his latest informant's shack.

Now he sat by his fire, looking at the stars and sipping coffee. He chuckled to himself when he heard a coyote bark not far away. He wondered what that coyote would think if the myths about him (or her) were read aloud?

"Not much!" said a voice. The anthro was startled, he hadn't heard anyone approach. "Not much, maybe just a cup of coffee and some of that cake I see sitting there." Then into the campfire light stepped an old man, but not a man. He had long, furry ears sticking

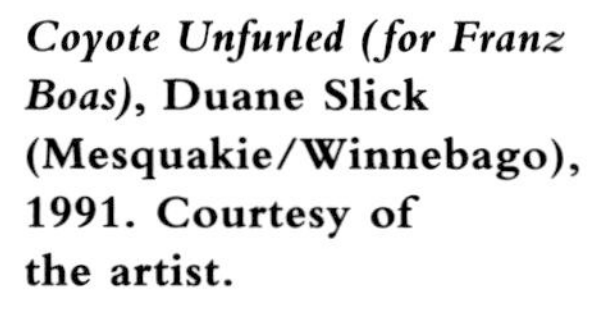

***Coyote Unfurled (for Franz Boas)*, Duane Slick (Mesquakie/Winnebago), 1991. Courtesy of the artist.**

thru his felt hat, and he had a long, bushy tail hanging from beneath his greatcoat. He leaned on his walking stick and grinned.

Good God! The anthro was stunned: it was Coyote Old Man himself. But it couldn't be; he was a myth!

"Not always," Coyote said, as the anthro closed his eyes and shook his head violently from side to side. When he opened his eyes, Coyote was leaning toward him, his head cocked sideways, listening. He nodded, "Yes, I heard them there in your head. Sounded like pebbles. Is that how you anthro's make music?"

The anthro knew he must be hallucinating. Better go along with it, he thought frantically, and maybe it'll go away. "Uh, are you Coyote Old Man?" he asked.

"Do I look like Fox Young Man? And do you really want me to go away?" Coyote studied the anthro, then asked, "What time are you?"

The anthro raised his arm to look at his watch, "Well, it's exactly . . ."

Coyote interrupted, "Nothing's exactly. It's not tick-tock time I asked about. I just want to know what time you are." The anthro looked blank. "I thought so," said Coyote. "Well, let's have that coffee, then we can maybe figure things out."

So they sat drinking coffee, the anthro so excited he couldn't sit still. He reached for his tape recorder, then looked at Coyote, "Uh, do you mind if I turn this on?"

"Why not? Do you pet it or sing to it? Will it dance?"

Once he'd turned on his tape recorder, he felt more confident. He was, after all, an anthropologist. He picked up his notebook and pencil, and began, "I'll pay you for your time, of course," he said.

"It's not really mine I'm worried about, it's yours I'm here for. How can you pay me for my time when you don't know what your own is? How about this time? Yes, this time put a little more sugar in my coffee." Coyote laughed at himself, then looked seriously at the anthro; "I'm a doctor, you know. I'm here to help you. Now then, how can I help you?"

"Well, actually, it's the stories I'm most concerned with. The reasons behind the reasons, if you follow me: interrelationships, the problem of spatial paradox, sexual taboos, those kinds of things. I want to create a whole fabric of thought, a completed tapestry, no loose threads. Know what I mean?"

"Parrot Boxes, huh? Sex shell tables and follow-youse: what's all that? That how you talk about pussy in college? You know, you sound like my tapeworm, and he never did make any sense. How about just one question to begin with, huh?"

"Well, let's start with the Creation myth, cutting to the core! What's the meat of it really, the true meaning?"

"My friend," said Coyote, "if you think Creation's a myth, you just might be in serious trouble. It's not the learning that's important, but the leaning. You must lean toward your questions, your problems; lean slowly so that you don't bend the solution too badly out of shape."

Coyote plucked a long hair from his tail and held it horizontally a foot from the ground. He whispered something to the hair, then let it go, and it floated there where he'd held it. He took a sip of coffee, then placed his cup on the hair. The anthro was incredulous: the cup sat on the hair above the ground. He blurted out, "But how did you do that? What's holding the hair up?"

"You're not studying your notes to this story very well, are you? If you'll just relook at the paragraph in front of this one you'll find that a foot from the ground is holding things up. Of course, you can't see the foot 'cause I just made up its measured guess. Something invisible is sleeping under this sand and only its foot is sticking out."

And so, because this story is getting too long, Coyote became somewhat impatient, and quickly finished his coffee. He stood up and beckoned the anthro, "Come on then, we got some leaning to do." And Coyote led him across the desert to a deep pool of water near some mountains.

A full moon was reflected in the water, shining as brightly as the one in the sky. Coyote sat down and began singing. Then, still softly singing, he leaned out over the water and touched the reflected moon. The water bent to his touch like rubber. Still singing he stepped onto the water moon, bouncing slightly. He jumped a bit and bounced up and down. Then he began bouncing in earnest, bounding into the sky, even doing a couple of back flips. He bounced as high as he could and grabbed the moon in the sky and hung there grinning at the anthro. "Hey, look at me," he said, "and I wasn't even sure I could do it."

He let go of the moon, did a double flip, bounced once and landed next to the anthro. "Okay," he said, "I got it all nice and rubbery. Go ahead and bounce a little."

So the anthro jumped from the bank, creating a great splash as he sank from view. He was gasping and spitting out water as he climbed from the pool.

"Well, well, look how you shattered the moon . . . You know, I thought only us coyotes were silly enough to try things we weren't sure of. And you, my friend, forgot to sing."

OPPOSITE: *We All Look Alike*, Jaune Quick-to-See Smith (Flathead/Shoshone/Cree), 1995. Courtesy of Steinbaum Krauss Gallery, New York, NY.

WE ALL LOOK ALIKE
AFTER THE DECLARATION OF INDEPENDENCE OUR FOUNDING FATHERS WROTE SOMETHING EVEN MORE IMPORTANT.
HOW A TRADITION BEGINS.
The most dramatic statement a man can make.
THE SHARPER IMAGE
BE ALL YOU CAN BE.
The Blessings of Liberty
BUILT IN AMERICA.
The Pilgrim's Slow Progress
the Vision Thing
The Stuff of Dreams
MAKES THE DREAM YOURS
It's More you.
OUR IDEA OF THE PERFECT THREE-PIECE SUIT.
Invest in America!
BRONZE
Design & Decoration
A Big Test for the Dollar
Never have so many done so much for so few.
No, it's not an import.
Discover the source.
EXOTIC SHOPPING
Envy.
PICK A COPIER YOUR OWN SIZE.
you would never suspect.
going going going
going going going
going going going
going going going
"The other guys do business with a bill of sale. We do it with a Bill of Rights."
BUFFALO PLAID
MOVIES SPORTS ADS

Marriage

❖ ❖ ❖ ❖ ❖

Stories of lust and love lead, in any tradition, to marriage, and this section begins with the power of song to bring back a quarreling lover and transform him into a bright star. Storytelling too is like song; both carry with them power as well as cautions. For example, in "Bridal Veil Fall," a leader of his people becomes so unbalanced with love that he forgets the tribe's well-being; only his lover's prayer brings fertility back to the Yosemite Valley.

Other problems also emerge from relationships. While the teller in "Weaver Spider's Web" relates clever stories about the creation of Coyote's "better half," he has a long way to go before he can win over women with his cute tales. In another selection, a young man courts a woman for the wrong reasons: Not Enough Horses has too much pride and arrogance for the girls in his village, and so he ends up marrying Coyote not once, but twice.

Stories can reveal the qualities in husbands and wives that people admire. In "Legend of the White Plume," a good provider with an honest and perceptive spouse evens the score, showing us how impostors eventually trick themselves and pay for their dishonesty. "Tolowim Woman," who is so flighty that she first abandons her child and then fails to hold tight to her husband, conveys the ideal of steadfastness, even if it is in a negative way. And there are always the lessons to be learned: fate decrees that animals and humans cannot marry, even if the animal is a shape-shifting Coyote as in "Coyote and the Woman," or even if the magic of love transforms a couple so that a buffalo woman can marry a man. Nature remains unchanged. The truth will eventually be revealed, in the next generation, if not before.

Once a person has married, there are stories to teach the proper treatment of spouses. "The Loon Story" portrays a woman who resents having to care for her blind husband, tries to abandon him, and ends up abandoned herself. Character revealed is not character changed, and the lack of compassion emanating from her people seems appropriate. And the wonderful Sia story, "Men and Women Try Living Apart," tells us quite plainly that men and women belong together, that without each other, they grow thin, dissatisfied, and unhappy.

OPPOSITE: ***Charlo Series*, Jaune Quick-to-See Smith (Flathead/Shoshone/Cree), 1985. Courtesy of the artist.**

Nettie Reuben's Evening Star's Song

❖ *Karuk* ❖

Sung by Nettie Reuben, translated by William Bright

Evening Star lived there,
along with his lover.
And for a long time they lived beautifully.
But one day they had a quarrel,
oh, they got cranky,
they had a quarrel.
And he went home,
Evening Star did.
And finally he went all the way around,
around the whole world,
he went off far away.
And the woman thought,
"Oh, my lover!
How will I ever see him again,
my sweetheart?"

Oh, she was lonely,
she sat back down on the doorstep.
"Oh, how lonely I am!
Oh, how he left me!"
she thought.
So once more the next day,
at evening she sat back down there.
"Whatever shall I do?"
And she thought,
"Perhaps I'll make a song,
that way I'll get to see him again,
my lover."
And again the next day,
she sat back down on the doorstep.
And she sang a song,
she thought,
"That way I'll get to see him again."

Ii ii ii iiya
aa ii ii iiya
aa ii ii iiya
oh, he left me
oh, my lover . . .

"Oh, let's be together again
oh, let's be together again
oh, my lover
oh, I'm lonely
oh, my lover" . . .

When she finished it,
singing the love song,
then Evening Star thought,
"Oh, I'm lonely,
I'm thinking of my lover,
let me go see her again!"
In fact his heart was lost,
but he would find his heart again.
In fact, here at the center of the earth,
the two would see each other again,
and so he would find his heart again
when Evening Star and his lover
embraced each other.

And she said this,
    the woman did,
  "When Humans come into existence,
  even though a woman is abandoned,
  she will find him again,
    by means of my song.
  He will come back from there,
    even though he's gone off to the
      end of the earth."

And Evening Star was transformed,
  into a big star in the sky.

***Starmakers*, Linda Lomahaftewa (Hopi/Choctaw), 1990. Courtesy of the artist.**

BRIDAL VEIL FALL

❖ *Miwok* ❖

RECORDED BY ALANSON SKINNER, ADAPTED BY ELLA CLARK

Hundreds of years ago, in the shelter of this valley, lived Tu-tok-a-nu-la and his tribe. He was a wise chief, trusted and loved by his people, always setting a good example by saving crops and game for winter.

While he was hunting one day, he saw the lovely guardian spirit of the valley for the first time. His people called her Ti-sa-yac. He thought her beautiful beyond his imagination. Her skin was white, her hair was golden, and her eyes were like heaven. Her voice, as sweet as the song of a thrush, led him to her. But when he stretched his arms toward her she rose, lighter than a bird, and soon vanished in the sky.

From that moment, the Chief knew no peace, and he no longer cared for the well-being of his people.

Without his directions, Yo Semite became a desert. When Ti-sa-yac came again, after a long time, she wept because bushes were growing where corn had grown before, and bears rooted where the huts had been. On a mighty dome of rock, she knelt and prayed to the Great Spirit above, asking him to restore its virtue to the land.

He granted her plea. Stooping from the sky, the Great Spirit above spread new life of green on all the valley floor. And smiting the mountains, he broke a channel for the pent-up snow that soon melted. The water ran and leaped far down, pooling in a lake below and flowing off to gladden other land.

The birds returned with their songs, the flowering plants returned with their blossoms, and the corn soon swayed in the breeze. When the Yo Semitee people came back to their valley, they gave the name of Ti-sa-yac to what is now called South Dome. That is where she had knelt.

Then the Chief came home again. When he heard what the beautiful spirit maiden had done, his love for her became stronger than ever. Climbing to the crest of a rock that rises three thousand feet above the valley, he carved his likeness there with his hunting knife. He wanted his tribe to remember him after he departed from the earth.

Tired from his work, he sat at the foot of Bridal Veil Fall. Suddenly he saw a rainbow arching over the figure of Ti-sa-yac, who was shining from the water. She smiled at him and beckoned to him. With a cry of joy, he sprang into the waterfall and disappeared with his beloved.

The rainbow quivered on the falling water, and the sun went down.

OPPOSITE: *Supernatural Flower World*, Mario Martinez (Yaqui), 1995. Courtesy of American Indian Contemporary Arts, San Francisco, CA.

WEAVER SPIDER'S WEB

❖ *Mohawk* ❖

TOLD BY PETER BLUE CLOUD

Coyote was starving and freezing, and here it was only mid-winter. He'd forgotten to gather firewood and food. He'd planned on singing a very powerful song to make the winter a mild one, easy to live with, but he'd forgotten to sing the song.

The reason he'd forgotten was that he was fascinated by Weaver Spider who'd moved into the entrance of Coyote's roundhouse and, there, had begun to weave the most intricate web imaginable.

Now Weaver Spider knew that Coyote was watching him, and he really showed off. He'd work on a tiny section of web, turning it into miniature landscapes with mountains and plants and creatures running all around. And Coyote just sat there on his butt watching the work in progress and making up little stories to go with each picture.

Yes, Coyote thought, this is very important to watch: I am learning many things in my head.

Weaver Spider was of course doing all this so that Coyote would starve and die. He wanted Coyote's house so he could get married and raise a family. And so he kept weaving to hypnotize Coyote, stopping only to eat an occasional bug. Whenever a bug got stuck in his web, he would sing, "Tee-vee-vee-vee," a song which put the bug to sleep and, so, ready to eat.

"Cousin, you're looking very skinny and sick. And it's sure cold in here!" said Grey Fox when he stopped by one day. Coyote agreed, but insisted that watching Weaver Spider was very important. "I am becoming much smarter," he said.

Grey Fox watched the weaving, but being a practical person, it didn't much move him. Instead he became suspicious of the spider, convinced that he was up to no good.

Grey Fox felt pity for Coyote and went home to get food and his axe for firewood.

Coyote ate the pinenuts and deer jerky while Grey Fox cut firewood. Then Grey Fox built a warming fire and suggested that maybe Coyote wanted to borrow the axe.

But Coyote just sat there, eating up all the food and saying, "Yes, I am becoming much smarter."

Grey Fox got fed-up with this nonsense. He sang a sleep song and a dream song, and soon Coyote was snoring away.

"Now," Grey Fox said to Weaver Spider, "I know you're up to no good. I want you to pack up and leave right now; if you don't, I'm going to have you for a snack." Weaver Spider got scared and quickly left.

Grey Fox tore away the spider's web and woke Coyote up. Coyote looked at the clear sky where the web had been and saw how beautiful it all was. This new clarity, he assured

***Red Man's Path*, Linda Lomahaftewa (Hopi/Choctaw), 1994. Courtesy of the artist.**

his cousin, had been brought about from watching the spider. And again he said, "Yes, I am much smarter now."

Grey Fox was angry with Coyote. "I'm going to make you twice as smart!" he said. "I'm going to give you a wife, then you can have children to pass your great wisdom on to." And Grey Fox picked up his axe and cut Coyote in half, from head to asshole. Then he sang a song and brought the halves alive. The better half turned out to be Coyote Woman.

"Now you are twice as smart," said Grey Fox. And Coyote Woman looked all around, then turned to Coyote, "Why don't you go catch some mice for dinner? And while you're out there, cut some firewood, too."

And Coyote went out to do her bidding. After he'd gone, she turned to me and sort of looked me over before saying, "I suppose you think you'll be winning over women with your cute stories, huh? Well, let me tell you, you got a long way to go yet."

COYOTE MARRIES A MAN

❖ *Plains Cree* ❖

ADAPTED BY BARRY LOPEZ

One time Coyote was going along and he came on a village. There were a lot of people living there and there was plenty to eat so Coyote decided to stay for a while. There was a good-looking man named Not Enough Horses living in the village who wanted to get married but he wouldn't have anything to do with the girls living there. He said they weren't the right kind for him, not good enough.

When Coyote heard this he decided to change himself into a woman and get this man for his husband. He changed himself that way and became very beautiful. He came back into the village on a sled with his tipi and other belongings on it and two wolves pulling it. When Not Enough Horses saw her he liked her right away.

Not Enough Horses told his mother, "My Mother, she is handsome. She's the kind I want. You must invite her over."

The old woman said she would do this. She went over to where the girl was living.

"Niece, you must come over to my house."

"Ho, what for?"

"My son wants to see you."

"I will come then."

"My son desires to marry you," said the old woman.

"You know, so many men wanted to marry me I ran away and came here," said the young woman. "My elder brother said to me, 'Go away'."

"Oh, my son ran away, too, and came here! There were so many women who wanted to marry him. That is why he ran away and came here."

"Oh, that is very interesting," said the young woman.

They went to where the old woman lived and there she saw the young man. He was very handsome. They got married and lived together for some time. Young Woman was a good worker and this made the man happy. Then Young Woman decided to go away. She had had children but she had not let anyone see them. When she left, she left the children behind and when the old woman and her son went in to see them they saw they were wolf puppies.

"Oho!" cried the old woman. "That person was Coyote!"

She was laughing as she wrapped the wolf puppies up in blankets. These were what Not Enough Horses had got for children. All the people in the village were now laughing at him.

They said, "Truly, this is a great thing this man has accomplished. This conceited young man has managed to take a man for his wife! Now we will have something to laugh about!"

They had such a laugh over all this that the young man left the village. He was ashamed.

While he was traveling along he said to himself, "I don't care what sort of woman I

***Chish Yah XV*, Rick Bartow (Yurok), 1992. Courtesy of Froelick Adelhart Gallery, Portland, OR.**

marry, what she looks like. Coyote has put me to such great shame."

In a little while he came to a lodge. He stood outside until the woman inside said, "Come in."

"I have come to take you for my wife," he said.

She was too skinny and not good-looking at all. It was dark inside the lodge and he couldn't see well, but he took that woman for his wife. When they slept together he felt very bad because he could feel how bony she was.

In the morning they loaded up her sled with all the things from her lodge and they left that place. They went back toward his village. He was ashamed of the way this woman looked, but he thought at least no one would laugh at him any more for having married Coyote now that he had married this ugly woman.

When they got into the village, his wife got out of the sled. But she wasn't skinny any more. It was Coyote again.

He said, "Hey, young man, are you the same one who married Coyote that other time?"

Everyone in the village began laughing. Coyote got that young man twice.

White Feather, Duane Slick (Mesquakie/Winnebago), 1993. Courtesy of the artist.

Legend of the White Plume

❖ *Iowa* ❖

Recorded by Alanson Skinner, adapted by Ella Clark

ong ago, near what is now Iowa City, lived a flourishing Iowa Indian tribe. The Chief of the Iowas was very proud of his two beautiful daughters. He was secretly hoping for one of them to marry the handsome hero White Plume, so called because he always wore one in his black hair.

One day, the Chief smeared his daughters' faces with charcoal and took them into the woods for them to fast and pray that one of them might attract the White Plume. The girls were most unhappy, crying until all the animals heard them and came running to find out what was the matter.

Each animal in turn asked, "Am I the one you are looking for?"

"What do you do for a living?" they asked. "What animals do you kill for your food?" In this way they learned the nature of the animals. When the girls said, "No, you are not the one," that animal ran away.

On another day, a man came wearing a white plume. He announced, "Surely I am the one you are seeking. I hunt for deer, elk, bear, turkey, and all the other good things you like to eat."

Without hesitation, Older Sister decided to marry the man-who-wore-the-white-plume. Next morning, Younger Sister said, "You have married the wrong man. Today the real White Plume will come." Older Sister was very cross and declared emphatically that she was certain she had married the true hero, White Plume.

In the middle of that day, birds began to chatter and sing, "White Plume is coming! White Plume is coming!" Even the meadowlarks, whom the Iowas say are really persons in disguise, were broadcasting loudly, "White Plume! White Plume!" Finally White Plume arrived.

"I believe that I am the one you have been seeking," he said to the two sisters.

Older Sister did not believe him, but Younger Sister welcomed him warmly. That same day, the two men each claiming to be White Plume went hunting. The real White Plume killed bear and deer, soon returning with his game.

The other hunter brought back only a few rabbits. Again and again the two men hunted, each returning with the same kind of game as before.

In a few days, the Chief of the Iowas came to visit his daughters. When he judged the results of the hunt, he was convinced that the first man who married Older Sister was an imposter. The Chief believed that the man who was the good provider was the real hero, White Plume.

Older Sister began to have some doubts about her husband, and asked, "Why do you not kill larger game for us?" Her husband gave a poor excuse, "I do not think the larger game provide such good meat."

Again the two men hunted together, arriving in a valley where they saw a raccoon. The imposter tricked White Plume into chasing the raccoon into a bog. Now it happened that the imposter had the power to change people; so he changed White Plume into a dog.

Later, when the imposter returned to his lodge with the dog following him, he announced, "I found this dog in the woods. White Plume must have hunted in a different direction."

That night the dog slept in the lodge of Younger Sister. She fed him and made a comfortable place for him to sleep. Next day she took the dog with her into the woods to look for White Plume.

The dog soon killed a sleeping bear and other animals. Together the girl and dog hunted many times, always with success. One day when they were alone in the woods, the dog said to Younger Sister, "Take me to a hollow log and put me in it, then help pull me out at the other end." This she did. From the other end of the log she pulled out the real White Plume!

When the two of them returned to the lodge, the imposter said to the real White Plume, "You must have been lost in the woods." White Plume's answer was casual but pleasant. Later he told his wife, "Sometime, I will even the score."

In a few days, the two hunters started out for more game. White Plume killed a buffalo. They built a campfire, intending to camp there for the night. A sudden snowstorm came upon them. "Watch yourself," said the imposter. "This kind of a moon will burn your clothes."

That evening, they told many stories at the campfire, after which they prepared their blankets for a good night's sleep. Later in the night, White Plume called out to the imposter, but hearing no response, he quietly exchanged his own clothes, which he used for a pillow, with those of the imposter.

Much later in the night, the imposter awoke and stole the clothes from under White Plume's head and tossed them into the fire.

Next morning was bitter cold. White Plume grabbed for his clothes but they were not under his pillow. "Brother, my clothes are gone," he shouted, shivering with cold.

"Did I not tell you that this is the moon that burns your clothes?" said the imposter. Then he reached for his own clothes, only to discover that they were White Plume's clothes! The imposter had burned his own clothes!

Soon they started for home, with White Plume in the lead dragging the frozen buffalo. Somewhere along the way, the imposter must have frozen to death.

White Plume returned to his wife and Older Sister. He supplied them well with plenty of meat for the entire winter. Then he told them and the Chief of the Iowas that he was really an eagle.

"When your supplies run low, I shall return. When your Iowa hunters wish plenty of game, always they should wear an eagle's white plume in their hair," said White Plume with this parting blessing. Instantly he became a beautiful large eagle and flew far away.

OPPOSITE: *Rage of the Changing Moon*, Margarete Bagshaw-Tindel (O-Je-Gi-Povi), 1994. Courtesy of the artist.

TOLOWIM WOMAN AND BUTTERFLY MAN

❖ *Maidu* ❖

RECORDED BY ROLAND DIXON, ADAPTED BY ALFONSO ORTIZ AND RICHARD ERDOES

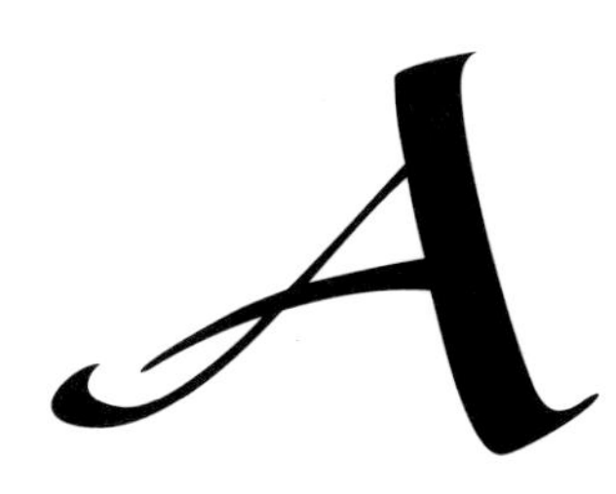

A Tolowim woman went out to gather food. She took her child with her, and while she worked, she stuck the point of the cradleboard in the ground and left the child alone. A large butterfly flew past, and she started after it and chased it for a long time. She would almost catch it, and then just miss. She thought, "Perhaps I can't run fast enough because of this heavy thing," and she threw away her deerskin robe. But still she never could quite overtake the creature. Finally she threw away her apron too and hurried on, chasing the butterfly till night came. Then, her child forgotten, she lay down under a tree and went to sleep.

When she awoke in the morning, she found a man lying beside her. He said, "You have followed me this far; perhaps you would like to follow me always. If so, you must pass through a lot of my people." Without thinking of her child at all, the woman rose and followed the butterfly man. By and by they came to a large valley, whose southern side was full of butterflies. When the two reached the edge of the valley, the man said, "No one has ever before come through this valley alive. But you'll be safe if you don't lose sight of me. Follow closely."

They traveled for a long time. "Keep tight hold of me; don't let go," the butterfly man said again and again. When they came halfway through the valley, other butterflies swarmed about them in great numbers. They flew every way, all around the couple's heads and in their faces, for they wanted to get the Tolowim woman for themselves. She watched them for a long time, holding tightly to her new husband. But at last, unable to resist, she let go of him and reached out to seize one of the others. She missed that one and she tried to grab now one, now the other, but always failed, and so she wandered in the valley forever, dazed and lost.

She died there, and the butterfly man she had lost went on through the valley to his home. And now when people speak of the olden times they say that this woman lost her lover, and tried to get others but lost them, and went crazy and died.

RIGHT: ***Man's Butterfly Luck Charm*** **(Crow). Courtesy of America Hurrah Archive, New York, NY.**

OPPOSITE: ***Butterfly Maiden Kachina*** **(Hopi). Courtesy of The Denver Art Museum, Denver, CO.**

Coyote and the Woman

❖ *Coeur d'Alene* ❖

Told by Lawrence Aripa, adapted by Rodney Frey

One time, . .
a long time ago, . . .
the Coyote . . was out enjoying himself, . .
and he . . running up the
Spokane River, . .
really having fun . .
He was running in the . . *sand*
on the rocks,
and just enjoying himself,
really having a good time . . .

And all of a sudden . . he stops, . .
and he sees a camp . . .
And there are tipis
and smoke
and people *all* over . .
And he looked, . .
and on the shore . . there was a group
of . . people . .
Some were fishing.
Some were cleaning fish . .
And he watched.
And as he watched,
he saw them,
really busy
cleaning a *lot* of fish
They were preparing for the winter.
So they had a *lot* of fish that they were
cleaning . .
And as they cleaned
there was . . one young lady . . that
stood out . .
The Coyote kept looking at her.
And as he looked he says,
"Oh my gosh . . that is the most
beautiful creature that I have
ever seen! . ."
And as he watches, . .
the other women and the men . . are
all singing.
They are singing because they are happy
that they have enough fish . . for the
winter . . .
They come here every year to *fish*
and get a lot of fish for the winter . . .
And so they were happy,
as they sang,
and as they worked . . .

And the Coyote,
he couldn't keep his eyes off this
beautiful creature . . .
He kept watching her,
her movements were something . .
were something to look at.
And he just kept watching her,
and watching.

Fish in the Hand is Worth Two in the Bush,
George C. Longfish (Seneca/Tuscarora), 1985. Courtesy of the artist.

And finally he couldn't stand it anymore . . .
So he runs into the camp, . .
and he asks for the chief . . .
And he tells the chief, . .
"I have seen the most beautiful woman
that I have ever . . set my eyes on, . .
and I want her . . .
I want her to be mine forever!" . .
The chief looked at him with a surprised look
and he started to laugh . . .
And then . . the Coyote says,
"What are you laughing at?
What is so funny?" . .
The chief says,
"You are a *coyote*!
You are not *human* . . .
You can't take care of a human being.
You are only a *coyote*!" . .
And the Coyote says,
"Well, . . what I can do is
I can . . *dance*
and I can pray
and the Great Animal
Spirit . . will change
me . . .
He will change me into a handsome . .
man."
But the chief says
"No-o-ho . . no-o!"
He says, . .
"You know,
I know,
and my daughter knows, . .
that you are a *coyote* . . .
You'll *always* be a coyote.
And . . *no* that can't happen!"
So he says,
"No,
you get out.
Leave this camp.
Don't bother us." . .

So the Coyote left the camp.
But he was angry . . .
and he says,
"I have to have that woman.
I have to have her." . .
He says,
"I will get the help from *another*
tribe." . .

So he goes to the Kalispel . . .
And he tells the Kalispel, . .
"You people . . you fish on the river, . .
and you get salmon."
And the Kalispel chief says,
"Yes we do.
We go there
and we join the . . Spokanes,
and the Coeur d'Alenes,
and we all get salmon
There is enough salmon for everybody."
And the Coyote says
"Well, . . I want to ask a favor . . .
I will bring you *more* salmon if you will
help me.
Go and talk to the Coeur d'Alene
chief, . .
and tell him to let me have his daughter,
let me have that beautiful creature."
And the Kalispel chief started to laugh.
He laughed and laughed.
And the Coyote says
"What are you laughing about?" . .
And he says
"You are a *coyote*!
You can't marry a human!"
And the Coyote says
"I will change myself to a handsome . .
man!"

And then the Kalispel chief says, . .
"*Well* I will *know* that you are a coyote.
You'll *always* be a coyote.
No, . . I won't help you."
So he goes to the Spokane tribe . . .
And he tells the Spokane chief,
"You fish out of the same river as the
Kalispel
and the Coeur d'Alene . . .
You get a lot of salmon . . .
If you will help me
I will get you more salmon!" . .
And so the chief says
"Well how can you do that?"
And he says
"I have the power,
and I can do it." . .

***Salmon Tale*, Rick Bartow (Yurok), 1995. Courtesy of Froelick Adelhart Gallery, Portland, OR.**

And he says
"All I want you to do is *help* me." . .
And the Spokane chief says
"What is it you want?" . .
He says
"I want that *woman*.
I want that beautiful woman as my mate." . .
And the Spokane chief . . began to
laugh . .
He laughed and he laughed.
And the Coyote got angry.

And other . . people from the council *came* in.
And the Spokane chief told them what the
Coyote had said,
and *they* started to laugh.
They laugh and laugh.

And he left the camp while they were still
laughing . . .

And so . . he says
"I will teach them.
I will teach them a lesson . .
They can't laugh at me."
He says
"That isn't right.
But I'm going to have that woman." . .

So he goes
and he started *praying*
and he *dances*
and then . . he asks for the
Great Animal Spirit . .
All of a sudden the Animal Spirit appears,
and he says
"Yes, . . what is it?" . .
And the Coyote says, . .
"You owe me a favor, . .
and I am asking for it now." . .
And so . . the Animal Spirit says
"*What* is it?" . .
He says
"I want you to give me . . the power of
strength . . .
I want to be *strong*,
and be able to . . move about . . in
the *air*
and everything." . .
And so the Animal Spirit didn't know what
it was for.
So he says
"Yes, . . you can." . .

And so . . the Coyote . . . went to the
rocks
he went to the mountains
He got big rocks, . .
he got mud, . .
dirt, . .
little rocks.
And he moved them *all* to the river . . .
He pushed them into the river,
and by doing that he created . . *falls*, . .
he created Spokane Falls,
Post Falls.
He created other *streams*,
that run away from the river . . .
And then . . he went back to the . .
Coeur d'Alene chief . . .
And he says
"There are no more salmon coming up
that river . . .
And the only way to get salmon
again . . is to let me have your
daughter." . .
And the Coeur d'Alene chief says
"No-o-o! . .
It is not possible
and I will not do it!" . .
And so . . the Coyote says
"Well, . . you will not have any
salmon . . .
You will no longer have salmon until . .
you tell me I can have her,
then I will let the salmon come
back up again.
Otherwise . . you will not get
salmon." . .

And as he started to leave
a young man
who had been . . more or less courting the
young lady
he too was a very important man,
he was part of the chief's line,
and so he followed the Coyote . . .

And so . . the Coeur d'Alene chief . .
waited and waited.
He says,
"He will not . . keep the fish from us
We will get it." . .
But there was no sign of the Coyote . .
And the Chief says
"When he comes back
we will tell him no
We can't do it." . .
And then the people started to talk . . .
"We have no fish.
The fish stopped coming . . .
We need *more* fish, . .
and we must get it." . .
So the chief says
"Well, . . the next time the Coyote
comes back
then we will talk.
And maybe something can be worked
out." . .

But they waited, . .
and waited . . .
And the young man
who had been *courting* . . the lady . .
never said anything
but he was glad
He was walking around *smiling*
and dancing
and being *happy* . . .

And all of a sudden word came
they found the Coyote.
He was dead . . .

And so the spell was never taken away . . .
And to this day, . .
the Coeur d'Alenes,
the Spokanes,
the Kalispels,
the Colvilles,
we . . have . . no . .
salmon . . .
The Coyote never came back.
And he never broke the spell.
So ever since then . . . we have no more
salmon. . . .

"An-tu-terq'w" Spring Salmon **(Colville/Puyallup). Courtesy of Thomas Burke Memorial Washington State Museum, Seattle, WA.**

BUFFALO WOMAN, A STORY OF MAGIC

❖ *Caddo* ❖

ADAPTED BY DEE BROWN

now Bird, the Caddo medicine man, had a handsome son. When the boy was old enough to be given a man's name, Snow Bird called him Braveness because of his courage as a hunter. Many of the girls in the Caddo village wanted to win Braveness as a husband, but he paid little attention to any of them.

One morning he started out for a day of hunting, and while he was walking along looking for wild game, he saw someone ahead of him sitting under a small elm tree. As he approached, he was surprised to find that the person was a young woman, and he started to turn aside.

"Come here," she called to him in a pleasant voice. Braveness went up to her and saw that she was very young and very beautiful.

"I knew you were coming here," she said, "and so I came to meet you."

"You are not of my people," he replied. "How did you know that I was coming this way?"

"I am Buffalo Woman," she said. "I have seen you many times before, from afar. I want you to take me home with you and let me stay with you."

"I can take you home with me," Braveness answered her, "but you must ask my parents if you can stay with us."

They started for his home at once, and when they arrived there Buffalo Woman asked Braveness's parents if she could stay with them and become the young man's wife. "If Braveness wants you for his wife, we will be pleased," said Snow Bird, the medicine man. "It is time that he had someone to love."

And so Braveness and Buffalo Woman were married in the custom of the Caddo people and lived happily together for several moons. One day she asked him, "Will you do whatever I may ask of you, Braveness?"

"Yes," he replied, "if what you ask is not unreasonable."

"I want you to go with me to visit my people."

Braveness said that he would go, and the next day they started for her home, she leading the way. After they had walked a long distance they came to some high hills, and all at once she turned round and looked at Braveness and said: "You promised me that you would do anything I say."

"Yes," he answered.

"Well," she said, "my home is on the other side of this high hill. I will tell you when we get to my mother. I know there will be many coming there to see who you are, and some may provoke you and try to make you angry, but do not allow yourself to become angry

OPPOSITE: ***Beginning of New Warmth*, Dan Lomahaftewa (Hopi/Choctaw), 1992. Courtesy of Jan Cicero Gallery, Chicago, IL.**

with any of them. Some may try to kill you."

"Why should they do that?" asked Braveness.

"Listen to what I am about to tell you," she said. "I knew you before you knew me. Through magic I made you come to me that first day. I said that some will try to make you angry, and if you show anger at even one of them, the others will join in fighting you until they have killed you. They will be jealous of you. The reason is that I refused many who wanted me."

"But you are now my wife," Braveness said.

"I have told you what to do when we get there," Buffalo Woman continued. "Now I want you to lie down on the ground and roll over twice."

Braveness smiled at her, but he did as she had told him to do. He rolled over twice, and when he stood up he found himself changed into a Buffalo.

For a moment Buffalo Woman looked at him, seeing the astonishment in his eyes. Then she rolled over twice, and she also became a Buffalo. Without saying a word she led him to the top of the hill. In the valley off to the west, Braveness could see hundreds and hundreds of Buffalo.

"They are my people," said Buffalo Woman. "This is my home."

When the members of the nearest herd saw Braveness and Buffalo Woman coming, they began gathering in one place, as though waiting for them. Buffalo Woman led the way, Braveness following her until they reached an old Buffalo cow, and he knew that she was the mother of his beautiful wife.

***Buffalo Kachina Doll* (Hopi). San Diego Museum of Man, San Diego, CA.**

For two moons they stayed with the herd. Every now and then, four or five of the young Buffalo males would come around and annoy Braveness, trying to arouse his anger, but he pretended not to notice them. One night, Buffalo Woman told him that she was ready to go back to his home, and they slipped away over the hills.

When they reached the place where they had turned themselves into Buffalo, they rolled over twice on the ground and became a man and woman again. "Promise me that you will not tell anyone of this magical transformation," Buffalo Woman said. "If people learn about it, something bad will happen to us."

They stayed at Braveness's home for twelve moons, and then Buffalo Woman asked him again to go with her to visit her people. They had not been long in the valley of the Buffalo when she told Braveness that the young males who were jealous of him were planning to have a foot-race. "They will challenge you to race and if you do not outrun them they will kill you," she said.

That night Braveness could not sleep. He went out to take a long walk. It was a very dark night without moon or stars, but he could feel the presence of the Wind spirit.

"You are young and strong," the Wind spirit whispered to him, "but you cannot outrun the Buffalo without my help. If you lose, they will kill you. If you win, they will never challenge you again."

"What must I do to save my life and keep my beautiful wife?" asked Braveness.

The Wind spirit gave him two things. "One of these is a magic herb," said the Wind spirit. "The other is dried mud from a medicine wallow. If the Buffalo catch up with you, first throw behind you the magic herb. If they come too close to you again, throw down the dried mud."

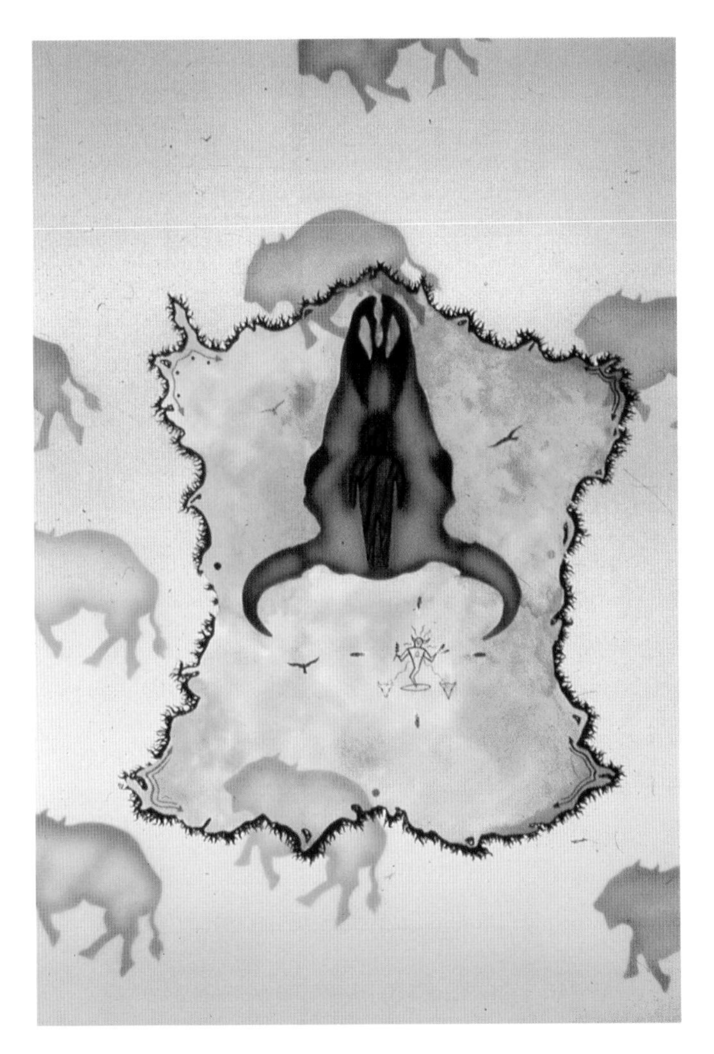

Buffalo Days, Buffalo Nights, **Jeffrey Chapman (Ojibwa), 1992. Courtesy of the artist.**

The next day was the day of the race. At sunrise the young Buffalo gathered at the starting place. When Braveness joined them, they began making fun of him, telling him he was a man-buffalo and therefore had not the power to outrun them. Braveness ignored their jeers, and calmly lined up with them at the starting point.

An old Buffalo started the race with a loud bellow, and at first Braveness took the lead, running very swiftly. But soon the others began gaining on him, and when he heard their hard breathing close upon his heels, he threw the magic herb behind him. By this time he was growing very tired and thought he could not run anymore. He looked back and saw one Buffalo holding his head down and coming very fast, rapidly closing the space between him and Braveness. Just as this Buffalo was about to catch up with him, Braveness threw down the dried mud from the medicine wallow.

Soon he was far ahead again, but he knew that he had used up the powers given by the Wind spirit. As he neared the goal set for the race, he heard the pounding of hooves coming closer behind him. At the last moment, he felt a strong wind on his face as it passed him to stir up dust and keep the Buffalo from overtaking him. With the help of the Wind spirit, Braveness crossed the goal first and won the race. After that, none of the Buffalo ever challenged him again, and he and Buffalo Woman lived peacefully with the herd until they were ready to return to his Caddo people.

Not long after their return to Braveness's home, Buffalo Woman gave birth to a handsome son. They named him Buffalo Boy, and soon he was old enough to play with the other children of the village. One day while Buffalo Woman was cooking dinner, the boy slipped out of the lodge and went to join some other children at play. They played several games and then decided to play that they were Buffalo. Some of them lay on the ground to roll like Buffalo, and Buffalo Boy also did this. When he rolled over twice, he changed into a real Buffalo calf. Frightened by this, the other children ran for their lodges.

About this time his mother came out to look for him, and when she saw the children running in fear she knew that something must be wrong. She went to see what had happened and found her son changed into a Buffalo calf. Taking him up in her arms, she ran down the hill, and as soon as she was out of sight of the village she turned herself into a Buffalo and with Buffalo Boy started off toward the west.

Late that evening when Braveness returned from hunting he could find neither his wife nor his son in the lodge. He went out to look for them, and someone told him of the game the children had played and of the magic that had changed his son into a Buffalo calf.

At first, Braveness could not believe what they told him, but after he had followed his wife's tracks down the hill and found the place where she had rolled he knew the story was true. For many moons, Braveness searched for Buffalo Woman and Buffalo Boy, but he never found them again.

THE LOON STORY

❖ Tanaina (Dena'ina) ❖

ADAPTED BY BILL VAUDRIN

There was an old blind man in the village who had a wife and one son. They had to lead him around everywhere he went. He could see a little outside on a bright day, but not inside or in the dark.

One morning he said to his wife, "Let's go into the woods and hunt. Maybe you'll get a spruce chicken or something."

Game was scarce and they had to go a long way from the village. After a three-day trip the family made camp in some flat country far from home.

Unknown to the rest of the village, the woman had been starving her husband for a long time. Many of the people had been giving her what food they could spare, because they knew her husband couldn't hunt any more and they respected him. However, the old man never got any of the food. She cooked it for herself and the boy, and threw her husband the bones. Since he was blind, he never knew. He just figured that times were hard and food was scarce.

One day while they were in camp his wife said to him, "Let's go for a walk in the woods."

"You know I'm blind," he said. "How can I walk in the woods, when I can't see?"

"We'll guide you," she said.

So they walked out of their little camp and hiked way off into the woods. By and by she told him to sit down on a stump to rest.

"Let's leave your daddy there for a while," she whispered to the little boy. "We'll come back for him after he's rested."

Then she took the boy and started for home.

After a while the old man began to suspect that she had abandoned him. He was hungry, so he took out some dry fish eggs that he had in his pocket and ate them. That filled him up, but now he was thirsty. He couldn't see anything, so he got down on his hands and knees and began crawling along the ground in search of water.

He didn't know how long he crawled, because he couldn't tell the difference between night and day, but he was terribly tired and hungry and thirsty, and it was cold and damp on the ground. Once he thought he could see daylight.

When his thirst was getting so bad he thought he would die the old man heard a loon. So he turned and began crawling in

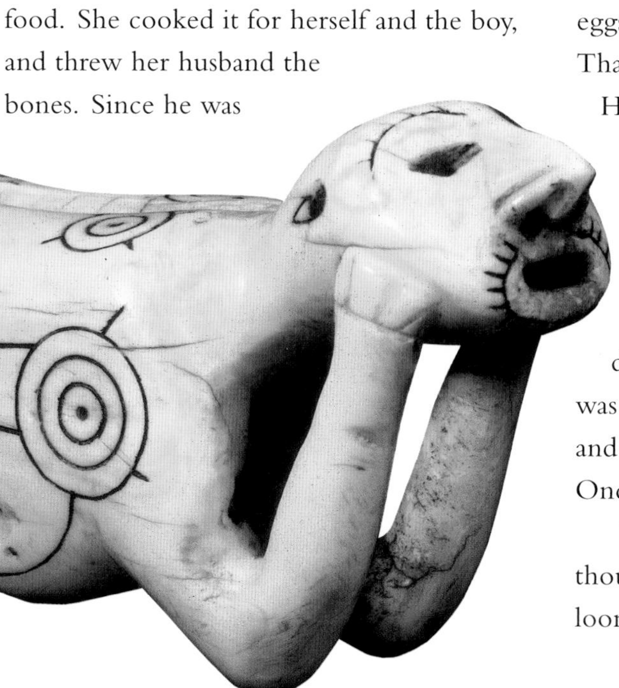

Toggle **(Southwestern Eskimo). Thaw Collection, Fenimore House Museum, Cooperstown, NY.**

the direction of the sound. Soon he felt stones under him like on a beach, and at last he came to water. As he put his face down into the water and began drinking, he felt ripples on the surface and knew that the loon was coming toward him. He finished drinking and waited. Finally, the loon came near him on the beach, and as it stepped out of the water it turned into a man.

Shell Bird Effigy **(Santo Domingo Pueblo). From the Collection of the Dayton Museum of Natural History, Dayton, OH.**

"What's the trouble?" he asked the blind old-timer.

So the old man told him his story.

"Here," said the loon-man coming closer. "Put your head under my arm."

As the old man did this, the loon jumped back into the lake and began swimming around. When he had circled it three times he dived underwater, pulling the old man down with him.

When they came up, the loon let go of him and said, "Now, open your eyes and take a look."

"I can see," said the old man. "But not good."

So the loon did the same thing again. He swam around the lake two or three times with the old man under his arm, then dived. When they surfaced that time, the old man could see clearly.

"What should I do now?" he asked.

"Take your little boy and leave your wife," was the answer.

"Well," said the old-timer, "I feel sorry for her, but I guess she doesn't feel sorry for me."

So he thanked the loon and headed back for camp. Just before he got there he stopped and whittled out a birch cane. Then he stumbled into camp pretending that he still couldn't see.

When the little boy saw him coming, he was happy and ran to meet him. But the wife was irritated and wondered how he ever found his way home.

"I'm thirsty," said the old man. "Give me a drink of water."

His wife went to fetch him water out of an old stagnant basin full of bugs. When she brought him a cup, however, he looked at it and said, "Here! I'd like to see you drink this."

His wife was stunned. "How did you know?" she asked.

"I can see just as good as you can now," he said.

She was really mad, but the boy was happy over it.

"Do you want to stay with your mother?" the old man asked him. "Or would you rather come along with me?"

The boy wanted to go with his father, so the two of them headed back to the village together.

When they arrived, the people wondered how he got back his sight, so he told his story to them, and they were all happy for him and angry with the wife.

Later, when she came back to the village complaining because he had thrown her out, nobody felt sorry for her, and from then on she didn't get along very well with the people.

The old man and his boy were always happy, however, and both of them made it a point never to shoot loons after that.

MEN AND WOMEN TRY LIVING APART

❖ *Sia* ❖

RECORDED BY MATILDA COX STEVENSON, ADAPTED BY RICHARD ERDOES AND ALFONSO ORTIZ

efore Ut'set, Mother of the People, left this world, she selected six Sia women and sent one to the north, one to the west, one to the south, one to the east, one to the zenith, and one to the nadir, and told them to make their homes at these points for all time. That way they would be near the cloud rulers of the cardinal points, and they could intercede for all the people of Ha'arts. Ut'set told her people to remember these women in times of need, and they would appeal to the cloud people for them.

***Four Directions*, Linda Lomahaftewa (Hopi/Choctaw), 1990. Courtesy of the artist.**

The Sia alone followed the command of Ut'set and took the straight road, while all other pueblos advanced by various routes to the center of the earth. After Ut'set's departure the Sia traveled some distance and built a village of beautiful white stone, where they lived, declared, for a long duration. At one time all the parents suffered tragically at the hand of the *ti'amoni*, who, objecting to the increase of his people, caused all children to be put to death. The Sia had scarcely recovered from this calamity when another serious difficulty arose.

The Sia women worked hard all day, grinding meal and singing; and at sundown, when the men returned to the houses, the women would often abuse them, saying: "You are no good; you do not care to work. All you want to do is be with women all the time. If you would allow four days to pass between, the women would care more for you."

The men replied: "You women really want to be with us all day and all night. If you could have the men only every four days, you would be very unhappy."

The women retorted: "It is you men who would be unhappy if you could be with the women only every four days."

And the fight grew angrier and angrier. The men cried: "Were it ten days, twenty days, thirty days that we remained apart from you, we'd never be unhappy." The women replied: "We think not, but we women would be very contented to remain away from you men for sixty days." And the men said: "We men would be happy to remain apart from you women for five moons." The women, growing more excited, cried: "You do not speak the truth; we women would be contented to be separated from you ten moons." The men retorted: "We men could remain away from you women twenty moons and be very happy." "You do not speak the truth," said the women," for you wish to be with us all the time, day and night."

Three days they quarreled and on the fourth day the women finally took themselves to one side of the pueblo, while the men and boys gathered on the other side, each forming their own kiva, or ceremonial chamber. The women had a great talk and the men held a council. They were both furious with one another.

The *ti'amoni*, who presided over the council, said: "Perhaps you will each be contented if you and the women try living apart." And on the following morning he had all the men and male children who were not being nourished by their mothers cross the great river which ran by the village, the women remaining in the village. The men departed at sunrise, and the women were delighted. They said: "We can do all the work; we understand the men's work and we can work like them." The men said to each other: "We can do the things the women did for us." As they left the village the men called to the women: "We leave you to yourselves, perhaps for one year, perhaps for two, and perhaps longer. Who knows how it will work out? After all, men are not so amorous as you."

It took a long time for the men to cross the river, as it was very wide. The *ti'amoni* led the men and remained with them. The women were compelled by the *ti'amoni* to send their male infants over the river as soon as they ceased nourishing them. For two moons the men and women were very happy. The men were busy hunting and had all the game they could eat, but the women had no animal food. The men grew stout and the women very thin. At the expiration of the first ten moons, some of the women were sad away from the men. As the second year passed, more of the women wanted the men, but the men seemed perfectly satisfied with the way things were. After three years the women more and more wished for the men, but the men were only slightly desirous of the women.

When the fourth year was half gone, the women called to the *ti'amoni*, saying, "We want the men to come to us." The female children had grown up like reeds; they had no flesh on them. The morning after the women begged the *ti'amoni* for the return of the men, they recrossed the river to live again with the women, and in four days after their return the women had recovered their flesh.

***The Four Directions; Vision*, Kay WalkingStick (Cherokee/Winnebago), 1995. Courtesy of the artist.**

ÖGWEHÖWE:KA:?
Jemison

Children and Community

❖ ❖ ❖ ❖ ❖

Marriage produces family, and family enlarges and extends into community. And the complexities of community, the needs it fulfills, and the obligations it carries are considered in the stories here. Sometimes the community is threatened, as is the case in the poignant story of "Stone Boy," who not only restores the uncles to his family, but also learns and transmits the lessons of the sweat lodge, the sacred rituals and ceremonies that may be used "for purification, for life, for *wichosani*, for health." By following these ceremonies, people preserve life and become a tribe. When bands join together to form a tribe or a confederation, people must first learn, above all, to treat words as sacred. Then they need law and government and a place in which to hold council; these are the concerns facing Hiawatha and Deganawidah in "The Origin of the Long House."

Although any community will include members who are, by nature, mean, and who hurt others, in the Coeur d'Alene community, this selfishness results in exile and in the tribe's testing of "Cosechin" to see just how much he is able to survive without the help of others. We learn from "Cosechin" how much we need other people: how we need a community to come from and live in, and how thoroughly loneliness can change someone's behavior. But Cosechin's realization that he needs his people only changes him temporarily; he reverts to his old ways and it is then that he disappears. No one ever does find out what happens to him. The story suggests that without an ability to participate in the community, Cosechin is gone, and forever. Whoever does not participate positively is not only lost but loses his or her identity and function, his or her ability to survive.

The powerful poem "Tongue" underscores the need for speaking rightly and well. It emphasizes the need for understanding, and for the separation that comes when the people who are transformed and restored through one man's careful adherence to ritual fail to appreciate what he has done. The people respond out of ignorance and scold the restorative hero until his "heart" becomes "bad," and his mother must tell them, "Now we shall make our separation." It is also separation, perhaps, that in "The Legend of Godasiyo" explains how strife and argument cause the people to divide into different tribes, speaking different languages, unable to understand each other.

Ultimately, in the Native American world, community is, if not everything, then most everything. Even though an individual like Swift-Runner can, through youthful ignorance or by accident, lose his sacred costumes to a trickster tarantula, the community can still join to restore and preserve their rituals, their sacred costumes and ceremonies, and their identities. Beauty matters, and sometimes that beauty comes from following communal ideals, such as those of the Laguna people and their relation to the sun. Finally, in "First Eagle Story," two youthful boys, who do not understand the seriousness of transformation, fall into trouble and need the strength and help of their elders to keep them alive.

OPPOSITE: ***Ongwehonwekaa (Indian Way of Life)*, G. Peter Jemison (Cattaraugus/Seneca), 1993. Courtesy of the artist.**

STONE BOY

❖ *Brule Sioux* ❖

TOLD BY HENRY CROW DOG, RECORDED BY RICHARD ERDOES

ack in the great days of the Indians, a maiden and her five brothers lived together. People in those times had to look for food; it was their main occupation. So while the sister cooked and made clothes, the brothers spent their days hunting.

It happened once that this family moved their tipi to the bottom of a canyon. It was a strange, silent place, but there was water in a creek and the hunting was good. The canyon was cool in the summer and shielded from wind in the winter. Still, when the brothers went out hunting, the girl was always waiting for them. Waiting and listening, she heard noises. Often she thought they were footsteps, but when she looked outside, no one was there.

Then one evening, only four of the five brothers came back from hunting. They and the sister stayed awake all night, wondering what could have happened to the other. The next day when the men went hunting, only three returned. Again they and the sister stayed awake wondering. The next evening only two came home, and they and the girl were afraid.

In those early days the Indians had no sacred ceremonies or prayers to guide them, so it was hard for the maiden and her two brothers to watch through the night in that ghostly place. Again the brothers went out in the morning, and only a single one returned at night. Now the girl cried and begged him to stay home. But they had to eat, and so in the morning her last and youngest brother, whom she loved best of all, went out to hunt. Like the others, he did not come back. Now no one would bring the maiden food or water, or protect her.

Weeping, the girl left the canyon and climbed to the top of a hill. She wanted to die, but did not know how to. Then she saw a round pebble lying on the ground. Thinking that it would kill her, she picked it up and swallowed it.

With peace in her heart the maiden went back to the tipi. She drank some water and felt a stirring inside her, as if the rock were telling her not to worry. She was comforted, though she could not sleep for missing her brothers.

The next day she had nothing left to eat except some pemmican and berries. She meant to eat them and drink water from the creek, but she found she wasn't hungry. She felt as if she had been to a feast, and walked around singing to herself. The following day she was happy in a way she had never been before.

On the fourth day that the girl had been alone, she felt pain. "Now the end comes," she thought. "Now I die." She didn't mind; but instead of dying, she gave birth to a little boy.

"What will I do with this child?" she wondered. "How did it come? It must be that stone I swallowed."

The child was strong, with shining eyes. Though the girl felt weak for a while, she had

***Hunter*, Joe Herrera (Cochiti), 1954. Museum of Indian Arts & Culture/Laboratory of Anthropology, Santa Fe, NM.**

to keep going to care for the new life, her son. She named him Iyan Hokshi, Stone Boy, and wrapped him in her brothers' clothes. Day after day he grew, ten times faster than ordinary infants, and with a more perfect body.

The mother knew that her baby had great powers. One day when he was playing outside the tipi, he made a bow and arrows, all on his own. Looking at his flint arrowhead, the mother wondered how he had done it. "Maybe he knows that he was a stone and I swallowed him," she thought. "He must have a rock nature."

The baby grew so fast that he was soon walking. His hair became long, and as he matured his mother became afraid that she would lose him as she had lost her brothers. She cried often, and though he did not ask why, he seemed to know.

Very soon he was big enough to go hunting, and when she saw this, his mother wept more than ever. Stone Boy come into the tipi.

"Mother, don't cry," he said.

"You used to have five uncles," she said. "But they went out hunting. One after another, they did not come back." And she told him about his birth, how she had gone to the top of the hill and swallowed a stone, and how she had felt something moving inside her.

"I know," he said. "And I am going to look for your brothers, my uncles."

"But if you don't return," she sobbed, "what will I do?"

"I will come back," he told her. "I will come back with my uncles. Stay in the tipi until I do."

So the next morning Iyan Hokshi started walking and watching. He kept on till dusk, when he found a good place to sleep. He wandered for four days, and on the evening of the fourth day he smelled smoke. Iyan Hokshi, this Stone Boy, he followed the smell. It led him to a tipi with smoke coming from its smoke hole.

This tipi was ugly and ramshackle. Inside Iyan Hokshi could see an old woman who was ugly too. She watched him pass and, calling him over, invited him to eat and stay the night.

Stone Boy went into the tipi, though he was uneasy in his mind, and a little timid. He looked around and saw five big bundles, propped up on end, leaning against the tipi wall. And he wondered.

The old woman was cooking some meat. When it was done he ate it, though it didn't taste good. Later she fixed a dirty old buffalo robe for him to sleep on, but he sensed danger and felt wide awake.

"I have a backache," the woman said. "Before you go to sleep, I wish you would rub it for me by walking up and down my back. I am old and alone, and I have nobody to help with my pain."

She lay down, and Stone Boy began walking on her back. As he did, he felt something sticking up under her buckskin robe, something sharp like a knife or a needle or the point of a spear. "Maybe she used this sharp tool to kill my uncles," he thought. "Maybe she put poison from a snake on its point. Yes, that must be so."

Doll **(Cheyenne). Courtesy of America Hurrah Archive, New York, NY.**

Iyan Hokshi, having pondered, jumped high in the air, as high as he could, and came down on the old woman's back with a crash. He jumped and jumped until he was exhausted and the hag was lying dead with a broken back.

Then Iyan Hokshi walked over to the big bundles, which were wrapped in animal hides and lashed together with rawhide thongs. He unwrapped them and found five men, dead and dried like jerked meat, hardly human-looking. "These must be my uncles," he thought, but he didn't know how to bring them back to life.

Outside the ugly tipi was a heap of rocks, round gray stones. He found that they were talking and that he could understand them. "Iyan Hokshi, Stone Boy, you are one of us, you come from us, you come from Tunka, you come from Iyan. Listen; pay attention."

Following their instructions, he built a little dome-like hut out of bent willow sticks. He covered it with the old woman's buffalo robes and put the five dead, dried-up humans inside. Out in the open he built a big fire. He set the rocks right in the flames, picked up the old woman, and threw her in to burn up.

After the rocks glowed red-hot, Stone Boy found a deer antler and used it to carry them one by one into the little hut he had made. He picked up the old woman's water bag, a buffalo bladder decorated with quillwork, and filled it with water. He drew its rawhide tie tight and took it inside too. Then he placed the dried humans around him in a circle.

Iyan Hokshi closed the entrance of his little lodge with a flap of buffalo robe, so that no air could escape or enter. Pouring water from the bag over them, he thanked the rocks, saying, "You brought me here." Four times he poured the water; four times he opened the flap and closed it. Always he spoke to the rocks and they to him. As he poured, the little lodge filled with steam so that he could see nothing but the white mist in the darkness. When he poured water a second time, he sensed a stirring. When he poured the third time, he began to sing. And when he poured the fourth time, those dead, dried-up things also began to sing and talk.

"I believe they have come to life," thought Iyan Hokshi, the Stone Boy. "Now I want to see my uncles."

He opened the flap for the last time, watching the steam flow out and rise into the sky as a feathery cloud. The bonfire and the moonlight both shone into the little sweat lodge, and by their light he saw five good-looking young men sitting inside. He said, "*Hou, lekshi,* you must be my uncles." They smiled and laughed, happy to be alive again.

He also told them: "The rock saved me, and now it has saved you. Iyan, Tunka—rock—Tunka, Iyan. Tunkashila, the Grandfather Spirit, we will learn to worship. This little lodge, these rocks, the water, the fire—these are sacred, these we will use from now on as we have done here for the first time: for purification, for life, for *wichosani*, for health. All this has been given to us so that we may live. We shall be a tribe."

***Blue Shadow Spirit*,**
Frank LaPena
(Wintu/Nomtipom), 1991.
Courtesy of American
Indian Contemporary Arts,
San Francisco, CA.

THE ORIGIN OF THE LONG HOUSE

❖ *Seneca* ❖

TOLD BY DELOS B. KITTLE, ADAPTED BY ARTHUR PARKER, EDITED BY W. S. PENN

Chief Big Kittle relates the following story of the origin of the League of the Five Nations.

Where the Mohawk river empties into the Hudson in ancient times there was a Mohawk village. The people there were fierce and warlike and were continually sending out war parties against other villages and returning would bring back long strings of scalps to number the lives they had destroyed. But sometimes they left their own scalps behind and never returned. They loved warfare better than all other things and were happy when their hands were slimy with blood. They boasted that they would eat up all other nations and so they continued to fight against other tribes.

Now among the Mohawks was a chief named Dekana-wi'da, a very wise man, and he was very sad of heart because his people loved war too well. So he spoke in council and implored them to stop. But the young warriors did not hear him. They laughed at his words, but he did not cease to warn them. At last, despairing of moving them by ordinary means, he turned his face to the west, weeping as he journeyed away from his people. At last he came to a lake whose shores were fringed with bushes, and being tired he lay down to rest. As he lay there, he heard the soft spattering of water sliding from a skillful paddle, and peering out from his hiding place, he saw in the red light of sunset a man leaning over his canoe and dipping into the shallow water with a basket. When he raised it up, it was full of shells, the shells of the periwinkles that live in shallow pools. The man pushed his canoe toward the shore and sat down on the beach where he kindled a fire. Then he began to string his shells and finishing a string would touch the shells and talk. Then, as if satisfied, he would lay it down and make another until he had a large number. Dekana-wi'da watched the strange proceeding with wonder. The sun had long since set but Dekana-wi'da still watched the man with the shell strings sitting in the flickering light of the fire that shadowed the bushes and shimmered over the lake.

After some deliberation he called out, "Kwe, I am a friend!" and stepping out upon the sand stood before the man with the shells. "I am Dekana-wi'da," he said, "and come from the Mohawk."

"I am Haiowent'ha of the Onondaga," came the reply.

Then Dekana-wi'da inquired about the shell strings, for he was very curious to know their import and Haiowent'ha answered, "They are the rules of life and laws of good government. This all white string is a sign of truth, peace and good will; this black string is a sign of hatred, of war and of a bad heart; the string with the alternate beads, black and white, is a sign that peace should exist between the nations. This string with white on either end and black in the middle is a sign that wars must end and peace be declared." And so

Water, **Leatrice Mikkelsen (Navajo), 1992. Courtesy of the College of Wooster Art Museum, Wooster, OH.**

Haiowent'ha lifted his strings and read the laws.

Then said Dekana-wi'da, "You are my friend indeed, and the friend of all nations. Our people are weak from warring and weak from being warred upon. We who speak one tongue should combine against the Hadiondas instead of helping them by killing one another, but my people are weary of my advising and would not hear me."

"I, too, am of the same mind," said Haiowent'ha, "but Tatodaho slew all my brothers and drove me away. So I came to the lakes and have made the laws that should govern men and nations. I believe that we should be as brothers in a family instead of enemies."

"Then come with me," said Dekana-wi'da, "and together let us go back to my people and explain the rules and laws."

So when they returned, Dekana-wi'da called a council of all the chiefs and warriors and the women, and Haiowent'ha set forth the plan he had devised. The words had a marvelous effect. The people were astonished at the wisdom of the strange chief from the Onondaga, and when he had finished his exposition, the chiefs promised to obey his laws. They delegated Dekana-wi'da to go with him to the Oneida and council with them, then go onward to Onondaga and win over the arrogant, erratic Tatodaho, the tyrannical chief of the

Gustoweh or Cap **(Iroquois). Courtesy of W. E. Channing & Co., Santa Fe, NM.**

Onondaga. Thus it was that together they went to the Oneida country and won over their great chief and made the people promise to support the proposed league. Then the Oneida chief went with Haiowent'ha to the Cayugas and told them how by supporting the league they might preserve themselves against the fury of Tatodaho. So when the Cayuga had promised allegiance, Dekana-wi'da turned his face toward Onondaga, and with his comrades went before Tatodaho. Now when Tatodaho learned how three nations had combined against him, he became very angry and ran into the forest where he gnawed at his fingers and ate grass and leaves. His evil thoughts became serpents and sprouted from his skull and waving in a tangled mass hissed out venom. But Dekana-wi'da did not fear him and once more asked him to give his consent to a league of peace and friendship, but he was still wild until Haiowent'ha combed the snakes from his head and told him that he should be the head chief of the confederacy and govern it according to the laws that Haiowent'ha had made. Then he recovered from his madness and asked why the Seneca had not been visited, for the Seneca outnumbered all the other nations and were fearless warriors. "If their jealousy is aroused," he said, "they will eat us."

Then the delegations visited the Seneca and the other nations to the west, but only the Seneca would consider the proposal. The other nations were exceedingly jealous.

Thus a peace pact was made and the Long House built and Dekana-wi'da was the builder but Haiowent'ha was its designer.

Now moreover the first council of Haiowent'ha and Dekana-wi'da was in a place now called Albany at the mouth of a small stream that empties into the Hudson.

COSECHIN

❖ *Coeur d'Alene* ❖

TOLD BY LAWRENCE ARIPA, ADAPTED BY RODNEY FREY

Cosechin was one of our . . ancestors,
and he lived way up at the mouth . .
of the St. Joe
where it is very small yet,
he was a *me-e-an, me-e-an* man.
He hated everything.
He would do anything to hurt people,
he'd live by himself,
he was just *cruel* . . . to animals.
He would knock down trees
and not use them.
He would grab leaves from the trees in the
springtime
and scatter them *to* try to *kill* the trees.
And you know it's the custom of the Indian
that when they're going to use
something from a tree
or . . even fish or hunt,
they . . ask permission first . . .
"Mr. Tree may I use some part of you
or I need it . . for warmth
for my children,"
and that type of thing.
Well he didn't think that way.
He was just mean,
no good.

He'd even . . go to bed, go to sleep at night
and he'd lay along the bank . . of the river
and he'd have . . a rawhide rope that
tied across . . the water.
And if anybody came up at night in a canoe
or tried to get by,
he'd just start shooting with his bow
and arrow
no matter who it was.
And so . . he was, he was just . . *mean*
just awful.

And so . . the people would go and tell him,
"Please take it easy,
try, try and have patience
try and be kind to the animals
to your . . neighbors."
And he'd just say
"Heck with it
I don't have to."
He'd say
"I am Co-o-sechin (slow deliberate voice)
and I'm going to take care of myself
and heck with everybody." . .

And then . . . one day they got together.
And so they called him
and they brought him in front of their . .
council.
And they told him, . . .
"You tell us that you . . are above all of us,
You look down at us.
We are nothing compared to you.
You hate everything . .

Alright, you said you could take care of
yourself,
but if . . you do one . . more . .
bad . . thing,
we are going to . . *get rid* of you.
We won't kill you yet,
but we will kill you later . . if you
don't . . change.
So what we will do is we will *banish you*,
we will turn you loose in the mountains
let you . . take care of yourself
and let's see how far you
can go by yourself."
And so . . he thought about it . . .
And he thought . . . .(long deliberate pause)
"They are *right*! . .
I can't live out there . . by myself.
I have to depend on others."
So he did change . . .

So . . . they . . . thought it was funny . . .
when they saw him petting a dog, petting a horse
talking to people,
telling stories to children . . .

And . . he was just . . . . completely
different! . .
And they couldn't . . couldn't believe it!

And then . . all of a sudden . . without any warning . . .
he went back to his old ways like.
And then . . all of a sudden . . he disappeared . . .
And . . for years and years . . they've said,
"Somebody *killed* him!" . .
And others say
"No . . . he just *ran* off."
And others say
"No! . . . he . . . he just . . got *chewed up* by
something,
something killed him,
No."
And so . . for years and years . . nobody knew.
Nobody *ever did* find out about what happened to
Cosechin! . .

***Moving Camp*, Jim Yellowhawk (Cheyenne River Sioux/Iroquois), 1991. Courtesy of the College of Wooster Art Museum, Wooster, OH.**

TONGUE

❖ *Clackamas (Chinook)* ❖

TOLD TO MELVILLE JACOBS BY VICTORIA HOWARD

RETRANSLATED BY DELL HYMES

It was right here they lived,
had their village.
All the time they would play.

Now their headwoman died,
now she was put away,
she was hung up.

Now it became night,
now something just like fire was seen.
It came out high up from one side of
the river.

Then now, two were brought,
they stayed,
they watched from both sides
(as) the thing comes.
(Their name was 'cutfish,'
from the river.)

Soo---n (while) they are there,
now something comes like fire.

Now they are there,
there they watch:
strai---ght whe---re that dead one hangs it goes,
strai---ght there that thing gets;
now its tongue,
now it carries all of it,
it is lying on its tongue;
now the two clip the tongue,
now that thing draws all the way back.
now the people go,
they go to take the dead one;
now the dead one is put away again.

Now they lived on (there).
Now that thing,
in fact its name is 'Tongue,'
now da---y,
night,
"Give me back my tongue."

Now---he made them tired,
now they said,
"Let's give it back to him."

Now then they gave it back to him,
now he put an end to the village,
he ate a---ll the people.

Only one woman was gone away,
she went to dig button-camas.
In the evening she came back,
she sat down:
no---people.
"Where, I wonder, did the people go?"
O---nly at her house was there smoke,
rising at her house.
Now she---went down,
she went to her house,
Now something is there,
there is a dangerous being!

Now that thing told her,
he informed her,

"*I* ate *all* the people"
Now she did not tell it anything,
she was afraid of it.
Now she fixed those camas of hers.
Now she gave them to him to eat,
he ate.
It became night,
now she went to bed.

In the morning, yes,
again she goes for camas.
In fact she is pregnant,
now her belly is getting large.

Now the two stayed there, (she and) that.
Now she thought,
"Now it's nearly time for my labor,
"now I'll carry in moss."
Now she carried in wood also,
she filled up her house.

Now to be sure,
now she went into labor,
now she brought out a baby boy.
Now it dawned five times,
now she bathed.

Now they lived on there steadily.
Now he became big.
Now she made him a little bow.

Now he played about.
Now he told her:
"Mother! I saw something,
"If my bow were a little bigger,
"I could kill it."

Now in the morning,
now she told that thing,
the dangerous being,
"Make a bow for him.
"He saw something."
Now he made him a little bigger bow.

Now the boy goes,
now he kills a rabbit.
He brings it back,
now he says to her,
"Mother! Now I've
brought it."
She told him,
"Yes--. Its name is 'rabbit'."

Now she skinned it,
she roasted it.
Now it was done,
she gave it to him to eat.
That thing there took it,
he just gulped it down.

Now again he goes about,
now he hunts.
Now again he comes back,
now he says to her,
"Mother! If only my bow were a little bigger,
"I could kill something big,
spotted all over."
"O---,"
she told him.

Now again (to) that thing,
"Now make a big bow for him."
Now he made him one a little bigger.
Now in the morning the boy goes,
he truly hunts.

In a little while,
now he gets back,
he brings back a fawn.
Now the two give half to that thing.
Now again he just gulps it down.

Now again he goes,
now the boy hunts all the time.
Now he would bring back deer,
sometimes he would kill two deer.
Now she would take a little of it,
now she would give all (the rest) to it.

Now they lived on there.
Now that is how they handled him.
Now her son became a man.

Now he asked his mother,
"How does it happen we are the only
ones?"
She told him,
"ã^{n}---
"I had not thought it would be soon,
(but) after a little while,
before I would tell you about it."

House Post
(Tlingit/Stikine). Courtesy of Thomas Burke Memorial Washington State Museum, Seattle, WA.

Now she told him all about it.
She told him,
"That thing you look at there is not a person.
"He devoured our village,
he ate all the people,
when you were not yet a
person."
Now he told her,
"How could you not have told me
about it already?"
Now she told him.
He told her,
"Now I will go from here.
"I will not get back for a day or two.
"I will camp overnight
before I get back."

Now he camped out two nights.
Now he went,
he went back home.

Now he did not carry them,
the deer he killed,
a few perhaps.

He arrived,
he told his mother,
"You will tell him,
"He will go for them."
Now she told him.
"Yes---,"
he told her.

Now he showed him (the way to) them.
Now the dangerous being went,
he went for them,
he carried them back.
She told him,
"Now you butcher them yourself!
"Eat them!"

Now the young man went to sweat-bathe.
He got there,
Now his heart was not good.
Several times he camped overnight.

Now again he told his mother,
"Now again I will go in the morning,
"I will go a long time."
Now he goes,
morning,
now he goes,
now there----he is in the mountains,
now he trains to the end.

Now when he has fin--ished all of it
now he comes back home.
Now he gathers together rotten wood,
now he transforms it.
Now that rotten wood a--ll becomes deer,
as many as are heaped up there.

Now he comes back home,
he goes along,
now he says to his mother,
"Now tell him,
"Now he shall carry in the deer."
Now she told him,
now--,
"Now you will carry in the deer."
Now he got ready.
"Yes---,"
he told her,
"I will carry them in."

Now he goes,
now he packed some,
two,
three,
he would bring.
All day long;
he ceased;
now he had brought them all.
Now she told him,
"It's yours, yes,
"now eat it!"

Now he ate,
now all night long he ate.
Now it is nearly sunrise,
now he nodded sleepily.

Now she told him,
"Eat!
"Your deer are just ly---ing there!"
Now no---,
now he sleeps on.
Soon now he fell backward,
he slept.

Now the two took their possessions.
Now they set the house afire.
Now they stayed outside,
they watched it,
that thing there burned.
Now it was every bit consumed.
Now they made a different house.

Now there they stayed.
Now he began to hunt regularly.
Now he would bring back a deer,
he would bring it to his mother,
she smoke-dried the meat.

Now he told her,
"Now then,
"now I will leave you."
Now he goes to the mountains.
He did not tell his mother
where he goes.
Now he is working in the mountains,
he is seeking,
he collects feathers;
he is seeking bones,
various kinds of animal bones.

LEFT: *Jar*, Lucy Lewis (Acoma). Courtesy of the School of American Research, Santa Fe, NM.

OPPOSITE: *Calvario Series #166*, Marty Avrett (Coushatta/Choctaw/Cherokee), 1994. Courtesy of the artist.

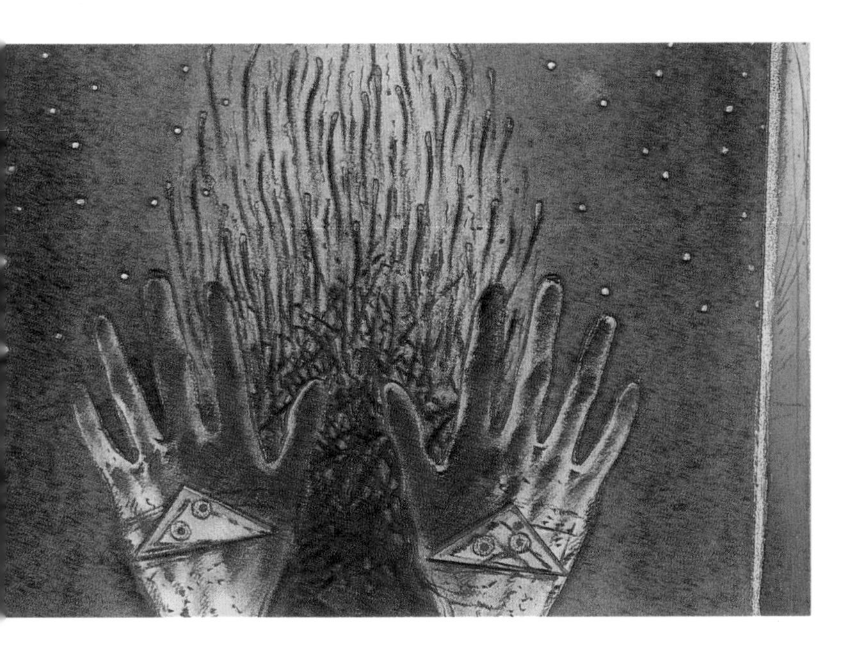

Now--- I do not know how long,
a long time,
he gathers together feathers of every kind of bird.
Now he gathered them together.
Now he counted out how many people,
that many bones;
he fixed the feathers,
he laid them out.

Now he counted out according to whence these came,
on this side he gathered them together.
Now he counted out how many were their villages.
One feather that was different he fixed for his father.
Now also he laid out feathers for canoes.
He said,
"These feathers will be for canoes."
He finished a----ll of it.

Then now, he transformed them,
they became people.
Those feathers,
bones,
they became people.
Those different feathers were for
canoes.
Now they became people.

All those persons, those people,
now they got into their canoes,
now they went.

Now he followed them.
They reached the falls,
now they truly worked.

Now he stood,
he watched,
he saw his father,
it was he who was showing them
(how to fish).

Now they would pass by him,
now they would scold him,
"How does he come to stand idly by?"
As for some, they would say nothing to him.

Now--- his heart became bad.
Now he went,
he waded.

Now his mother saw him,
going.
Now she ran,
she scolded the people,
"It is he himself who has made you.
"He brought you back here."

Now in vain he was followed,
he was told
"Come back!"
No.
He went further.

Now he wept,
Now there he stood in the water.

Now his mother wept.
Now she told the people,
"Now then.
"Had you not done like that to him,
"You would have lived on here.
"Now then.
"Now we shall make our separation."

THE LEGEND OF GODASIYO

❖ *Seneca* ❖

RECORDED BY JEREMIAH CURTIN AND J.N.B. HEWITT, EDITED BY W. S. PENN

In the beginning of time, when the earth was new, when the inhabitants of it spoke but a single tongue, when these good people dwelt in perfect harmony and peace, and when the several settlements lived in such manner that there were no quarrels or contentions among them, there dwelt in one of these settlements, or villages, Godasiyo, a woman who was the chief of her village.

The village which Godasiyo led occupied both sides of a large river. It was the custom of her people to cross the river to attend dances and exchange goods—meat, venison, skins, furs, roots, bark, and dried fruits and berries. But the assembly lodge was on one side of the river, and that caused considerable traveling across and back. This river was large and rapid, and the people crossed it by means of a bridge made of saplings and limbs of trees fastened together. After a long time, trouble arose over a white dog which belonged to the chief, Godasiyo. The dissension became serious, and there was great danger that the factions would become involved in a fight over the matter. The great river divided the two parties.

Finally, Chief Godasiyo, after long deliberation, decided that the only way in which a deadly contest could be avoided would be by the removal of her own adherents to some other place. Having decided to do this, she told her adherents of her resolution to remove westward by going up the stream on which they were living. She invited all who had taken her part to follow her, and they all agreed to go with her. She told them that they would ascend the river in canoes of birch bark, and this would enable them to transport their small belongings with ease. So the people set to work to construct the canoes. Two canoes of birch bark of suitable size were made. These were fastened together by strong saplings, so they supported a kind of platform extending over the canoes and the space between them

Canoe Model **(Passamaquoddy). Thaw Collection, Fenimore House Museum, Cooperstown, NY.**

This platform was for the sole use of the chief, Godasiyo. Then, the followers of Godasiyo proceeded to construct birch-bark canoes for themselves.

They all embarked with Chief Godasiyo in the lead and paddled upstream. The flotilla of canoes was very large, covering the water as far as the eye could see up and down the river. After they had paddled a long way, the people came in sight of forks in the river, and then it was that they began to talk together—the two divisions of canoes, one on each side of Godasiyo—as they paddled upstream. One side chose one of the forks as the way to their new settlement. The other side chose the other fork. Each side gave reasons for the choice it had made, and this gave rise at last to a heated discussion. This strife continued to the point where, if it persisted, the people would become permanently separated. Still they argued. At last, the leaders of each side turned their canoes into the forks they had chosen, and they began to separate.

The two men paddling the two canoes that supported Chief Godasiyo disagreed as to the course they should take. Each chose the fork branching off on his side of the stream, and the two canoes became separated. Chief Godasiyo's platform slipped off its support and fell into the water, carrying the chief with it. The people drew near, and looking into the water to see what had become of their chief, they saw that she had sunk to the bottom, where she had become a great fish.

The people of the two sides tried to talk together, but their language had become changed, and they could not understand each other. It was in this way that the people became divided into different tribes that speak different languages.

COYOTE GOES GAMBLING

PART TWO *from* COYOTE AND EAGLE'S DAUGHTER

❖ *Tonkawa* ❖

TOLD BY JOHN RUSH BUFFALO, RECORDED BY HARRY HOIJER, RETRANSLATED BY DELL HYMES

Then, they say, they made Coyote marry a
beautiful girl.
Then, after staying a while, to that woman.
"I'll go to the other camp over yonder,"
they say he said, Coyote.
Then that woman.
"Oh!" they say she said.
"Don't go!" they say she said.
Then Coyote,
"I won't stay long," they say he said.
"In two days I'll come back," they say he said.
Then that woman,
"All right," they say she said.

Then, they say, Coyote went off.
And, getting to a large camp,
they say he stayed for a long while.

It was then that woman went after them, they say;
getting to that large camp,
"And Coyote?" they say she said.
Then,
"He's joined a bunch of gamblers over
there," they say they said.

Then she got to a place nearby, and entering
the tipi,
"Water," they say she said.

OPPOSITE: ***Blue Woman*, Emmi Whitehorse (Navajo), 1989. Courtesy of the artist.**

Then,
"There is none," they say they said.

Then she picked up the bucket, and,
they say, she went to get water.
As she did so, one young man at the
gambling place:—
"Oh!" they say he said.
"Coyote's wife!" they say he said.
"She comes this way!" they say he said.
Then Coyote saw her, and,
they say, he was laughing.
Then the young man,
"We heard that you left her," they say they said.
Then Coyote,
"No," they say he said.
"Watch me!" they say he said.
"She'll give me water to drink," they say
he said.

And then, getting to where that woman was,
they say, he touched her.
Then that woman, seeing Coyote,
"Leave me!" they say she said.

Then Coyote,
"Give me water to drink!" they say he said.
Then, that woman, not giving him water to drink,
went off, they say.

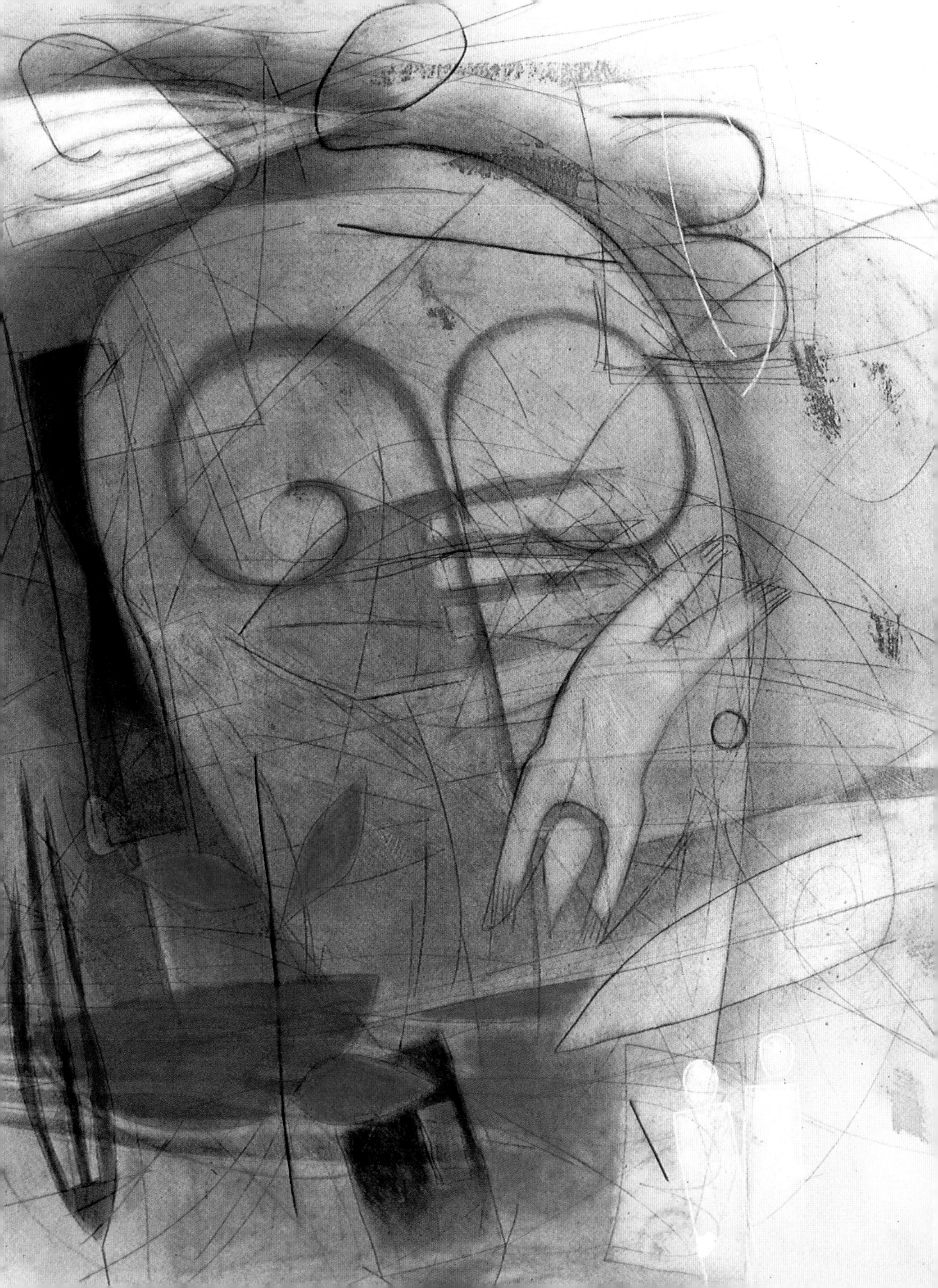

When night came, he came to that woman,
and as he talked with her, the young men,
"Let's not let Coyote sleep tonight," they
say they were saying.
"Let's steal that woman," they say they were saying.
And then that night, they say, they danced with him.
And, they say, they didn't let him sleep until
daylight, Coyote.
Then, they say, that woman was angry;
And,
"I'll go," they say she said.

Then Coyote,
"I'll go to gamble in the north," they say he said.
And, they say, he went away, Coyote.

And he got to a large camp, and
"I go to gamble in the north," they say he said.
And then, going away,
they say, he got to a large camp.

And the next day,
"I go to gamble in the north," they say he
said, Coyote.
The next day, they say, he went off;
getting to a large camp,
they say, he joined a bunch of gamblers.

While he did, that woman,
"I'll go after Coyote," they say she said.
And, they say, she went after him;
getting to a large camp,
"And Coyote?" they say she said.
Then,
"He's gone to gamble in the north," they
say they said.

Then, they say, that woman went after him.
And again, getting to a large camp,
"And Coyote?" they say she said.
Then,
"He's gone to gamble in the north," they
say they said.

Then, they say, that woman went after him.
And getting to a large camp,
"And Coyote?" they say she said.
Then,
"He's gone to gamble in the north," they
say he said.

Then, they say, that woman went after him.
And getting to a large camp,
"And Coyote?" they say she said.
Then,
"He's gambling here," they say they said.

Then,
"Go to him, and
"Tell him,
"Come!" they say she said.

Then, going to him,
"Your wife is summoning you," they say he said.
Then Coyote,
"You're lying," they say he said.
Then,
"I speak the truth," they say he said;
"Now come!" they say he said.

Then Coyote went with him, they say;
the two got to the tipi, they say;
"She is staying here," they say he said.
Then, they say, Coyote peered inside.

Then that woman,
"Come in!" they say she said.
Then Coyote, they say, not going in,
was laughing.

Eagle Dancer, **Pablita Velarde (Santa Clara Pueblo). Courtesy of the School of American Research, Santa Fe, NM.**

Then again,
"Come in!" they say she said.
Then Coyote, they say, not going in,
was laughing.

Then again, that woman,
"Come in!" they say she said.
Then Coyote, they say, not going in,
was laughing.

Again as he peered in,
"Come in!" they say she said.
Then when Coyote laughed, that woman,
"I shall go away," they say she said.
"Back," they say she said;
Going outside, she flew away, they say.

Then Coyote peering in,
"And my wife?" they say he said.
Then,
"She has gone away," they say they said.

Then, they say, Coyote came running,
back.
As he did, that woman was getting home;
"I left him," they say she said.

Then her father and mother,
"You are doing the right thing," they say
they said;
"Let us go," they say they said.
And, they say, she flew away with them up
into the air.
She was an Eagle, they say.

So it is.

SWIFT-RUNNER AND TRICKSTER TARANTULA

❖ *Zuni* ❖

ADAPTED BY DEE BROWN

In the long ago time there was only one Tarantula on earth. He was as large as a man, and lived in a cave near where two broad columns of rock stand at the base of Thunder Mountain. Every morning Tarantula would sit in the door of his den to await the sound of hornbells which signaled the approach of a young Zuni who always came running by at sunrise. The young man wore exceedingly beautiful clothing of red, white and green, a plaited headband of many colors, a plume of blue, red and yellow macaw feathers in his hair knot, and a belt of hornbells. Tarantula was most envious of the young man, and spent much time thinking of ways to obtain his costume through trickery.

Swift-Runner was the young Zuni's name, and he was studying to become a priest-chief like his father. His costume was designed for use in sacred dances. To keep himself strong for these arduous dances, Swift-Runner dressed in his sacred clothing every morning and ran all the way around Thunder Mountain before prayers.

One morning at sunrise, Tarantula heard the hornbells rattling in Swift-Runner's belt. He took a few steps outside of his den, and as the young Zuni approached, he called out to him: "Wait a moment, my young friend, Come here!"

"I'm in a great hurry," Swift-Runner replied.

"Never mind that. Come here," Tarantula repeated.

"What is it?" the young man asked impatiently. "Why do you want me to stop?"

"I much admire your costume," said Tarantula. "Wouldn't you like to see how it looks to others?"

"How is that possible?" asked Swift-Runner.

"Come, let me show you."

"Well, hurry up. I don't want to be late for prayers."

"It can be done very quickly," Tarantula assured him. "Take off your clothing, all of it. Then I will take off mine. Place yours in front of me, and I will place mine in front of you. Then I will put on your costume, and you will see how handsome you look to others."

If Swift-Runner had known what a trickster Tarantula was, he would never have agreed to this, but he was very curious as to how his costume appeared to others. He removed his red and green moccasins, his fringed white leggings, his belt of hornbells, and all his other fine clothing, and placed them in front of Tarantula.

Tarantula meanwhile had made a pile of his dirty woolly leggings, breech-cloth and cape—all of an ugly gray-blue color. He quickly began dressing himself in the handsome garments that Swift-Runner placed before him, and when he was finished he stood up on his crooked hind

Knifewing Dancer Pin **(Zuni). Courtesy of W. E. Channing & Co., Santa Fe, NM.**

legs and said: "Look at me now. How do I look?"

"Well," replied Swift-Runner, "so far as the clothing is concerned, quite handsome."

"You can get a better idea of the appearance if I back off a little farther," Tarantula said, and he backed himself, as only Tarantulas can, toward the door of his den. "How do I look now?"

"Handsomer," said the young man.

"Then I'll get back a little farther." He walked backward again. "Now then, how do I look?"

"Perfectly handsome."

"Aha!" Tarantula chuckled as he turned around and dived headfirst into his dark hole.

"Come out of there!" Swift-Runner shouted, but he knew he was too late.

Tarantula had tricked him. "What shall I do now?" he asked himself. "I can't go home half naked." The only thing he could do was put on the hairy gray-blue clothing of Tarantula, and make his way back to the village.

When he reached home the sun was high, and his father was anxiously awaiting him. "What happened?" his father asked. "Why are you dressed in that ugly clothing?"

"Tarantula who lives under Thunder Mountain tricked me," Swift-Runner replied. "He took my sacred costume and ran away into his den."

His father shook his head sadly. "We must send for the warrior-chief," he said. "He will advise us what we must do about this."

When the warrior-chief came, Swift-Runner told him what had happened. The chief thought for a moment, and said: "Now that Tarantula has your fine costume, he is not likely to show himself far from his den again. We must dig him out."

And so the warrior-chief sent runners through the village, calling all the people to assemble with hoes, digging sticks, and baskets. After the Zunis gathered with all these things, the chief led the way out to the den of Tarantula.

They began tunneling swiftly into the hole. They worked and worked from morning till sundown, filling baskets with sand and throwing it behind them until a large mound was piled high. At last they reached the solid rock of the mountain, but they found no trace of Tarantula. "What more can we do?" the people asked. "Let us give up because we must. Let us go home." And so as darkness fell, the Zunis returned to their village.

That evening the leaders gathered to discuss what they must do next to recover

***Moccasins* (Kiowa, Umatilla, and Woodland). San Diego Museum of Man, San Diego, CA.**

Swift-Runner's costume. Someone suggested that they send for the Great Kingfisher. "He is wise, crafty, and swift of flight. If anyone can help us, the Great Kingfisher can."

"That's it," they agreed. "Let's send for the Kingfisher."

Swift-Runner set out at once, running by moonlight until he reached the hill where Great Kingfisher lived, and knocked on the door of his house.

"Who is it?" called Kingfisher.

"Come quickly," Swift-Runner replied. "The leaders of our village seek your help."

And so Kingfisher followed the young man back to the Zuni council. "What is it that you need of me?" he asked.

"Tarantula has stolen the sacred garments of Swift-Runner," they told him. "We have dug into his den to the rock foundation of Thunder Mountain, but we can dig no farther, and know not what next to do. We have sent for you because of your power and ability to snatch anything, even from underwater."

"This is a difficult task you place before me," said Kingfisher. "Tarantula is exceedingly cunning and very sharp of sight. I will do my best, however, to help you."

Before sunrise the next morning, Kingfisher flew to the two columns of rock at the base of Thunder Mountain and concealed himself behind a stone so that only his beak showed over the edge. As the first streaks of sunlight came over the rim of the world, Tarantula appeared in the entrance of his den. With his sharp eyes he peered out, looking all around until he sighted Kingfisher's bill. "Ho, ho, you skulking Kingfisher!" he cried.

At the instant he knew he was discovered, Kingfisher opened his wings and sped like an arrow on the wind, but he merely brushed the tips of the plumes of Tarantula's head before the trickster jumped back deep into his hole. "Ha, ha!" laughed Tarantula. "Let's have a dance and sing!" He pranced up and down in his cave, dancing a tarantella on his crooked legs, while outside the Great Kingfisher flew to the Zuni village and sadly told the people: "No use! I failed completely. As I said, Tarantula is a crafty, keen-sighted old fellow. I can do no more."

After Kingfisher returned to his hill, the

leaders decided to send for Great Eagle, whose eyes were seven times as sharp as the eyes of men. He came at once, and listened to their pleas for help. "As Kingfisher, my brother, has said, Tarantula is a crafty, keen-sighted creature. But I will do my best."

Instead of waiting near Thunder Mountain for sunrise, Eagle perched himself a long distance away, on top of Badger Mountain. He stood there with his head raised to the winds, turning first one eye and then the other on the entrance to Tarantula's den until the old trickster thrust out his woolly nose. With his sharp eyes, Tarantula soon discovered Eagle high on Badger Mountain. "Ho, you skulking Eagle!" he shouted, and Eagle dived like a hurled stone straight at Tarantula's head. His wings brushed the trickster, but when he reached down his talons he clutched nothing but one of the plumes on Tarantula's headdress, and even this fell away upon the rocks. While Tarantula laughed and danced in his cave and told himself what a clever well-dressed fellow he was, the shamed and disappointed Eagle flew to the Zuni council and reported his failure.

The people next called upon Falcon to help them. After he heard of what already had been done, Falcon said: "If my brothers, Kingfisher and Eagle, have failed, it is almost useless for me to try."

"You are the swiftest of the feathered creatures," the leaders answered him. "Swifter than Kingfisher and as strong as Eagle. Your plumage is speckled gray and brown like the rocks and sagebrush so that Tarantula may not see you."

Falcon agreed to try, and early the next morning he placed himself on the edge of the high cliff above Tarantula's den. When the sun rose he was almost invisible because his gray and brown feathers blended into the rocks and dry grass around him. He kept a close watch until Tarantula thrust out his ugly face and turned his eyes in every direction. Tarantula saw nothing, and continued to poke himself out until his shoulders were visible. At that moment Falcon dived, and Tarantula saw him, too late to save the macaw plumes from the bird's grasping claws.

Tarantula tumbled into his den, sat down, and bent himself double with fright. He wagged his head back and forth, and sighed: "Alas, alas, my beautiful headdress is gone. That wretch of a falcon! But what is the use of bothering about a miserable bunch of macaw feathers, anyway? They get dirty and broken, moths eat them, they fade. Why trouble myself about a worthless thing like that? I still have the finest costume in the Valley—handsome leggings and embroidered shirt, necklaces worth fifty such head-plumes, and earrings worth a handful of such necklaces. Let Falcon have the old head-plumes."

Meanwhile, Falcon, cursing his poor luck, took the feathers back to the Zunis. "I'm sorry, my friends, this is the best I could do. May others succeed better."

"You have succeeded well," they told him. "These plumes from the South are precious to us."

Then the leaders gathered in council again. "What more is there to be done?" Swift-Runner's father asked.

"We must send your son to the land of the gods," said the war-chief. "Only they can help us now."

They called Swift-Runner and said to him: "We have asked the wisest and swiftest and strongest of the feathered creatures to help us, yet they have failed. Now we must send you to the land of the gods to seek their help."

Swift-Runner agreed to undertake the dangerous climb to the top of Thunder Mountain where the two war-gods, Ahaiyuta and Matsailema, lived with their grandmother. For the journey, the priest-chiefs prepared gifts of their most valuable treasures. Next morning, Swift-Runner took these with him and by midday he reached the place where the war-gods lived.

He found their grandmother seated on the flat roof of their house. From the room below came the sounds of the war-gods playing one of their noisy games. "Enter, my son" the grandmother greeted Swift-Runner, and then she called to Ahaiyuta and Matsailema: "Come up, my children, both of you, quickly. A young man has come bringing gifts."

The war-gods, who were small like dwarfs, climbed to the roof and the oldest said politely: "Sit down and tell us the purpose of your visit. No stranger comes to the house of another for nothing."

"I bring you offerings from our village below. I also bring my burden of trouble to listen to your counsel and implore your aid."

He then told the war-gods of his misfortunes, of how Tarantula had stolen his sacred clothing, and of how the wisest and swiftest of the feathered beings had tried and failed to regain them.

"It is well that you have come," said the youngest war-god. "Only we can outwit the trickster Tarantula. Grandmother, please bestir yourself, and grind some rock flour for us."

While Swift-Runner watched, the old grandmother gathered up some white sandstone rocks, broke them into fragments, and then ground them into a powder. She made dough of this with water, and the two war-gods, with amazing skill, molded the dough into two deer and two antelope which hardened as quickly as they finished their work.

They gave the figures to Swift-Runner and told him to place them on a rock shelf facing the entrance to Tarantula's den. "Old Tarantula is very fond of hunting. Nothing is so pleasing to him as to kill wild game. He may be tempted forth from his hiding-place. When you have done this, go home and tell the chiefs that they should be ready for him in the morning."

That evening after Swift-Runner returned to his village and told how he had placed the figures of deer and antelope on the rock shelf in front of Tarantula's den, the chiefs summoned the warriors and told them to make ready for the warpath before sunrise. All night long they prepared their arrows and tested the strength of their bows, and near dawn they marched out to Thunder Mountain. Swift-Runner went ahead of them, and when he approached the rock shelf, he was surprised to see that the two antelope and the two deer had come to life. They were walking about, cropping the tender leaves and grass.

"I call upon you to help me overcome the wicked Tarantula," he prayed to the animals. "Go down close to his den, I beg you, that he may be tempted forth at the sight of you."

The deer and antelope obediently started down the slope toward Tarantula's den. As they approached the entrance, Tarantula sighted them. "Ho! What do I see?" he said to himself. "There go some deer and antelope. Now for a hunt. I might as well get them as anyone else."

He took up his bow, slipped the noose over the head of it, twanged the string, and started out. But just as he stepped forth from his den, he said to himself: "Good heavens, this will never do! The Zunis will be after me if I go out there." He looked up and down the valley. "Nonsense! There's no one about." He leaped out of his hole and hurried toward the deer, which were still approaching. When the first one came near he drew back an arrow and let fly. The deer dropped at once. "Aha!" he cried. "Who says I am not a good hunter?" He whipped out another arrow and shot the second deer. With loud exclamations of delight, he then felled the two antelope.

"What fine game I have bagged today," he said. "Now I must take the meat into my den." He untied a strap which be had brought along and with it he lashed together the legs of the first deer he had shot. He stooped, raised the deer to his back, and was about to rise with the burden and start for his den, when *cachunk!* he fell down almost crushed under a mass of white rock. "Mercy!" he cried. "What's this?" He looked around but could see no trace of the deer, nothing but a shapeless mass of white rock.

Detail from *Pair of Trousers* (Sioux). Courtesy of W. E. Channing & Co., Santa Fe, NM.

"Well, I'll try this other one," he said, but he had no sooner lifted the other deer to his back when it knocked him down and turned into another mass of white rock. "What can be the matter?" he cried.

Then he tried one of the antelope and the same thing happened again. "Well, there is one left anyway," he said. He tied the feet of the last animal and was about to lift it when he heard a great shouting of many voices.

He turned quickly and saw all the Zunis of the village gathering around his den. He ran for the entrance as fast as his crooked legs would move, but the people blocked his way. They closed in upon him, they clutched at his stolen garments, they pulled earrings from his ears, until he raised his hands and cried: "Mercy! Mercy! You hurt! You hurt! Don't treat me so! I'll be good hereafter. I'll take this costume off and give it back to you without making the slightest trouble if you will only let me alone." But the people closed in angrily. They pulled him about and stripped off Swift-Runner's costume until Tarantula was left unclothed and so bruised that he could hardly move.

Then the chiefs gathered around, and one of them said: "It will not be well if we let this trickster go as he is. He is too big and powerful, too crafty. To rid the world of Tarantula forever, he must be roasted!"

And so the people piled dry firewood into a great heap, drilled fire from a stick, and set the wood to blazing. They threw the struggling trickster into the flames, and he squeaked and sizzled and hissed and swelled to enormous size. But Tarantula had one more trick left in his bag. When he burst with a tremendous noise, he threw a million fragments of himself all over the world–to Mexico and South America and as far away as Taranto in Italy. Each fragment took the shape of Old Tarantula, but of course they were very much smaller, somewhat as tarantulas are today. Some say that Taranto took its name from the tarantulas, some say the tarantulas took their name from Taranto, but everybody knows that the wild dance known as the tarantella was invented by Tarantula, the trickster of Thunder Mountain, in the land of the Zunis.

Twilight Meets Dawn,
Margarete Bagshaw-Tindel (O-Je-Gi-Povi), 1994. Courtesy of the artist.

CHILD OF THE SUN

❖ *Laguna* ❖

TOLD BY LEE FRANCIS

Several months before she passed on, my mother, T'du-u-eh-t'sah (or Ethel), and I were talking about her sleepless nights. *"All I have to do now is get through the night. I guess I'm just a child of the sun."*

The sun had just set when mother passed on several months later, and I understood about her being a child of the sun and why she chose to pass on at sunset from the story I was told when I was young.

And so it is said . . . in the long-ago time . . . that one day Kochininako was strolling through the woods and over the hills near the village. Somewhat tired, she sat down under a mighty oak tree. It was a warm spring day and she soon went to sleep.

As she lay sleeping, light from the sun glittered on her from between the leaves. Osrats Paitummu, the Great Sun, seeing Kochininako asleep, came down on a beam of sunlight to look at her more closely. It was then that Kochininako awoke. In that first instant, she was extremely afraid. But Osrats Paitummu began speaking in a soothing way as he dazzled within the ray of sunlight and soon Kochininako was laughing and her fear was completely gone. When the sun began to set behind Blue Mountain, Osrats Paitummu departed and Kochininako walked back to the village.

Every day after that first meeting, Kochininako returned to the oak tree and every day Osrats Paitummu returned on a beam of sunlight only to leave when the sun began to set. Finally, after they had spent many days together under the oak tree, Kochininako and Osrats Paitummu were married.

Fearing that the people of her village wouldn't understand, Kochininako decided to keep her marriage secret. Because Osrats Paitummu had the power to remain invisible to those he did not want to have see him, keeping the secret of their marriage was very easy for Kochininako.

And while Kochininako was very happy being married to Osrats Paitummu, the people of the village were suffering. They were starving because there was no rain for the corn to grow. To avoid the horror of starvation, the people decided that they would all move south to a better land.

A little after sunset on the night before the departure of all the people of the village, a child was born to Kochininako. Because the boy's birth would reveal the secret of her marriage to Osrats Paitummu, Kochininako decided her only choice was to remain in the now-empty village.

Unable to find enough food for herself and her child, the mother became weaker and weaker until she finally died. But her infant son, who was fed by the birds that came every morning bringing grain and seeds, continued to live and soon grew into a young man.

Every day the young man would wander across the land in search of game. He would also work every day in the field, tending to the corn which grew green and tall because the rains had returned to nourish them. Since his earliest childhood, the young man was especially attentive to his duties and would scatter corn meal before the door every morning at sunrise as an offering.

One morning while he was scattering corn meal, he noticed a smooth black stone in the container, which held the corn meal. Carefully, he picked the stone out of the container, and as he held it in his hand, a voice began to speak from the stone.

"I am your grandmother and I live in the stone. Kochininako, the daughter of the sovereign of the village, was your mother. Osrats Paitummu, the sovereign of the sky, is your father."

Throughout that long day, the young man thought about the strange event which had occurred. He tried to remember if he had ever heard the sound of any voice other than his own since being born, but he could not. As the day stretched into night, he was overwhelmed by loneliness. Finally he went to sleep engulfed in his need for companionship.

The next morning, the young man began to scatter corn meal as he had always done at sunrise, but the sun seemed to have come extremely close to the earth. Rising from a high mountain in the east close to the place where the young man lived, the sun dazzled him, and he fell on the ground filled with wonder and fear. Then he heard the sun calling to him.

"Sah-mu-tii." (My son.)

"Ny-s-tii-ah!" (My father!) the young man exclaimed.

Then the sun continued to speak to the young man. *"When I rise from the east four times, I shall take you with me because I have wanted to show you to the people and prove to them that I have a son. From this time forward you will be called Paischun-nimoot (child of the sun)."*

When the fourth day finally arrived, the Osrats Paitummu rose from behind the eastern mountain where he waited for Paischun-nimoot. The young man quickly climbed the mountain and was welcomed by Osrats Paitummu. Then they traveled together until noontime when they arrived in the middle of a great realm where all the peoples of the earth were gathered.

Osrats Paitummu spoke. *"My people, this is my son, Paischun-nimoot. I have brought him for you to see and welcome among you."*

They talked among themselves, and after a time said to Osrats Paitummu, *"We shall examine him to see if he is indeed the child of the sun."*

First they took the young man into a chamber in the north which was filled with bees. Paischun-nimoot caught the bees and took their honey, but they did not sting him. Then he was taken into a chamber in the west that was filled with *Wa-waka*, who are fierce water animals. These he caught as he had the bees and was unharmed. Then they took Paischun-nimoot to a room in the south where the most ferocious of captive bears were held. Not once was he attacked or bitten as he rode the bears in that great room. Finally, Paischun-nimoot was taken to a room in the east filled with lions who stopped their roaring after he petted and stroked all of them in turn.

When the people of the earth saw all this, they spoke with one voice: *"This is indeed Paischun-nimoot, the child of the sun."*

OPPOSITE: *Sun God*, Milland Lomakema (Hopi), 1968. Courtesy of the School of American Research, Santa Fe, NM.

MILLARD LOMAKEMA "Hopi 68"

FIRST EAGLE STORY

❖ *Tanaina (Dena'ina)* ❖

ADAPTED BY BILL VAUDRIN

The two brothers were young and handsome. They were the desire of all the girls in the village and could have had their pick of any of them. But they were young and didn't care much about girls.

Often the two of them would slip out of the village and run off deep into the woods. Far from home, they had cached two eagle skins in a tree. Draping these over their bodies, they would begin to shake furiously. (There is an Indian word for what they did—*co doz zle schish,* or "he shakes himself.") Then the two brothers would turn into their *jonchas*—a pair of eagles. They would rise into the air and glide for hours above the woods or out over the sea, hunting. They were proud of their young strength and beauty.

As the months passed, an older woman in the village who had not yet married was attracted to the boys and wanted them. First she tried to get one, and then the other. But they wouldn't have her. She wasn't an ugly woman—in fact, she was very good-looking—and was hurt and insulted when the boys kept on ignoring her. She would get even, she promised herself.

So one afternoon when the boys slipped off into the woods, she followed them. And she was there watching when they turned into their *jonchas.*

As she watched them fly away a plan formed in her mind. She waited until they were almost out of sight, then switched to her own *joncha,* a sparrow hawk, and followed them.

The brothers flew farther and farther away from the village, until they were out over the waters of Cook Inlet. And still they didn't stop, but flew far out from land in search of beluga whales.

Then, when the eagles were miles out from shore, the hawk attacked. She charged right into them, slashing first one, then the other, knocking their feathers off and cutting them with her beak. The eagles tried to fight, but they were too young and not nearly as fast as the hawk, and they didn't have a chance. They kept trying to get back to shore, but as soon as they turned their backs on her, the hawk would slash them from behind. They grew weaker and weaker, and the hawk knew she was winning.

Far away, back at the village, the boys' father began to feel uneasy. He couldn't lose the feeling. Finally, when he could stand it no longer, he ran out of the village and turned into his *joncha.* Then, as a huge eagle, he climbed into the air and circled higher and higher, while the feeling in his heart grew stronger.

***Net Gauge* (Wishram/The Dalles). Courtesy of Thomas Burke Memorial Washington State Museum, Seattle, WA.**

Then, suddenly, unexplainably, he knew his boys were in trouble, and that he must go to them.

Out over the ocean the battle was almost over. The young eagles had lost too many feathers, and were barely keeping themselves above the water. The hawk was taunting and slicing at them. A few minutes more and it would be all over.

Suddenly the hawk was smashed from behind and went reeling off into space. She turned to see a third eagle, larger and fiercer than the other two. It was the last look she ever got. The older, more experienced bird ripped her wide open, and she plunged into the inlet dead.

Then, with his wounded sons clutched to his back, the father winged his way back to the village and home.

Old Age and Elder Wisdom

❖ ❖ ❖ ❖ ❖

Almost all stories told and re-told by Native American peoples have multiple meanings. Because most can be told to audiences of all ages and experiences, the stories in Old Age and Elder Wisdom greatly resemble some of those included in Adolescence. Nonetheless, some stories do seem to teach what can only be learned by long life and careful meditation on the world inside and outside of the self. Some stories, in other words, seem to exist to be told by elders to all of the people—reminding them of what they know, of who they are, and of how they must be in the world. Sometimes, these stories describe the still contemporary and still contradictory and indefinable Coyote; other times, they remind us to be careful of what we wish for, lest we end up like the man in "The Black Bear Story," who gets what he wants but doesn't want what he gets.

In "Coyote and Crow," Coyote teaches us to beware of our pride and sense of self-importance; if we are too filled with ourselves, we can be tricked out of our very sustenance by false compliments and inflated appellations—a lesson it never hurts to relearn. And even Coyote can begin to think too much of himself; when "Never Grows Bigger" gives him a small bite, he blows up like a buffalo bladder—a metaphorical representation of the way in which Coyote puffs himself up with his size and his arrogant attitude toward smaller animals, who have more power in their bites than one might suspect. Like Coyote in "The Wolves and the Dogs," we need to remember to rely on and trust our elders, and to take their advice about the riddle that is life and perception. Even elders may have difficulty interpreting and solving the riddles of life (such as the "black rope" in "Speaks-in-Riddles and Wise Spirit," which suggests braided buffalo hair used by the Pawnees to belt their robes in place).

If the riddles of life can be difficult for elders, then every member of every band or tribe needs to remember the lesson of Prairie Dog, whose inherent nature is to be cautious and to warn the rest of his people when he smells danger. In "Coyote and Skunk" we learn that to be incautious or not abide by one's nature, it seems, threatens the very survival of both the individual and the group. On the other hand, if one's nature is, like Coyote's, to be greedy for more than one's share, one runs the risk of losing it all, much to other's uncompassionate enjoyment. So it is with the white man, in "Enough Is Enough," who forgets warnings, abuses what he's learned, and sticks himself up in a tree no longer able to free himself.

***Ancient Ones*, Chethlahe Paladin (Navajo), 1966. Courtesy of James T. Bialac Collection.**

THE BLACK BEAR STORY

❖ *Tanaina (Dena'ina)* ❖

ADAPTED BY BILL VAUDRIN

Late one fall two villagers went bear hunting on a mountain a few miles upriver from their home. They'd just worked their way above and along the timberline about a mile when they spotted three black bears—two old ones and a cub. The hunters sneaked up on them while the bears were playing in a rock slide. When they came within range, one of the hunters said to himself, "I'm going to marry that black bear."

So he turned and killed his partner. Then he shot the male bear.

He had a tough time making up with the female after that, but he disguised himself as a black bear, and by the first snowfall went into hibernation with her and the cub.

Sometimes she would wake up and look around and sniff.

"What's the matter?" he'd ask.

"I smell something strange."

"There're no men in here," he'd say.

The disguised villager stayed with the bears all that year and the next. But by the following spring he'd begun to tire of that life. He decided that he really didn't care for it, after all. So he left the bears and went back home.

Years later, two villagers were squirrel hunting on the same mountain. One was setting snares and really working hard, but the other one just sat around eating berries. They were supposed to be partners, so the first one said to the other one, "Why don't you work hard?"

"Oh, I don't know," said the second hunter as he filled his mouth with berries. "I just don't want to."

One day a few weeks later the hard-working partner found it necessary to go back down the mountain to the village, and leave the snares for the lazy one to watch.

It was some time before he was able to

RIGHT: *Bear Carving* (Eskimo). San Diego Museum of Man, San Diego, CA.

OPPOSITE: *Untitled*, Jeffrey Chapman (Ojibwa), 1992. Courtesy of Jan Cicero Gallery, Chicago, IL.

***Bears at Cornstalk* (Yakima). Courtesy of America Hurrah Archive, New York, NY.**

return, and when he did he had a surprise waiting for him. On his way up to the camp he passed several of their snares and traps, and they were all full. His partner hadn't checked them since he'd left.

When he finally reached camp, he found his partner sitting around eating berries.

"Why didn't you run the traps?" he asked.

"Oh," said the partner, as he scooped in another armload of berries, "I just didn't want to."

The first hunter was still puzzled and a little bit angry when, several days later, he heard his berry-eating partner singing off in a field beside some trees. He had an idea. With the greatest care he sneaked up on him. When he got right up close, he suddenly jumped up and screamed.

The partner in the berry patch was so surprised and scared that he jumped up and turned into a black bear and ran away.

It was the same man who had killed his partner years before so he could marry a black bear. Now he was one.

He got what he wanted, but he didn't want what he got.

COYOTE AND CROW

❖ *Yakima* ❖

ADAPTED BY ELLA CLARK

Coyote traveled through the country, fighting monsters and making the world ready for the people who were to follow. He crossed the Cascade Mountains and came into the Puget Sound country. He was hungry, very hungry.

He saw Crow sitting on the peak of a high cliff, with a ball of deer fat in his mouth. Coyote looked at Crow with this fat and thought how good it would taste. Becoming hungrier and hungrier, he wondered how he could get the fat for himself. He thought hard. Then he laughed.

"I know what to do. I know how I can get the fat from Crow."

Then Coyote came close to the base of the cliff and called. "Oh, Chief! I hear that you can make a good noise, a pleasing noise with your voice. You are a big chief, I know. You are a wise chief, I have heard. Let me hear your voice, Chief. I want to hear you, Chief Crow."

Crow was pleased to be called chief. So he answered, "Caw!"

"Oh, Chief Crow," called Coyote, "that wasn't much. You can sing better than that. Sing a good song for me, Chief. I want to hear you sing loud."

Crow was pleased again. So he opened his mouth wide and called from the cliff in a loud voice, "C-a-a-w!"

Of course the ball of deer fat fell down from Crow's open mouth.

Coyote grabbed it quickly. Then he laughed.

"You are not a wise chief," said Coyote. "You are not a chief at all. I called you 'Chief' just to fool you. I wanted your deer fat. I am hungry. Now you can go hungry because of your foolishness."

The Tasks of Rabbit

❖ *Creek* ❖

Adapted by John R. Swanton

abbit went to the Master and asked him for wisdom. He said, "I haven't much sense and want you to give me more."

The Master gave Rabbit a sack and told him to fill it with small red ants. "Fill it," he said, "and I will teach you sense." The Master thought that if he did not have any sense he couldn't get one ant into the sack. Rabbit went to the anthill and said, "The Great Master has been saying that you could not fill this sack, but I said you could. What do you think about it?" They answered, "We will fill it," and as they were very anxious to show that they could do so, all went in, whereupon Rabbit tied it up and carried it to the Master. "Here it is," he said, "now give me some knowledge."

The Master said, "There is a big Rattlesnake over yonder. If you bring him here, I will impart to you some knowledge." He thought if Rabbit was really ignorant he would not know what to do. Rabbit went off, cut a stick, and went to find the snake. Then he said to it, "The Master says you are not as long as this stick, but I say you are longer." "I think I am longer. Measure me," said the snake. So Rabbit measured him by laying the stick beside him with its sharp end toward his head and as he was doing so ran the point into his head and killed him. He carried him back to the Master on the end of the stick.

Next the Master said, "There is an Alligator over yonder in the lake. Bring him to me and I will give you knowledge." So Rabbit went to the lake and called out, "Halpata hadjo, halpata hadjo" ("Alligator hadjo" is an honorary name bestowed on the reptile). The Alligator came up in the middle of the lake and poked his head above the water. "What's the matter?" he said. "An ox has been killed for the Master and they want you to come and get timbers for a scaffold on which to roast it." So Alligator came out of the water and followed Rabbit. Before they had gone far Rabbit turned round and struck him with a club. The Alligator started for the lake and although Rabbit pursued him, beating him all the way, he got safely back into the water.

After that Rabbit went off and lay down on the hillside in the sunshine for some time. Then he went and called to the Alligator once more, "Halpata hadjo, halpata hadjo, halpata hadjo." The Alligator came out in the middle of the lake as before and said, "What's the matter?" "Pasikola (story name of Rabbit) was sent here some time ago and nothing has been seen of him, so they told me to come and see what had happened to him." The Alligator answered that someone had come to him before with such a story and had beaten him. "They thought he might have done something of the sort," said Rabbit, "for he is a mean, devilish kind of person. They told him to get you to bring the forked pieces for a scaffold on which to roast an ox and as he didn't come back they sent me to find out what had happened." Upon that the

Alligator came out of the water again and they set out. As they went along Rabbit said, "That Pasikola is very bad and they ought not to have sent him. He has no sense. Did he beat you very badly?" "He beat me a great deal, but did not hit a dangerous place." "If he had hit you in a dangerous spot would you have lived?" "No; it would certainly have killed me." "Where would one hit to hurt you?" "If one struck me across the hips it would finish me." And so, having learned what he wanted to know, Rabbit presently struck the Alligator across the hips and laid him out dead. Then he picked him up and took him to the Master. And when the Master saw him he said, "You have more sense now than I could impart to you."

The end.

Visiting, **Geronima Montoya, (San Juan Pueblo), 1961. Courtesy of the School of American Research, Santa Fe, NM.**

COYOTE AND NEVER GROWS BIGGER

❖ *Wichita* ❖

ADAPTED BY BARRY LOPEZ

One time Coyote met a very small snake called Never Grows Bigger.

"What a ridiculous thing you are," said Coyote. "Who would ever want to be as small as you are? Why are you this small anyway? You ought to be big like me. You can't do anything if you're that small. There must be something wrong with you."

The snake didn't say anything.

"Let me see your teeth," said Coyote.

The snake opened his mouth. Then Coyote opened his mouth and pointed at his teeth. "See? Look at these teeth of mine. What would happen if we bit each other? Your teeth are too small to hurt anyone, but I could bite you in half. Let's bite each other and you'll see what I mean."

So they bit each other and then Coyote said, "Let's move back a little and call out to each other." Coyote knew that he could tell by the way the snake called out how quickly he was dying. The snake gave a cry and then Coyote called out. Each time the snake called his voice was weaker. Coyote went off a little ways, lay down, and got ready to take a nap. Coyote was still calling out but he could hardly hear the snake. "It's no good to be that small," Coyote thought. "Now he knows."

Soon Coyote noticed that the place where the snake had bitten him was beginning to swell up. The swelling got bad very quickly and Coyote got very weak. He could hardly call out now and he was beginning to feel very dizzy and ill.

By this time the snake's wound had begun to heal. His voice got stronger. Coyote's calls grew weaker and weaker until finally there was no sound out of him anymore. Never Grows Bigger went over to where Coyote was laying down and saw he was dead. "This animal never learns," said Never Grows Bigger. He went away and left Coyote out there on the prairie all blown up like a buffalo bladder from that bite.

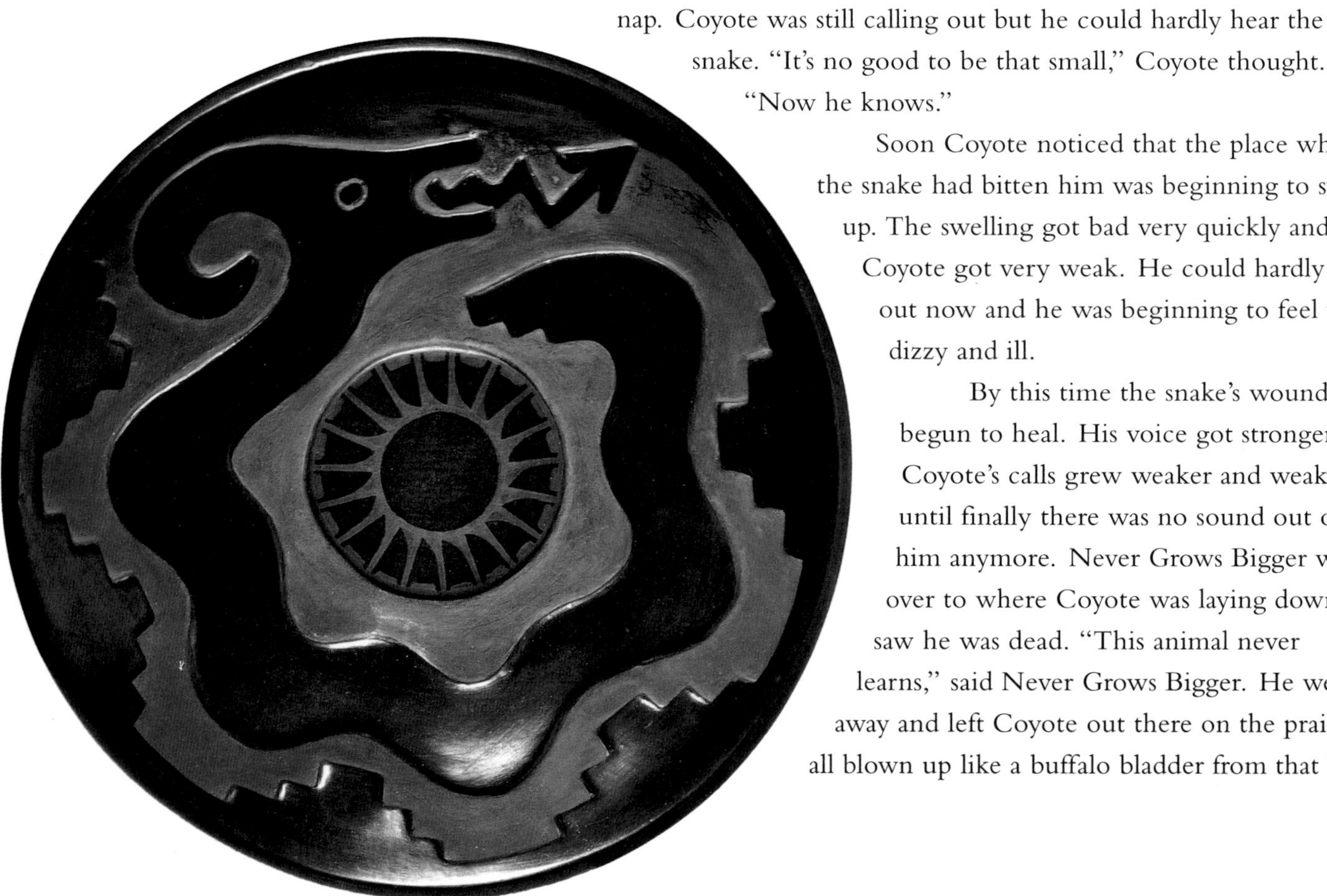

BELOW: *Ceramic Plate* (San Ildefonso). Courtesy of the School of American Research, Santa Fe, NM.

OPPOSITE: *Coyote Equation*, Duane Slick (Mesquakie/Winnebago), 1992. Courtesy of the artist.

2 XC X OX YKOXTXE = LIVES
not
DIES
NOT
DEAD
not
Dying
Coyote
COOY
YOT
E =
Coyote
LIVES
~~DIES~~
LIVES
~~DIES~~
LIVES
LIVES
LIVES

THE WOLVES AND THE DOGS

❖ *Creek* ❖

ADAPTED BY JOHN R. SWANTON

The Wolves used to go about with the Dogs, but men made the Dogs catch the young Wolves and kill them. Therefore the Wolves became angry and a great number held a consultation. They said, "Our children are often killed. Let us gather the Dogs together and kill them." All agreed, so they started off and came howling about the house where the Dogs lived. At the noise the Dogs howled back. Then the Wolves howled in return and the Dogs all assembled. While they were talking to each other the Wolves said to them, "We are going to have a big chicken dinner at noon. All of you come and eat with us." The Dogs answered, "All right." Then the Wolves went back and dug a hole in the ground, and they waited until the date fixed upon, which was the fourth day.

When this day arrived the Dogs prepared to go. A very old Dog wanted to go with them but they said to him, "You know you would not be able to travel around, so stay at home." But he answered, "I can eat too." While this Dog was still at the house the others all started off. Still the old Dog followed them. When they saw him coming they said to one another, "That old man ought to have stayed at home but he is coming."

When they got to the place a great number of Wolves were there waiting for them, and when all were together, they said,

Kachina Doll **(Hopi). San Diego Museum of Man, San Diego, CA.**

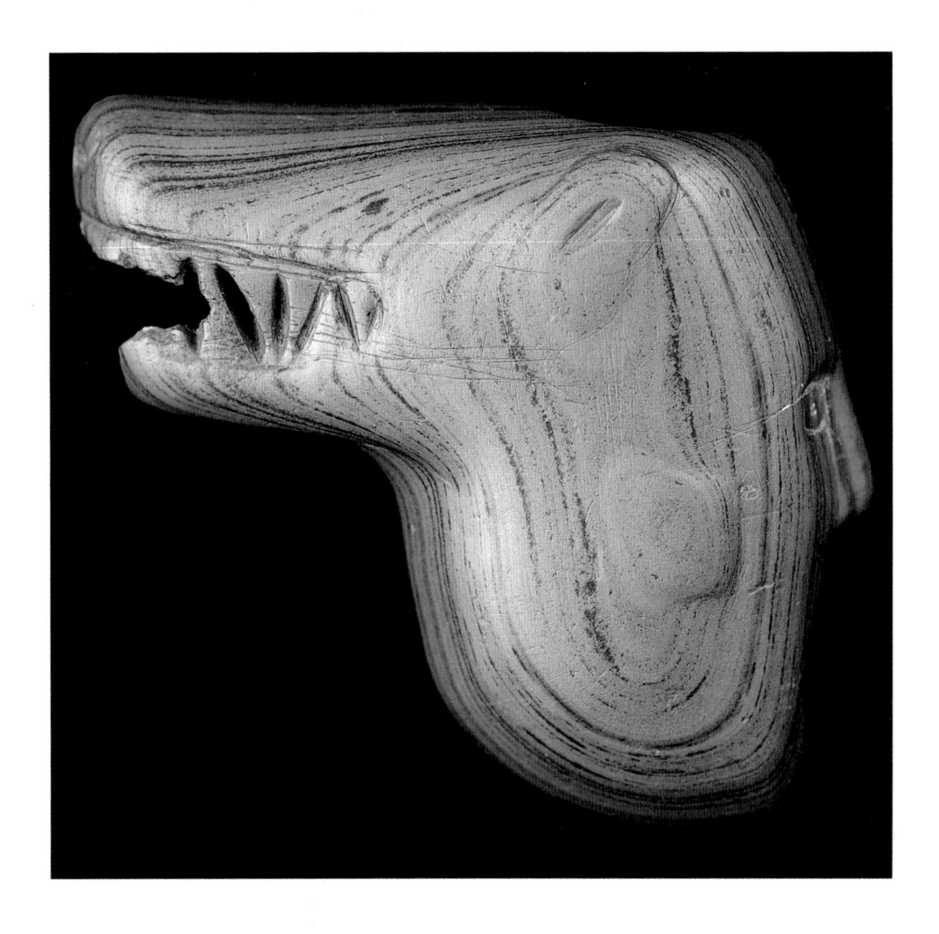

Wolf Man Pipe **(Fort Ancient Culture). From the Collection of the Dayton Museum of Natural History, Dayton, OH.**

"Go into that big hole in the ground and sit down there." When the Dogs got in, the Wolves said to them, "Are you all here?" "An old one is coming," they answered, and they waited for him. When the old male arrived they said, "You go in there too." So the old one went inside, and then one of four Wolves sitting round the door to the hole in the ground stood up and said, "We have been looking for this chance to get you. You have killed all of our beautiful children, and now we are going to kill all of you." One old Wolf talked in this manner and lay down. Another stood up and said the same thing. All spoke likewise. Then the Dogs cried and howled. But the old Dog to whom they had said, "You are fit for nothing and must remain in the house," the one that would not remain but went on, stood up and said, "I am the one who destroyed the children you said you lost and I am getting pretty old." He took out a Wolf's tail he had in his possession and said, "Here lies your tail, so kill me first of all." He shook the wolf tail at them and when the old Wolves saw it all jumped up and ran away. The Dogs, not waiting for one another, jumped over the wall of the hole, got out, and ran off. After they had disappeared the old Dog walked around and went out. When he got home the Dogs were already there and he said, "You couldn't help yourselves, but yet you said to me, 'Remain in the house; you are not able to travel around,' so you went along, but I set out and I saved all of you. From this time on rely upon the old people when you go about. If one older than the rest advises you, trust him. Take this advice. All of you remember to do this. Before long I shall be dead, but do not forget the advice I am giving you. Think, 'An old man who used to be with us saved our lives.'" He advised them in this manner and not long afterwards died.

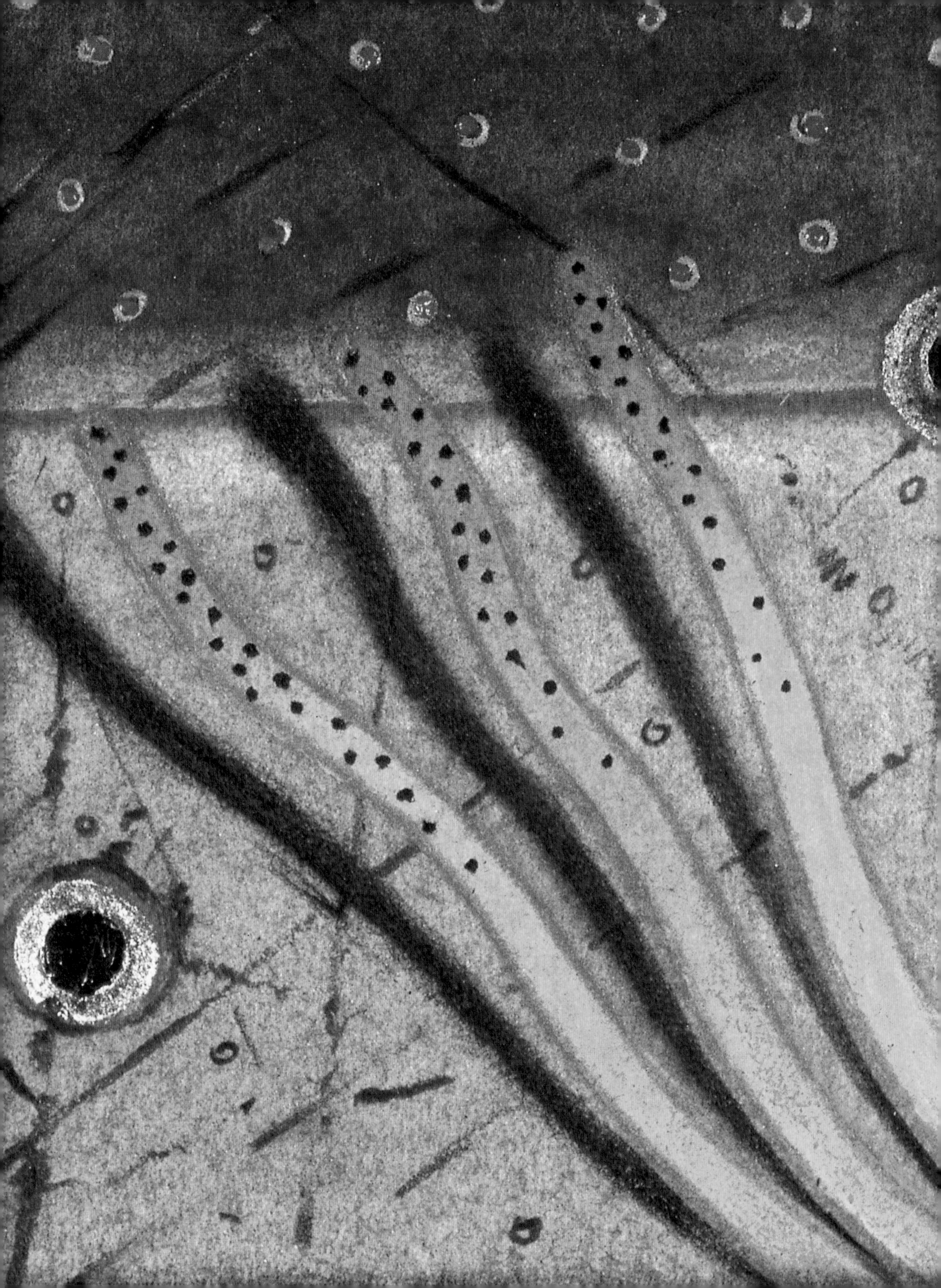

SPEAKS-IN-RIDDLES AND WISE SPIRIT

❖ *Skiri Pawnee* ❖

TOLD BY HARRY MAD BEAR,

RECORDED AND TRANSLATED BY DOUGLAS PARKS

There were two bands of Indians, and in one of the two there was a person who was very wise. They called him Wise Spirit. And living in the other band was another person, named Speaks-in-Riddles. And each of them wanted to see the other one, but the day had not yet come for them to meet.

And then eventually Wise Spirit thought, "Oh, I wish I could meet Speaks-in-Riddles."

Then Speaks-in-Riddles thought, "I wish I could meet Wise Spirit."

Now this is what Speaks-in-Riddles did: he went to see Wise Spirit. That band where he lived was camped not far away. And he arrived there.

Then he said, "I guess you have heard that I've come. I am Speaks-in-Riddles. I hear that you're named Wise Spirit. I've come looking for you. Now I want to say what I want to say. It won't take long, and then I'll go."

Then Wise Spirit said, "Now sit down there, and say what it is that you want to say!"

Now Speaks-in-Riddles sat down. "Now I'm going to tell you about things I saw on my way here. My, while I was coming along the bank of that rapidly flowing river, it seemed as if there were someone with me. And now after I crossed the river and looked back, there appeared to be dead red birds lying there on the ground.

"Well, after I came up the hill, I also saw these things. And again this is what I did: while I was watching things as I looked off into the wide valley, why, off in the distance in the wide valley, there appeared to be lines of black rope. Why, there appeared to be lines of black rope. Well, now, I looked around at the valley with many streams of water extending through it—with those streams spreading out in different directions—and there appeared to be tree roots sticking up out of the water in those streams that were spread out in different directions. And now there seemed to be roots sticking up out of the water.

"And in the distance I saw people walking around throughout the valley. Why, in the distance, in that wide valley, those people were standing all around by the water—they were standing there by the water. And this is what they were doing: it looked as though they were crying and wiping their tears—as if they were crying while they were returning to their village in the wide valley—wiping the water off themselves the way one does when perspiring, when a person breaks out all over in perspiration.

"And when the people were coming into their village from different directions, into that large village," he said, "why, what I saw was a truly unbelievable number of people! It seemed, as they say—it seemed as if they were bending over and whistling.

***Calvario Series #97*, Marty Avrett (Coushatta/ Choctaw/Cherokee), 1994. Courtesy of the artist.**

"Then this is what an old woman did—in front of those lodges, why, this is what a grandmother was doing: she was rocking back and forth—all the while sitting by the fire, rocking back and forth."

And he said, "And this is what I did when I got into the village. And this is what I did when I went into that lodge: I pushed the door open and went inside. And I looked all around. Why, there appeared to be human skulls scattered all around along the wall of the lodge. Now I saw the same thing throughout the rest of the village. I saw the same thing throughout that village. Well, then I came out.

"Now I kept walking until I arrived here where you're living. Now I'm going to go back to my village. In the meantime let's see if you can interpret a little of what I've said—of what I've told you."

Well, then this is what this person Wise Spirit did: he said, "Repeat what you said!"

Speaks-in-Riddles said, "No, I have already told you once."

"Just tell me again what you told me before! Just tell me again what you told me before." He repeated, "Just tell it. Say it again! Say it again!"

Now this is what Speaks-in-Riddles said. Then he said, "Now I'm leaving. I'll come back sometime." That is what he said.

Then he got up. Then he went off.

Now after he left, this man Wise Spirit pondered what he had said. Wise Spirit pondered it for days. Now he would not eat, and he would not even drink. My, all he would do was ponder it! Why, they say that he was the wisest person in this village—in this entire village. There was no one else like him here, and it was said that if someone did not know something, this Wise Spirit would know. That one knew everything.

"Now I certainly don't know the answer to this riddle! Now see if you can bring him back to me!"

Now they went to get Speaks-in-Riddles, and after a number of days he came.

And Wise Spirit said, "Well, now sit down! Why, I'm lying here truly at the end of my wits! My mind is totally exhausted. Why, what they say is true! You are rightfully named Speaks-in-Riddles. You are rightfully named that. Now interpret for me the meaning of what you said you saw!"

"First it seemed as if someone were with me while I was coming—while I was coming down through the valley along the bank of the river. Now I meant that it seemed as though there were someone with me as I came down through the valley while the sun was setting. Now my own shadow appeared in that rapidly flowing river, and it made it seem as though there were someone traveling along with me.

"Thereupon I crossed the stream, and on the other side, why, what appeared to be red birds were really ripe plums that must have fallen off the trees. They appeared to be red birds whose feathers had been plucked and were lying there spread out over the ground. The plums were *so* red!

"Well, then this is what I did: I came up the hill. After I came up it—when I was coming up to this village of yours—why, I looked back while I was coming along, and there in the distance in the wide valley through which I had come, there appeared to be lines of black rope on the ground. They were buffalo that looked like lines of black rope. And people were driving the buffalo into that stream, where they killed them. And a buffalo would fall in the water, and it would be lying on its back—and it would be lying on its back in the water with its hooves upright. And those buffalo lying in the water looked like tree stumps sticking up. Well, then people were picking them up. Then this is what they did: they came on foot, and then they apparently started butchering them. Then they packed them on their backs. Thereupon they carried them through the valley. While they were carrying them on their backs, they got hot and broke out in perspiration and were wiping the perspiration off while they were going into the village.

"And meanwhile the women were preparing everything by spreading the buffalo hides out and staking them." They say the women used to scrape the buffalo hair off them. They would also take all the flesh off. They would dry the hides to make them into robes after they were nice and dry.

"Why, now there was grandmother, rocking back and forth all the while. And by grandmother rocking back and forth, I mean first she made a hole in the ground and then took kettles of boiling bones off the fire. Then she poured the broth from a kettle into the hole and blew on it. And in that way it became marrow grease, or tallow, after it hardened. Now this is what people were doing: they would shape the marrow grease into balls and then take them into their lodges. And when they put those balls of tallow along the wall of the lodge, they would look like human skulls lying there.

"Well, now after I saw these things, I knew these people had plenty," he said, "and then I came here. I came to see you, Wise Spirit. Now I have told you about everything I saw while I was coming here. And these things are what I meant by the riddle."

And now Wise Spirit sat up, after he had made himself sick from worrying about its meaning. "Well, now, old woman, at least give him some coffee to drink! Well, at least bring some food! Now he and I will eat!

"Now sit down! We're going to eat. You have outdone me."

Now the gut extends. I have finished the story.

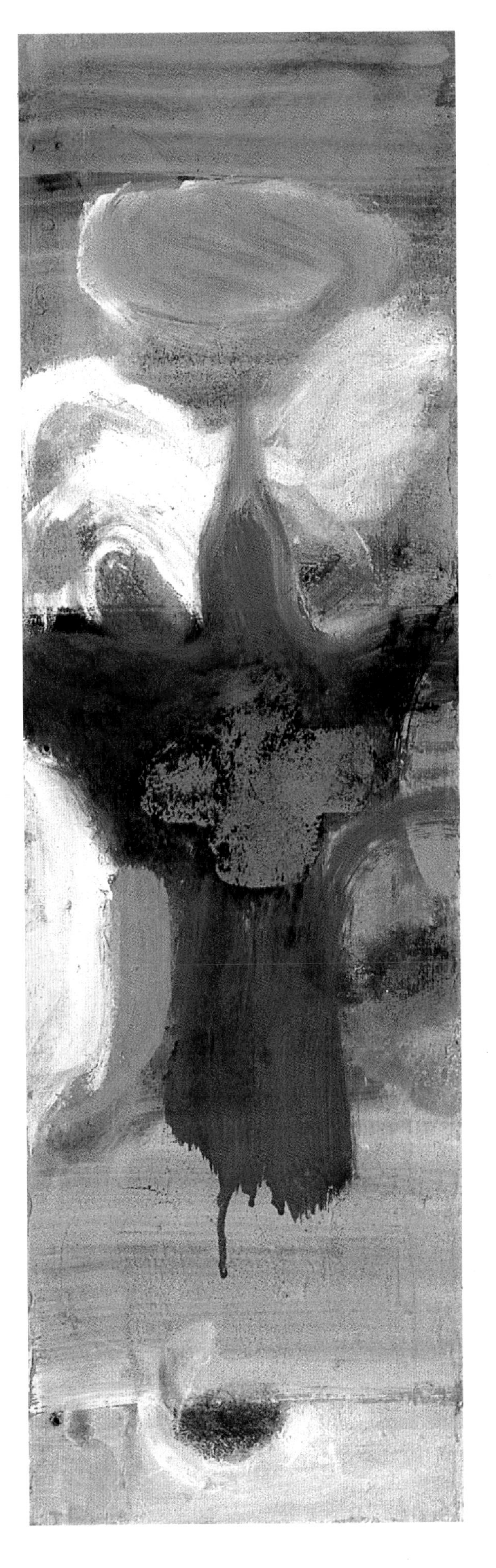

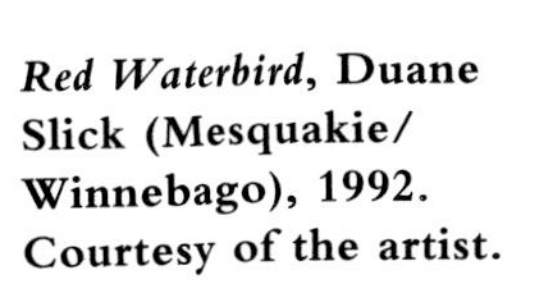

***Red Waterbird*, Duane Slick (Mesquakie/ Winnebago), 1992. Courtesy of the artist.**

COYOTE AND SKUNK

❖ *Navajo* ❖

TOLD BY TIMOTHY BENALLY, SR.

There was a dark spot moving along the vast desert valley, the plains stretching in every direction. Over the dark spot two vultures were circling high up in the sky.

Coyote could not escape from the midmorning sun on this flat desert, and there was not a speck of cloud in the sky. He was sweating and getting thirstier as he plodded along. Even the reptiles were seeking shelter from the hot sun.

Coyote had traveled for days and nights in this condition, without water and food. He could see the buzzards circling high above him and thought, "This may be the end of me finally." His mouth would not stay open by itself; so he had to work it to keep from choking.

"You can wish, but I am not your meal yet," he yelled hoarsely at the buzzards, continuing to drag his feet one after another. His progress was slow, and his destination, the mountain, was barely visible in the distance. "It should be cool upon those mountains," he thought. "I'll make it. I have been in worse situations than this. I was even ground into pieces once, and look at me now."

Thinking about his past gave him an idea. "A cloud ought to appear above him," it is said he said, and a cloud formed directly above him. "His underfeet ought to be moist while he trots," he said again, and it began to sprinkle, and the soles of his feet were moist as he trotted.

After cooling off, Coyote regained some strength and became more lively. He said, "Rainwater ought to gush out between his toes as he trots." It began to rain more heavily, and the water began to gush out between his toes. Then he said, "Water ought to reach his knees while he trots," and the rain became heavier, and the water rose till it reached his knees. Coyote trotted with the water splashing all around him, and he lapped and drank the rainwater as he went.

"Just his back ought to be above water as he trots," it is said he said again, and it started to rain much more heavily, until only his back was visible.

Again this he said, it is said: "One should float down the river, and one ought to wash ashore where prairie dogs, rabbits, squirrels, quails, and other edible beings are plentiful." And the water rose higher, till it began to carry him down the wash.

Coyote floated down the wash for quite some time. While he was floating, he was planning how he would lure the animals to him. He began to sing a song:

Prairie dogs, see me floating.
I am drowned, and soon I shall be washed ashore.
You will be so delighted by the reports of my

***Skunks*, Awa Tsireh (San Ildefonso), c. 1929.**

death,
that you will want to celebrate.
Gather around me
and sing songs of joy.

Coyote was washed ashore finally and played dead, just lying on the beach, barely breathing. He could hear the flies buzzing around him. After some while, he heard a rattle. The sound came closer and closer; then it stopped.

Coyote opened one eye and saw Skunk standing there looking at him, his mouth hanging open as if in surprise. Skunk had a jar in one hand, with a gourd dipper sticking out of it.

Coyote whispered to Skunk, "*Psst*, my cousin, my cousin. Come here. I need your help. Don't be afraid of me. I won't hurt you, I promise."

Skunk took several steps backward. Once he recovered from his initial surprise, he asked, "How can I help? You look like you are beyond help!"

"Come closer to me, my cousin," Coyote whispered. "I don't want anyone else to hear what I have to tell you."

"Well, all right," said Skunk as he reluctantly came closer to Coyote. "Now, what is it that's so important it has to be kept secret?"

Untitled, **Fred Kabotie (Hopi), 1922. Courtesy of the School of American Research, Santa Fe, NM.**

"I just want to tell you how we can get plenty to eat later this evening. I'm so hungry! I haven't eaten for several days now. Getting us both fed will require your help," said Coyote.

Skunk was still recovering from the shock of seeing Coyote lying on the riverbank half-dead, and he just listened as Coyote continued.

"The first thing I want you to do is pick some grass seeds from the fields and put those seeds around my mouth, eyes, ears, anus and between my toes. Arrange them so that they look like the larvae of the blue flies," Coyote instructed. "I'll tell you the rest when you've done that."

Skunk said suspiciously, "I don't see how that is going to get us fed."

"Well, I am not through yet, my cousin," replied Coyote. "When you tell the people in your community that Doo Yildiní is dead, they will be curious and want to check your story. That is why I can't move from the spot where I am lying. I don't want to leave my tracks all over the place."

"So, when they check my story, you'll lie there as you are now, playing dead? When they come near, you'll grab them and then eat them? What a clever idea, my cousin. OK, I'll do it for you," said Skunk.

"No! No! Nothing like that. If the first one who comes does not return, they will know you are lying to them. But when they hear the same reports from different individuals, they will believe your story. They will want to celebrate my death. *That's* when we'll make our move."

"Oh! That's when we'll grab them and eat them, huh?" asked Skunk.

"You stupid skunk," Coyote thought disgustedly. "You still don't see the whole thing do you?" "Look," he said, "we can't catch but a few that way. So when they gather to celebrate my death, here is what I want you to do." He whispered again.

Skunk was delighted by Coyote's clever plan. He said, "OK, OK! I'll do just that," and left his cousin on the riverside.

After some time Skunk returned with the grass seeds and started placing them according to Coyote's instructions. When he had finished, he admired the fine work he had done. "It looks real enough even for me," he said aloud.

"One more thing," Coyote instructed, "before you go, make four wooden clubs, and bury two in front of me and the other two behind me so that at the proper moment we can grab and use them to kill our feast."

When everything was ready, Skunk filled his jar with water and headed home. When he got home, he said, "I saw Coyote washed ashore down by the river. The flash flood from the morning's heavy rainfall must have gotten him!"

Some of Skunk's neighbors gathered around and asked, "How could Coyote be dead? That's impossible!"

Skunk said, "I saw him with my own eyes as I was getting water just before noon. I checked *very* carefully. The flies had already laid their larvae around his mouth and eyes. We should celebrate his death. After all, it will mean we no longer have to hide in fear of him."

"It's a trick," said Prairie Dog, looking sideways at Skunk. "We should not trust Coyote to be dead. I don't even trust the one telling this story."

Cottontail Rabbit said, "Yes, Coyote is clever all right. Let's send someone else there to check him out. We shouldn't just come to a conclusion and start celebrating even though it is good news for many of us."

"Who wants to volunteer to check on Coyote's death?" asked Raccoon. No volunteer.

"I would volunteer, but my legs are too short. Coyote could easily overtake me," said Prairie Dog.

"That's it," said Raccoon. "We need someone who can easily outrun Coyote, and that is Jackrabbit, the rabbit that is big."

Jackrabbit stood up from behind the crowd and said, "I am getting old and can't run fast anymore. Get someone else." There was silence for a period of time.

"Come on, Jackrabbit. What do you mean you're old?" said Raccoon. "Why, you'd outrun Coyote so fast he wouldn't know what to do!"

A big cheer went up from the crowd. "Yeah, yeah, Jackrabbit! We know you are the fastest runner in the area."

"Well, OK, I'll go," said Jackrabbit.

Another big cheer!

As Jackrabbit disappeared over the hill, Skunk smiled to himself thinking, "So they swallowed my story just like my cousin Coyote had predicted. I can taste my feast already!"

More animals had gathered around the two main speakers, Raccoon and Prairie Dog. Skunk thought, "The more the merrier!" One of the newcomers asked, "What's going on here? What's all the commotion about?"

Skunk replied, "Coyote is dead. He's washed ashore down by the river."

Prairie Dog interjected, "We just sent Jackrabbit to investigate the story. One just can't be too sure about these things, you know."

The newcomer, Quail, said, "It's a good idea to check it out to make sure. If it isn't true, lots of us would be at the mercy of Coyote."

Prairie Dog said, "True, true. We can't afford to take chances. Coyote is our worst enemy, and a very clever one too."

"What if Jackrabbit doesn't come back? Does that mean that Coyote still lives? What do we do then?" asked Ground Squirrel.

Skunk answered, "He'll come back! I was the one who reported Coyote was dead. I made sure he was *really* dead before I came back. I even kicked him in the stomach several times, and he didn't make a sound or make a move. I'm sure Jackrabbit will come back."

Prairie Dog thought Skunk seemed awfully sure of the answers he provided. He said, "If Jackrabbit does not get back, we will send someone else. And even if he comes back, we will check once more, just to be sure."

Skunk complained, "We should be celebrating the death of Coyote. What do we do instead? We check him out to see if he is really dead. I say let's celebrate and feast."

Just then Jackrabbit appeared in the distance. A loud cheer went up from the crowd, which had been growing in size since Skunk's return with the news. "It is true. Coyote is really dead, as Skunk reported," Jackrabbit shouted cheerfully. "He's dead! Coyote is dead! I jumped up and down on top of him, and he never moved at all. The larvae are all over his face now, as our friend Skunk had reported."

The crowd cheered louder at the news, and Prairie Dog had difficulties controlling them. He said, "I agree that is good news, but I am still not satisfied." The crowd was not listening to him.

Skunk took advantage of the situation. "Let's celebrate at the place where Coyote is lying dead," he said and started walking toward the river. Some started to follow him.

Prairie Dog shouted to the people, "Stop! Listen to me. We should send one more runner to check Coyote out. That way we will be certain that he is dead and that this is not a trick. Then you can celebrate if you like."

The followers stopped and returned to the main crowd.

Prairie Dog said, "Gopher, you go this time. Use your ability to dig fast in the ground for your getaway in case he is alive." Without any objections, Gopher took off toward the river and was gone.

"We could be celebrating right now," Skunk complained. "Instead, we have to listen to this worrier." He slunk off by himself and observed the discussions from a distance. He was forgotten.

Jackrabbit said, "When Gopher gets back, we ought to plan how to celebrate this special occasion, the death of Coyote."

The talk alerted Skunk once more, and he hurried back into the crowd and suggested, "Why wait till Gopher gets back? Let's start celebrating right now. I suggest that we go to the site and dance and feast for the rest of the day and all night!" A tremendous cheer went up again at the suggestion. "Bring your food, and we will share whatever we have," continued Skunk. "We no longer have to fear Coyote. He's dead! That calls for much celebration." More cheers!

Gopher in the meantime was approaching Coyote. He stopped at a distance, surveyed the situation carefully, and then decided to burrow his way. He didn't want to take the chance of being eaten. He burrowed right to the spot between the forelegs and the hind legs of Coyote and came up. He checked around and saw the larvae; then he bit into Coyote's ear. Nothing happened. He decided Coyote was dead just as had been reported by Skunk and Jackrabbit. Satisfied, he returned to the crowd and reported that Coyote was really dead.

"Yaaah!" the crowd yelled almost in unison as they started to move toward the river. Only Prairie Dog stayed behind. Once on the site, they formed four concentric circles around Coyote and began singing and dancing.

When they had really warmed up, Skunk moved a distance away from the crowd and pissed into the space above them. He yelled, "Look. Look. Look in the sky. There is something real pretty up there!" As they looked into the sky, Skunk's urine got into their eyes and momentarily obstructed their vision.

At that moment Skunk yelled to Coyote, "Now, my cousin, now!" Coyote sprang to his feet and grabbed the two clubs closest to him and started killing all the creatures who had been celebrating. Only a few got away after they recovered from the effects of Skunk's urine.

ENOUGH IS ENOUGH

❖ *Cheyenne* ❖

RECORDED BY GEORGE GRINNELL, ADAPTED BY ELLA CLARK

One Cheyenne man of long ago had a pointed leg. By running and jumping against trees he made his leg stick in them. When he said the magic word, he dropped again to the ground. Sometimes on a hot day he would stick himself high on the tree trunk for greater shade. However, he knew he could not do this trick more than four times in one day.

A white man came along, saw him perform, and cried out, "Brother, sharpen my leg!" Cheyenne man said, "That's not too hard. I can sharpen your leg." So the white man stood on a large log, and with an axe the Cheyenne sharpened his leg. "But you must remember never to perform your trick more than four times in one day, and keep exact count."

White man then went down toward the river and saw a large tree growing on the back. Toward this he ran, jumped, and thrust his leg into the tree, where it stuck. He called himself back to the ground. Again he jumped against another tree, but only counted one. The third time he only counted two. The fourth time, birds and animals stood by and watched as the white man jumped high and pushed his leg on the tree, up to his knee. But he only counted three.

Then coyotes, wolves, and other animals came to see him. Some asked, "How did the white man learn the trick?" They begged him to show them, so they could stick themselves to trees at night. The white man became even prouder from all of this admiration, and the fifth time he ran harder, jumped higher, and half his thigh entered the tree and there he stuck fast. Then he counted four.

He called and called to bring himself down to the ground again, but he still stuck fast. He called out all night and the next day—but nothing helped him. He asked his animal friends to find the Cheyenne who had taught him the trick, but no one knew whom to look for. The white man had forgotten the secret of freeing himself, and after many days stuck in the tree, he starved to death.

***Tale of Two Trees*, Duane Slick (Mesquakie/ Winnebago), 1992. Courtesy of the artist.**

COYOTE AND THE WHITE MAN

❖ *Coeur d'Alene* ❖

TOLD BY LAWRENCE ARIPA, ADAPTED BY RODNEY FREY

Coyote was going along, . . .
and all of a sudden . . . he heard a *man screaming*,
"*He-lp, help, help*!"
and he says
"That's a strange *voice*?"
He says,
"That isn't an Indian!
So he runs over and he looks,
and there . . . is a White Man,
the *first* one he's ever seen.
And the White Man . . is getting beat up . . by a group of Indians. . . .
And so they are just about ready to kill him
they are *really* going after him.

And the Coyote says
"*Well*, I still have a *little power*,
maybe I can chase them away?"

So Coyote goes to his tipi,
and makes some "Indian ice cream,"
from berries and what not.

It's all foamy
and he puts it all over his mouth.
(motions with hands over his mouth).
like he has *rabies*!

So he jumps up there,
and he *scares* them,
and he says,
"I will use my powers
and I will get rid of *all of you,*
you leave the man alone!"
So they did,
they left him alone . . .

And the man was grateful,
"Thank you,
I don't know who you are
but I am *grateful*,
thank you for what you've *done* for me."
And he says
"That's alright."
He says
"I'm the *Coyote*.
And I am lonely."

He says
"I can't . . use my powers anymore,
and people,
they ignore me now
they don't depend on me
and nobody will pla-a-y with me
nobody will listen to my stories!"

And he says,
"I am *getting lonely*!" . . .
And the man says,
"Well, . . . *I* can keep you company."
He says,
"I can do anything that will make you happy,
because you saved *my* life."
So the Coyote says,
"Well, stay with me!" . .
And he did.

A-a-ll summer long . . they enjoyed each
other's company,
they *had a lot* of fun,
they went swimming,
they went
and did all different kinds
of things.
And they had a-a-ll the *food* they
wanted.
And so the two of them got along real well.

And then all of a sudden . . the summer was gone.
The leaves turned,
and everything got *co-o-ld*.
And then it was winter time.
They didn't go out
and get food
and save it.
So here they were
no food, . . .
And they were starving . . . .
And so they said,
"*Well, what can we do*?
We have to do something to get *food*
otherwise we will both perish." . .
So the Coyote says
"Well, . . . about fifty miles up this way,
a . . they tell me that they're starting
a *trading post* over there."

He says
"Maybe we can go
and *trade*
and get some food from the
man *there*?"
So the man says
"Alright, so let's *go*!"

So they went and they started off,
and they were *v-e-ry hungry*,
almost starving.
They got close,
and the Coyote says
"Now, I have a plan."
He says,
"You tie my four legs together
and put me over your shoulder
and go up to the *trading post*
and tell the man that you want to
trade . . coyote hide . . for some
food!"
And he says
"And when you *get* the food,
you come back out and untie me.
and then we will just leave,
and we will have a-a-ll that food
and it will keep us, . . .
for most of the winter."
So the man says
"*Al*right, okay!"

So they get close
and then he ties up his legs
and puts him on his shoulder
and then he goes up
and all of a sudden the trader comes out,
"*O-o-o-oh, look at that,*
that's a be-e-autiful fur,
where did you get it?"

The man says,
"I got it
I trapped it,"
and says,
"I want to *trade*, . . .
if it's *possible*?"
And the man says,
"*Su-u-re*!"
He looked at it,
"I can give you about twenty dollars
worth of food."
And the man says
"Oh, good!"
So he lays the Coyote down
and they go into the trading post.

The Coyote is laying there
and listening . . .
All of a sudden he hears the man say, . . .
"I want that . . *sugar*
I want *coffee*,
I want bre-e-ad,
all of the good things,
G-e-e-z-z!"
Coyote is laying there,
and he is *gett-en' hungry*.
(laughter from audience)
"*A-a-h*," he says,
"He's getten' all the things that I like."
And he says,
"Boy, now when he comes out,
we can go and we will *eat*,
and we will both get our strength back,
and *everything will be fine*." . .

And then he heard the man make the deal,
and so . . . the man comes out,
and he and the trader . . . shake hands,
and then he comes by the Coyote.

Here he has . . a big . . . bundle of . . . *f-o-o-d*.
He has *a-a-ll the things* that the Coyote likes to eat.
And he comes by,
and then the Coyote *looks* at him,
"S-s-s-s-p, untie me!" (whispering voice)
And the man don't even look at him,
keeps walking.
"*S-s-s-p, hah, hah,*
you're suppose to untie me!" (much louder
and almost desperate voice)
The man keeps walking
don't even *hear him*,
he just keeps right on walkin'.

All of a sudden he's getting out there by himself
and the Coyote starts hollering
"*Hey, you come back here,*
you come back here,
or I'll catch up to you, . . .
and chew out . . your windpipe,
you come back here!" (desperate voice)
And . . the man didn't even hear him.

All of a sudden the door opens
and the trader come out,
and he looks,
"I thought I heard *voices*!" . . .
So he looked around
and he don't se-e-e anything.
And then he thought,
"Oh it's *that man*,
he's so happy to get *food* that he's singing,
He's *way up* there by himself
and he's *enjoying it*."

He says,
"Ah, I'm glad . . I was able to make that
man . . happy."

OPPOSITE: *Untitled*, Fred Kabotie (Hopi), 1922. Courtesy of the School of American Research, Santa Fe, NM.

He looks down,
and there's the Coyote.
The Coyote is, is *mad*,
and he's *scared*,
and he's laying there with his eyes shut.
And the man goes back into . . . the trading post,
and in a couple of minutes he comes out,
and he's got a sharpener,
and he's got a *la-a-rge knife*
and he's going
su-u-wsh, su-u-wsh, su-u-wsh,
su-u-wsh. (audience laughter)
He's sharpening it up.
And the Coyote looked up,
"*U-u-u-u-h*, . . . *I'm going to get it.*"
(a lot of audience laughter)
And he says,
"*You can't do that*!"
The man stops,
he looks around,
"I thought I heard a voice?"
(a few laughs)
And the Coyote says,
"*Don't kill me,*
don't, don't skin me!"
(pleading voice)
And the man goes down,
takes his knife,
he can't he-a-r.
So he . . goes right ahead,
and he skins the Coyote . . .

And the Coyote has *no* skin.
He looks *pi-ti-ful*, . .
He's already *skinny*! (audience laughter)
The man takes him,
throws him . . . in the pile of . . . brush
and everything.

And there's the po-or Coyote.
He can't *m-o-ve*
and he can't *hol-ler*
and he's *gone*! . .
And so . . that is the end . . . of the Coyote.
And he laid there
and *he* was just *dead*.

And all of sudden Mr. Fox comes by.
And Mr. Fox comes,
goes over,
and Mr. Fox is *wi-se*! . .
"Oh, that po-or thing." . . .
He says,
"Well, he's no good sometimes.
He's mischievous.
He has no respect for others.
But, *a-a-h*, sometimes he's *pretty good*!"
He says,
"Well, maybe I'll bring him back to life."

So he takes him,
and he lays him on the ground,
and then he prays, . . .
"Animal spirit, . . give me your *powers*,
help me so I can bring this foolish
thing back to life
. . . (chuckle by storyteller and
laughter by audience)
Maybe he don't deserve it
but he *is* . . . my friend.
And so *help* me."
So he dances around . . the body
and he goes around and sings
and then he goes over
and he *jumps* over . . once . .

And then when he *jumps over* he stops,
"*What* am I do-o-ing?
That Coyote is only goin' to raise . . .
a lot of *trouble* if I bring *him back*!"
And then he turns and he looks
"*Well*, . .
I guess I *can* . . . help him."

So he jumps over again.

But he is still puzzled,
"*I shouldn't do this,*
he's just a mischievous
a no-good . . . Coyote!"
And then he says,
"No, I have to do it."
So he jumps over the third time.

And the Coyote opens his eyes, . .
he stretches,
and "*A-a-a-a-h, I've slept a-a-long*
time!"
And the Fox looks at him,
"*Sleep*? . . .
You've been dead!
You *foolish* thing
don't you know that, that you did . .
something *wr-o-ong*?
And now you are . . are *go-o-ne*
but I have brought you back!"
And the Coyote sat there,
and he says
"*O-o-o-h, now I remember.*

He says
"*A-a-a-h that man*, . . .
that man, he's the one . . . that had me killed,
and he wouldn't help me
when . . he should of
and he took *a-a-ll* the *food*."
And he says,
"I'm going to catch up to him
and I'm going to *chew* his
windpipe."
Mr. Fox says,
"Wait, *wait*, Coyote, . . .
you were *dead*.
You have to be *thankful* that you are *a-live now*,
that you are able to *breathe*
you're going to be able to *eat*
you'll be able to . . . do *all the things*
that you did before.
And you should be *grateful*.
And I am telling you . . . as a friend,
don't, don't do anything, . . .
don't look for *revenge*.
Just live . . the way you have to live!"
And so he preached on and on.

And then . . . the Coyote says,
"Yes, . . . *you're* right."
He says,
"Okay, I *won't* chew out . . his windpipe,
I won't do anything.
Alright, I'll change.
I'll be a *go-o-d, go-o-d Coyote* from now on."
And Mr. Fox says,
"I'm glad you feel that way."
He says
"But let this be a lesson to you." . .
He says
"Now remember, . . .
from this time on . . . there are going to be
a-a lot of white men that come."

And he says
"And I want you to *remember*, . . .
now *remember* this, . . .
If you . . . give something to a white
man,
and it's going to do him some
good, . . .
he'll skin you alive! . . .
(slow deliberate voice, followed
by tremendous laughter from
audience)

And so that . . was another lesson that we
had to learn. . . .
And we haven't *yet*! . . .
(more laughter from both storyteller
and audience)

❖ ❖ ❖ ❖ ❖

As odd as it may seem, without death, life would become very boring; the forms and processes of life as we know it would have no meaning if they ran on forever. In reality, it is the end of life that draws the circle to a close, to completion, and in completion lets us achieve immortality in the memories and stories of our friends, our children, and our grandchildren. Native American people, like those of many other cultures, highly value speaking well during life, and being spoken well of after life. If you speak well in Nez Perce country while alive, you may be honored; you will certainly be admired and respected. Thus, oral historians and storytellers hold high position in Nez Perce culture. If you speak well and truly while alive, you may be spoken well and truly of after death; and the people always remember the great men and women through stories and legends. It is death, then, that allows people to say, "He was a good man or she was a good storyteller for good and always." If you try to live a good life, you earn the right to a good death. So if Death did not exist, well, someone would have to invent it.

Coyote (or among the Blackfeet, *Na'pi*, or Old Man) is often the one who accounts for the existence of death by recording its invention; usually the invention carries with it some regret on Coyote's part that he has succeeded in inventing it when someone from his own family dies. In "Dancing with Grief" Lizard and Cottontail do not mind if there are too many people, and they regret that people have to mourn the death of loved ones; and so it is that Cottontail reminds Coyote who is responsible for making people weep. In the Blackfoot legend, "Woman Chooses Death," she chooses it without really knowing what it is she is doing; when Coyote and Eagle visit the land of the dead, Coyote gets tired, fails, and then doesn't want to return once again in an effort to bring the spirits back to life. Perhaps this image of tiredness relates to life—in creating and keeping our names and identities, in participating in the life of our communities, in earning a good death, we wear out, grow weary of the processes. Perhaps like the spirits in the story—given the image of the afterworld in these stories—we, too, would fly back to the spirit world even though we were so close to the world of the living. Regardless, the Native perspective on death tends to be matter of fact and, as in the case of Albert Hummingbird driving a modified conversion van, almost amusing.

In some of these stories, spirit people offer lessons. A Mashpee Ghost offers a mother gold; but every time she digs her hoe into the ground, one of her sleeping children cries out. Of course, in the morning the gold is gone. At first she thinks she's lost her chance at riches, but she realizes that her children are her wealth; her long life with them is what she values. We find that the desires of the living conflict with the endless patience of the dead in "Memaloose Island" and that the joyous sensual feelings of Coyote are what cause his wife to remain in the land of the dead. But another story, "A Matter of Concentration," shows us that if one knows that Death is always there, he really becomes boring—especially to the old and wise whose concentration surpasses that of other human beings.

The simply beautiful Havasupai "The Farewell Song" highlights this entire section of stories about death and images of the afterworld. Wisdom requires the awareness of death, and in the final selection, "Telling About Coyote," Simon Ortiz tells us that only Coyote will "be back"—we assume and hope to teach our children and grandchildren as the cycle of human beings begins and ends again. Thus in the world I come from, a man or a woman journeys after death through an arid land until he finds his horse, which takes him

to his people. There he can wait patiently for his children who will come after him. A bad man takes a long, long time to find his horse, and a real bad man walks the hot places forever. In my world, then, only bad men have cause to fear the transformation to the other world that gets called "death."

***Coyote Lives*, Duane Slick (Mesquakie/Winnebago), 1992. Courtesy of the artist.**

DANCING WITH GRIEF
from SEX, FINGERS, AND DEATH

❖ *Yani* ❖

TOLD BY SAM BATWI, TRANSLATED WITH EDWARD SAPIR, ADAPTED BY WILLIAM BRIGHT

The people were very many,
the people were like blackbirds.
There was no one who died,
no poisoning by magic,
no one who wept.
The men grew old,
but didn't die.
The women grew old,
but didn't die.

It rained.
All the people went in the sweathouse together.
Then it snowed.
Now Coyote had a child.
Coyote said,
"Let's make people die!"
speaking to the three creators.
They were sitting there on the south side of
the sweathouse.
Lizard had his head hung down.
Cottontail was sitting there,
Gray Squirrel was sitting there,
All three had their heads hung down,
listening to Coyote's words,
"It will be good if people die."

Now they spoke,
Cottontail, Gray Squirrel, Lizard.
"Hm, hm, hm!" said Lizard.
"People shall not die,
so we won't weep when people die,"
said Lizard,
"In fact people will die,
but they will come back to life.
"We'll bury them when they die,
and they'll come back up.
"We won't bury them deep,
when we bury them,
when they die."
"Why should they come back to life?"
said Coyote.
"When they die, they'll die.
"When people die,
we'll weep,
'Boo-hoo,' people will say.
"People will weep,
when their brother dies,
when their sister dies,
when their child dies.
"Hoo! So they'll put pitch on their eyes,
so they'll put clay on their faces,
they'll mourn.
"'Wai! wai! wai!' they'll say,
when people weep."
What could Lizard say?
He was defeated.

OPPOSITE: *Moon Mask, Death Mask* (Heiltsuk). Courtesy of Donald Ellis Gallery, Ontario.

Now it was snowing,
the trees were all covered with snow.
They whispered together,
Lizard, Gray Squirrel, Cottontail.
The people were afraid to go out in the snow,
the people filled the sweathouse completely.
A man was sick,
Lizard himself had poisoned him.
The sick man died.
Coyote said nothing.

A man was dead,
but people did not weep.
"What shall we do with the dead man?"
said Cottontail.
"Let's bury him."
"Where shall we bury him?
"There's too much snow outside.
"Let's bury him here in the sweathouse,
in the floor on the south side."
Now they dug a pit,
now they laid him in the pit,
not very deep in the ground.
They covered him with earth,
while the snow was still falling.

When he'd been buried,
when he'd been laid in the pit,
he kept moving the gravestones around.
Coyote was sitting there like this,
looking at the gravestones.
The dead man did like this,
moving the gravestones around.
He was about to come back to life,
he who had died,
the dead man kept moving them
around.
Coyote was looking at him,
as he moved them around,
he kept watching him.
The dead man came up this far from the grave.

Coyote jumped up,
Coyote jumped on the dead man,
he pushed him down in the earth.
"Die!" said Coyote.
Coyote raised his foot,
he did like this,
he forced the dead man down with his foot.
"Why are you coming back to life?
"Die! Die!"
So he did,
forcing him down with his foot.
The people said nothing against it.
Coyote left him and returned to his seat,
he sat down again at the north side.
Again he looked at the gravestones,
they weren't moving around any more.

Truly, the man was now dead for good.
"Now!" said Coyote,
  "Cry! Weep!"
"Now the man is dead,
  now we'll never see him again.
"Come on! Put on white clay for mourning!
  Come on! Smear your faces with pitch!"

Well, now the people finished.
"Come on, let's go hunting deer!"
  said the people.
Coyote's young son went along,
  hunting the deer.
"What shall we do to him?
  Let's make Coyote weep!"
  so said the people.
The trail ran east,
  a yellow pine stood not far to the east,
  the trail ran near the yellow pine.
"What shall we do?
  Let's make a rattlesnake!"
"Yes!" said the people.
Now they made a rattlesnake in the east.
"Be coiled around the tree there!"
  they told the rattlesnake.
"Yes," it said.
They put it there where the yellow pine stood.

Now young Coyote came from the west on that trail.
Truly now there was a rattlesnake there,
  they had put it down for young Coyote.
Now young Coyote went up to the rattlesnake,
  suddenly it struck at young Coyote.
It curled around the coyote's legs,
  he was shouting,
  it was pulling him around and biting him.
The rattlesnake killed young Coyote,
  young Coyote died.

"Your child is dead,"
  so said all the people.
"Where is he?"
"He's dead in the east,
  he's been bitten by a rattlesnake."
Coyote said, "So!"
  now weeping,
  now dancing with grief.
Coyote was putting dirt on his face,
  acting like a crazy man.

People brought young Coyote back home.
Coyote said, "Friend,"
  talking to Lizard,
  dancing with grief.
"Wai! wai! wai!
"Friend, you said people should come back to life,
  after they die.
"Make my child come back to life.
"I don't like weeping so much.
"Make him come back to life!"

"Hm! hm!" said Cottontail.
"Cry, cry!
"You said people would cry.
"Weep, weep!
"Put white clay on your face,
  put pitch on your face!
"You said people would weep,
  if someone's brother died,
  so you said, you told me.
"Weep, weep!"

OPPOSITE: *Untitled*, Jeffrey Chapman (Ojibwa), 1989. Courtesy of the artist.

***Human Figure* (Salish).**
Courtesy of Thomas Burke
Memorial Washington State
Museum, Seattle, WA.

WOMAN CHOOSES DEATH

❖ *Blackfoot* ❖

RETOLD BY ALFONSO ORTIZ AND RICHARD ERDOES

ld Man decided that something was missing in the world he had made. He thought it would be a good thing to create a woman and a child. He didn't quite know how they should look, but he took some clay and mud and for four days tried out different shapes. At first he didn't like the looks of the beings he formed. On the fourth day, however, he shaped a woman in a pleasing form, round and nice, with everything in front and back, above and below, just right.

"This is good," Old Man said, "this is the kind of woman I like to have in my world." Then he made a little child resembling the woman. "Well," said Old Man, "this is just what I wanted, but they're not alive yet."

Old Man covered them up for four days. On the first day he looked under the cover and saw a faint trembling. On the second day the figures could raise their heads. On the third day they moved their arms and legs. "Soon they will be ready," said Old Man. And on the fourth day he looked underneath the cover and saw his figures crawling around. "They're ready now to walk upon my world," thought Old Man. He took the cover off and told the woman and the child: "Walk upright like human beings." The woman and the child stood up. They began to walk, and they were perfect.

They followed Old Man down to the river, where he gave them the power of speech. At once the woman asked: "What is that state we are in, walking, moving, breathing, eating?"

"That is life," said Old Man. "Before, you were just lumps of mud. Now, you live."

"When we were lumps of mud, were we alive then?" asked the woman.

"No," said Old Man, "you were not alive."

"What do you call the state we were in then?" asked the woman.

"It is called death," answered Old Man. "When you are not alive, then you are dead."

"Will we be alive always?" asked the woman. "Will we go on living forever, or shall we be dead again at some time?"

Old Man pondered. He said: "I didn't think about that at all. Let's decide it right now. Here's a buffalo chip. If it floats, then people will die and come back to life four days later."

"No," said the woman. "This buffalo chip will dissolve in the water. I'll throw in this stone. If it floats, we'll live forever and there will be no death. If it sinks, then we'll die." The woman didn't know anything yet, because she had been walking on earth for just a few hours. She didn't know about stones and water, so she threw the stone into the river and it sank.

"You made a choice there," said Old Man. "Now nothing can be done about it. Now people will die."

A MATTER OF CONCENTRATION

❖ *Nez Perce/Osage* ❖

TOLD BY W. S. PENN

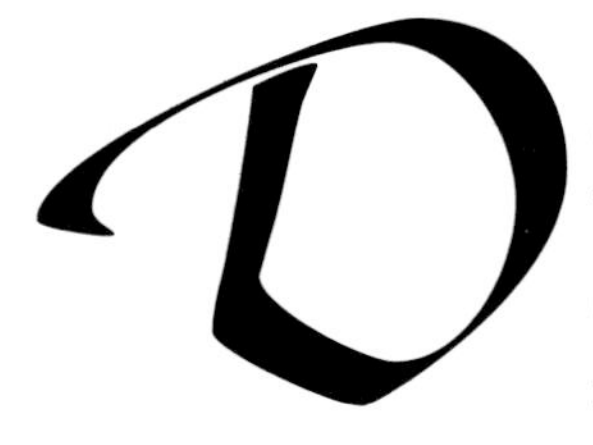

eath made Himself familiar to the Boy at birth, traveling by wagon, dressed in Eastern cloth and a hardhat with a little light on the forehead. "It's as if some people can't see where they're going," the Grandfather laughed.

Death had made the journey to the City of Angels to guard the body of a newborn child in its crib. The baby was His, but Death couldn't get into the crib to take him. The crib was in an oxygen tent, and no one but the doctors who poked and prodded the baby and then stood with the elk's head necklaces hanging from their necks consulting each other's ignorance was allowed to reach into the tent. So Death waited patiently, and watched. At moments, He would go out into the waiting room and sit beside the Father, who seemed to be reading his hands like some ancient text; or He would slip into the maternity ward and stroke the belly of the Mother, who knew from the conspiracy of silence that her baby was not well. Death couldn't help but smile when the doctors told the Father that the child would not live.

As Death waited, the Grandfather made the journey from Chosposi Mesa to the city. In his then new 1947 Plymouth, he made the fifteen-hour trip in eleven hours, never going above fifty miles per hour.

"It's not a matter of how fast you drive," he would say to explain how he did it. "It's a matter of concentration."

Without much imagination, the Boy could picture him virtually motionless behind the steering wheel, his gray eyes focused on the horizon, concentrating on reaching the white space between the hills and the blue sky, the big wheels of the Plymouth gobbling up an extra yard for every yard they rolled over. No one believed him, yet all he said was, "When you drive as far as the eye can see, you have to see farther."

So the Grandfather arrived at the hospital, the first time he had ever been in a hospital. He said little to the Father. Only went to the isolated crib in its plastic tent and observed the form of the baby boy who was, as he said years later,

***Doll Cradleboard* (Nez Perce). Courtesy of W. E. Channing & Co., Santa Fe, NM.**

Spirit Guide/Spirit Healer, **George C. Longfish (Seneca/Tuscarora), 1983. Courtesy of the artist.**

green: "Blue from no oxygen. Yellow from jaundice." The baby's fists, which no one had seemed to notice, were clenched tight as though they grasped a key, and it was the fists that seemed to satisfy the Grandfather.

"The baby will live," he told the Father, who was rapidly making extravagant promises to the God who tries to make all other gods unnecessary, and when he can't do that, enters a cosmic mitosis and calls himself the Trinity.

Then the Grandfather took a disappointed Death by the wrist, put Him in the passenger seat of the 1947 Plymouth, concentrated on the grayness as far away as his eyes could see, and arrived at Chosposi eleven hours later. To the Hopi woman he had married, he said, "The boy has it and won't let go."

The Grandmother, who lived with the Grandfather with a contention which could be mistaken for bitterness but was really a kind of boundless love, understood. She knew that Death had returned with the Grandfather.

"The child of the mission is sickly," she said.

The Grandfather simply nodded and, without taking off his cap, walked Death to the mission, where he left Him chained like a rabid dog beside the mission door.

Possibly, you could deduce that the Grandfather had just invented entropy for himself. But the Boy doubts that the Grandfather thought it through. He understood that for every child Death misses He finds a replacement. Besides, he had seen the mission child's hands, and they were loose and flabby, the fingers like baby Gilas, wiggling and mean. And he didn't particularly wish to have Death hang around his own door. As he said, "Death is so boring."

And he meant that, boring. The Grandfather wasn't frightened of Death. Death was an uninteresting companion. So, rather than wait, rather than make up some strange moral complication, he walked Death to the mission and left Him. Five days later, the once childless missionary was childless again, and when the Grandfather passed the building on his way to the trading post he retrieved the broken chain to take home and repair, in case he would need it again.

A Mashpee Ghost Story

❖ *Wampanoag* ❖

Told by Mabel Knight, adapted by Ella Clark,

edited by W. S. Penn

ne night on Cape Cod at Gay Head, a Mashpee woman and her children were alone in their wigwam. The children were sound asleep in their blankets and their mother sat knitting beside her central fire-pit. As customary, her door-flap was wide open. Suddenly she became aware of someone approaching her doorway, and went to see who it might be.

A sailor stood outside. She asked him, "What do you want?" He replied, "I'd like to come inside and warm myself by your fire, because my clothes are wet and I feel chilled to the bone."

She invited him inside and offered a place for him to sit beside the fire to dry out and warm himself. She placed another log on her fire, then resumed her knitting. As she watched the fire, she noticed that she could see the fire right through the sailor's legs, which were stretched out between her and the fire—as if he were a ghost!

Her fear of him increased, but since she was a brave woman, she kept on with her knitting while keeping a suspicious eye toward the visitor. Finally the sailor turned to the Indian woman and said, "Do you want any money?"

Her first thought was not to answer his question. Then he repeated, "Do you want any money?" She replied, "Yes."

The sailor explained, "If you really want a large amount of money, all you have to do is go outdoors behind your wigwam. Beside a rock there you will find buried a kettle full of money. I thank you for your hospitality. Good night." He went away.

The Mashpee woman did not go outdoors immediately, as she wanted to think about the sailor's proposal. She sat and knitted and thought for a while longer. Still, she felt frightened from the evening's experience and was reluctant to leave her wigwam. More knitting time elapsed. Then she thought, "I might as well go out and see if the sailor spoke the truth—to see if there really is a kettle of money out there."

She took her hoe and went outside to the back of her wigwam, and easily saw the place described by the sailor. She began to dig with her hoe. She realized that every time she struck her hoe into the ground, she heard her children cry out loudly, as if in great pain. She rushed indoors to see what was their trouble. They were soundly sleeping in their blankets.

Again and again she dug with her hoe; each time her children cried out loudly to her; each time she rushed in to comfort them, only to find them soundly asleep as she had left them.

After this had happened several times, the mother decided to give up digging for the night. She thought she would try again early next morning after bright daylight and her children were awake.

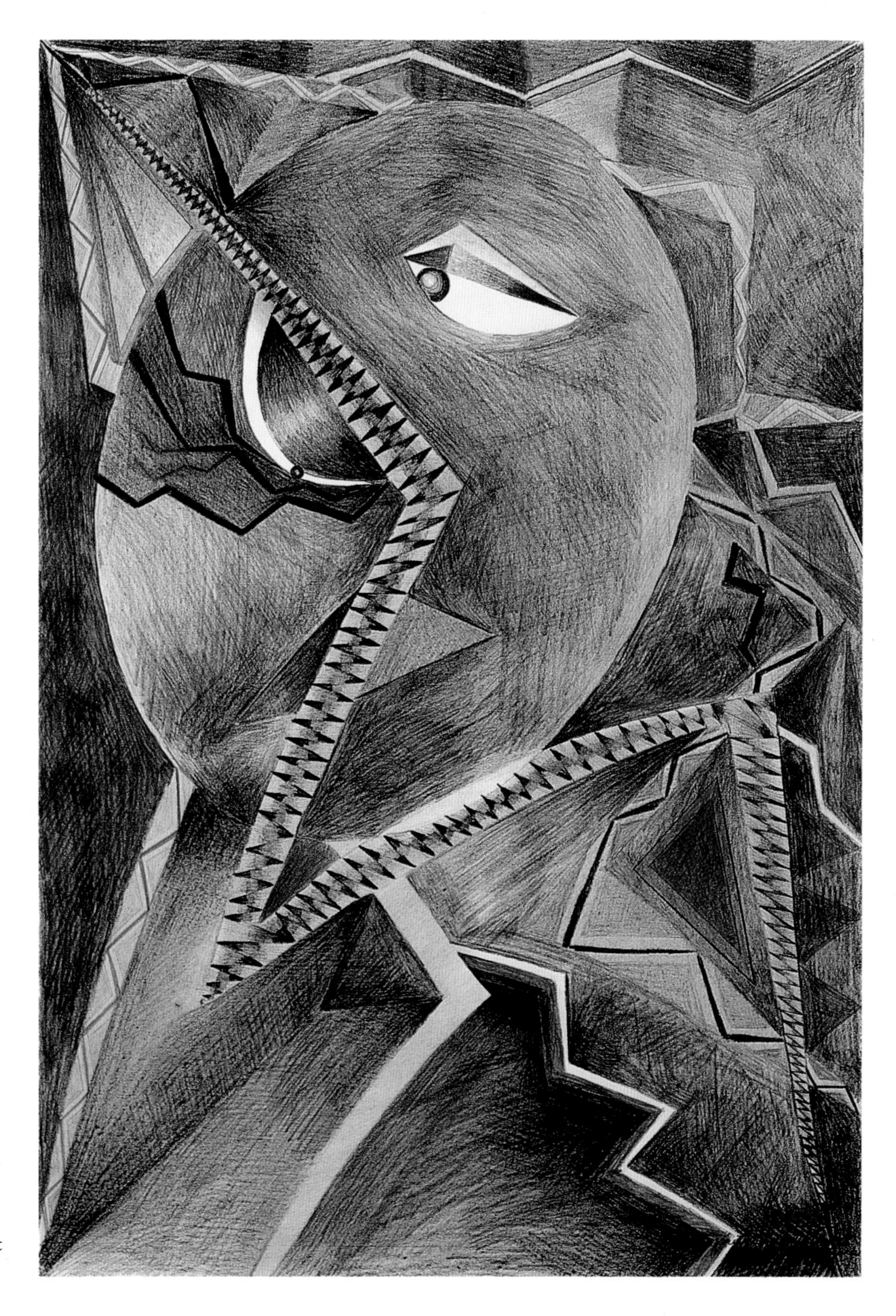

Spiritual Conflict, **Margarete Bagshaw-Tindel (O-Je-Gi-Povi), 1992. Courtesy of the College of Wooster Art Museum, Wooster, OH.**

Morning came, and she wondered if she had only dreamed last night's happenings. Her children were eating their breakfast when she went out to the digging place. There was her hoe, standing where she had left it. But she could see that someone else had been there in the meantime, and had finished digging while she slept.

Before her, she saw a big round hole. She knew someone had dug up the hidden treasure. She was too late for the pot of gold promised by the ghostly sailor. Again she thought and wondered, "Was I really too late?"

She thought that the sailor may have been the Evil Spirit in disguise—or even a real ghost. Perhaps he was tempting her to see if she cared more for her children, or more for he gold."

The Mashpee woman and her children continued to live in their village for a long, long time.

COYOTE AND EAGLE VISIT THE LAND OF THE DEAD

❖ *Yakima* ❖

RECORDED BY DR. G. B. KUYKENDALL, ADAPTED BY ELLA CLARK

In the days of the animal people, Coyote was sad because people died and went away to the land of the spirits. All around him was the sound of mourning. He wondered and wondered how he could bring the dead back to the land of the living.

Coyote's sister had died. Some of his friends had died. Eagle's wife had died and Eagle was mourning for her. To comfort him Coyote said, "The dead shall not remain forever in the land of the dead. They are like the leaves that fall, brown and dead, in the autumn. They shall come back again. When the grass grows and the birds sing, when the leaf buds open and the flowers bloom, the dead shall come back again."

But Eagle did not want to wait until spring. He thought that the dead should be brought back without any delay. So Coyote and Eagle started out together to the land of the dead, Eagle flying along over Coyote's head. After several days they came to a big body of water, on the other side of which were a great many houses.

"Bring a boat and take us across the water!" shouted Coyote.

But there was no answer—no sound and no movement.

"There is no one there," said Eagle. "We have come all the way for nothing."

"They are asleep," explained Coyote. "The dead sleep during the day and come out at night. We will wait here until dark."

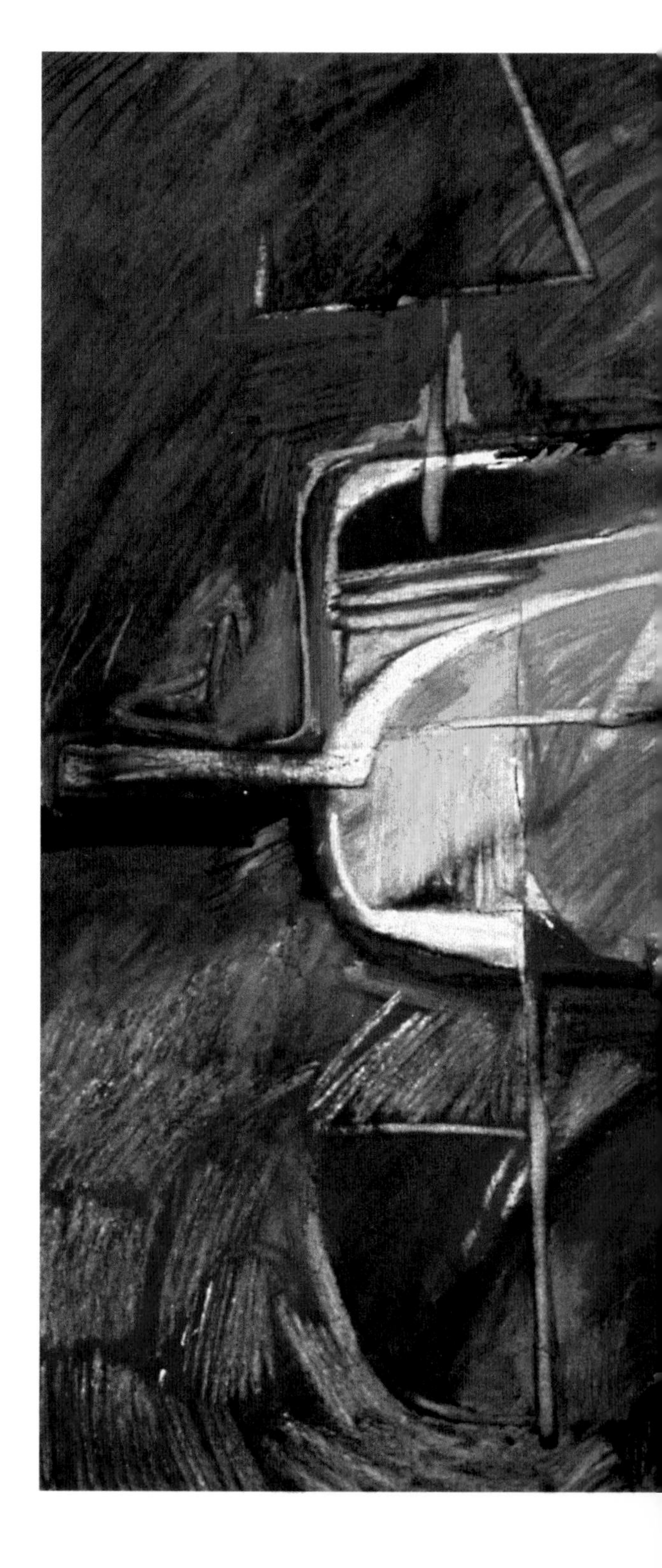

***Drifting VI*, Rick Bartow (Yurok), 1994. Courtesy of Froelick Adelhart Gallery, Portland, OR.**

After sunset, Coyote began to sing. In a short time, four spirit men came out of the houses, got into a boat, and started toward Coyote and Eagle. Coyote kept on singing, and soon the spirits joined him, keeping time with their paddles. But the boat moved without them. It skimmed over the water by itself.

When the spirits reached the shore, Eagle and Coyote stepped into the boat and started back with them. As they drew near the island of the dead, the sound of drums and of dancing met them across the water.

"Do not go into the house," warned the spirits as they were landing. "Do not look at the things around you. Keep your eyes closed, for this is a sacred place."

"But we are hungry and cold. Do let us go in," begged Eagle and Coyote.

So they were allowed to go into a large lodge made of tule mats, where the spirits were dancing and singing to the beating of

the drums. An old woman brought to them some seal oil in a basket bottle. Dipping a feather into it, she fed them from the oil until their hunger was gone.

Then Eagle and Coyote looked around. Inside the lodge everything was beautiful, and there were many spirits. They were dressed in ceremonial robes, beautifully decorated with shells and with elks' teeth. Their faces were painted, and they wore feathers in their hair. The moon, hanging from above, filled the big lodge with light. Near the moon stood Frog, who has watched over it ever since he jumped into it long ago. He saw to it that the moon shone brightly on the crowd of dancers and singers.

Eagle and Coyote knew some of the spirits as their former friends, but no one paid any attention to the two strangers. No one saw the basket which Coyote had brought with him. In this basket he planned to carry the spirits back to the land of the living.

RIGHT: ***Basket*** **(Yakima). Courtesy of Thomas Burke Memorial Washington State Museum, Seattle, WA.**

BELOW: ***Wishxam Totem,*** **Lillian Pitt (Yakima), 1996 Courtesy of the artist.**

Early in the morning, the spirits left the lodge for their day of sleep. Then Coyote killed Frog, took his clothes, and put them on himself. At twilight the spirits returned and began again a night of singing and dancing. They did not know that Coyote, in Frog's clothing, stood beside the moon.

When the dancing and singing were at their gayest, Coyote swallowed the moon. In the darkness, Eagle caught the spirit people, put them into Coyote's basket, and closed the lid tight. Then the two started back to the land of the living, Coyote carrying the basket.

After traveling a great distance, they heard noises in the basket and stopped to listen.

"The people are coming to life," said Coyote.

After they had gone a little farther, they heard voices talking in the basket. The spirits were complaining.

"We are being bumped and banged around," groaned some.

"My leg is being hurt," groaned one spirit.

"My legs and arms are cramped," groaned another.

"Open the lid and let us out!" called several spirits together.

Coyote was tired, for the basket was getting heavier and heavier. The spirits were turning back into people.

"Let's let them out," said Coyote.

"No, no," answered Eagle quickly.

A little later, Coyote set the basket down. It was too heavy for him.

"Let's let them out," repeated Coyote. "We are so far from the spirit land now that they won't return."

So he opened the basket. The people took their spirit forms and, moving like the wind, went back to the island of the dead.

Eagle scolded at first, but soon he remembered Coyote's earlier thought. "It is now autumn. The leaves are falling, just as people die. Let us wait until spring. When the buds open and the flowers bloom, let us return to the land of the dead and try again."

"No," replied Coyote. "I am tired. Let the dead stay in the land of the dead forever and forever."

So Coyote made the law that after people have died they shall never come to life again. If he had not opened the basket and let the spirits out, the dead would have come to life every spring as the grass and flowers and trees do.

Memaloose Island, The Island of the Dead

❖ *Yakima* ❖

Recorded by G.B. Kuykendall, *adapted by* Ella Clark

ong ago, a young warrior and a beautiful maiden were deeply in love and very happy. But sickness came to the warrior. He died, and his spirit went to the land of spirits. There he mourned for the girl, and she mourned for him in the earth world. A few nights after his death, a spirit from the land of the dead came to her in a dream and spoke to her.

"Your lover is longing for you," said the voice of the spirit. "Even though he is in the beautiful land of the spirits, he is unhappy without you. He cannot be happy again unless you come to him."

The girl was so troubled by the dream that she told her parents. They too were troubled and did not know what she should do. The next night, and again a third night, the spirit spoke to the girl in a dream. After the third vision, her parents decided that they would send their daughter to her lover, lest some harm come to them from the land of the spirits.

So in their canoe they took the girl down the river to the island where all the dead are gathered in the happy spirit land. Darkness was falling as they drew near. From the island came the sound of drums and of spirits singing as they danced to the music. Through the twilight haze, lights gleamed on the island.

***Spirit Dancing: The Practice of Our Ancestral Religion*, Ron Hilbert Coy (Tulalip), 1988. Courtesy of Thomas Burke Memorial Washington State Museum, Seattle, WA.**

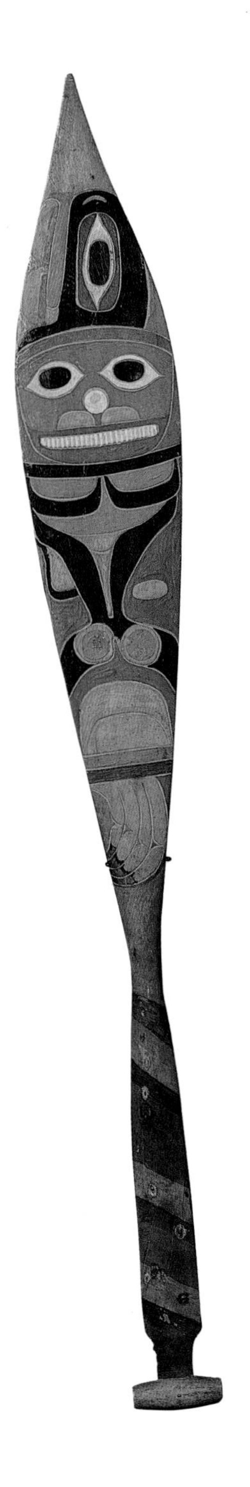

Four spirits met the family at the shore, helped the girl out of the canoe, and told her parents to return to their home among the living. The spirits guided the girl to a great dance house, a large lodge made of tule mats. There she saw her lover, more handsome and noble looking than he had been on earth and dressed with the richness found only in the land of the spirits.

All night the singing and dancing continued, and the young couple were among the happiest of the dancers. When dawn began to break and the first bird songs were heard, the spirits went to their rest. . . .

The maiden also closed her eyes on the joyful spirit world and went to sleep. But, unlike the spirits, she did not sleep soundly. When the sun was high above her, she awoke and looked around. Beside her lay the skeleton of her lover. His skull, with hollow eyes and grinning teeth, was turned toward her. All around her were skeletons and skulls. The air was filled with the smell of death, for the beautiful spirits of the night hours had become bones.

With a scream, the girl sprang from her bed and ran to the shore. After a little search she found a canoe and rapidly paddled back to her home village. But her family and friends were alarmed. They feared that the spirits would be offended by her leaving their land and that they would punish the village.

"You have done wrong to the spirit people," they told her. "You should have slept all day, as they do. You must go back to your lover, for he has claimed you."

So the maiden returned to the island that evening and again joined her lover at the dancing lodge. He was again a handsome and happy spirit. Next day, and every day after that, she slept until evening. When darkness came, she woke up and was happy with all the spirits.

In course of time a child was born to her, a child of unusual beauty, half human and half spirit. The young father was so eager for his mother on the earth to see the baby that he decided to send for her. He found a spirit messenger and gave him this message:

"Tell my mother that we are very happy in the spirit land and that we have a beautiful baby. We want her to see him. Ask her to come back with you. Then the baby and his mother will return home with her to the land of the living. I will soon follow, taking with me all the dead people so that they may live on earth again."

The message made the grandmother happy, and she gladly went to the island of the dead. Her son welcomed her but warned her that she could not see the baby yet.

"Not for ten days can you see him."

The grandmother waited patiently at first. But the longer she waited, the more eager she was to see her grandchild. After a few days she decided that she would peep at him. It would do no harm to anyone, she thought, if she should lift up the cloth covering the baby board and take one glance.

She lifted the cloth and saw the sleeping child. The punishment came swiftly, for the baby sickened and died. The spirit people were so displeased that they have never since permitted the dead to return to the living.

The grandmother was sent back to her village and never heard of the young couple again.

Painted Oars **(Haida). Courtesy of America Hurrah Archive, New York, NY.**

THE TWO JEEBI-UG

❖ *Ojibwa* ❖

ADAPTED BY MENTOR L. WILLIAMS

There lived a hunter in the North who had a wife and one child. His lodge stood far off in the forest, several days' journey from any other. He spent his days in hunting and his evenings in relating to his wife the incidents that had befallen him. As game was very abundant he found no difficulty in killing as much as they wanted. Just in all his acts, he lived a peaceful and happy life.

One evening during the winter season, it chanced that he remained out later than usual, and his wife began to feel uneasy, for fear some accident had befallen him. It was already dark. She listened attentively and at last heard the sound of approaching footsteps. Not doubting it was her husband, she went to the door and beheld two strange females. She bade them enter, and invited them to remain.

She observed that they were total strangers in the country. There was something so peculiar in their looks, air, and manner that she was uneasy in their company. They would not come near the fire; they sat in a remote part of the lodge, were shy and taciturn, and drew their garments about them in such a manner as nearly to hide their faces. So far as she could judge, they were pale, hollow-eyed, and long-visaged, very thin and emaciated. There was but little light in the lodge, as the fire was low, and served by its fitful flashes rather to increase than dispel their fears. "Merciful spirit!" cried a voice from the opposite part of the lodge, "there are two corpses clothed with garments." The hunter's wife turned around, but seeing nobody, she concluded the sounds were but gusts of wind. She trembled, and was ready to sink to the earth.

Her husband at this moment entered and dispelled her fears. He threw down the carcass of a large fat deer. "Behold what a fine and fat animal," cried the mysterious females, and they immediately ran and pulled off pieces of the whitest fat, which they ate with greediness. The hunter and his wife looked on with astonishment, but remained silent. They supposed their guests might have been famished. Next day, however, the same unusual conduct was repeated. The strange females tore off the fat and devoured it with eagerness. The third day the hunter thought he would anticipate their wants by tying up a portion of the fattest pieces for them, which he placed on the top of his load. They accepted it, but still appeared dissatisfied, and went to the wife's portion and tore off more. The man and his wife felt surprised at such rude and unaccountable conduct, but they remained silent, for they respected their guests, and had observed that they had been attended with marked good luck during the residence of these mysterious visitors.

In other respects the deportment of the females was strictly unexceptionable. They were modest, distant, and silent. They never uttered a word during the day. At night they would occupy themselves in procuring wood, which they carried to the lodge, and then returning the implements exactly to the places in which they had found them, resume their places without speaking. They were never known to stay out until daylight. They never laughed or jested.

The winter had nearly passed away, without anything uncommon happening, when, one evening, the hunter stayed out very late. The moment he entered and laid down his day's hunt as usual before his wife, the two females began to tear off the fat, in so unceremonious a way that her anger was excited. She constrained herself, however, in a measure, but did not conceal her feelings, although she said but little. The guests observed the excited state of her mind, and became unusually reserved and uneasy. The good hunter saw the change, and carefully inquired into the cause, but his wife denied having used any hard words. They retired to their couches, and he tried to compose himself to sleep, but could not, for the sobs and sighs of the two females were incessant. He arose on his couch and addressed them as follows:

"Tell me," said he, "what is it that gives you pain of mind, and causes you to utter those sighs. Has my wife given you offense, or trespassed on the rights of hospitality?"

They replied in the negative. "We have been treated by you with kindness and affection. It is not for any slight we have received that we weep. Our mission is not to you only. We come from the land of the dead to test mankind, and to try the sincerity of the living. Often we have heard the bereaved by death say that if the dead could be restored, they would devote their lives to make them happy. We have been moved by the bitter lamentations which have reached the place of the dead, and have come to make proof of the sincerity of those who have lost friends. Three moons were allotted us by the Master of Life to make the trial. More than half the time had been successfully passed when the angry feelings of your wife indicated the irksomeness you felt at our presence, and has made us resolve on our departure."

They continued to talk to the hunter and his wife, gave them instructions as to a future life, and pronounced a blessing upon them.

"There is one point," they added, "of which we wish to speak. You have thought our conduct very strange in rudely possessing ourselves of the choicest parts of your hunt. *That* was the point of trial selected to put you to. It is the wife's peculiar privilege. For another to usurp it, we knew to be the severest trial of her, and consequently of your temper and feelings. We know your manners and customs, but we came to prove you, not by a compliance with them, but by a violation of them.

***Black Ovals*, Duane Slick (Mesquakie/Winnebago), 1992. Courtesy of the artist.**

Pardon us. We are the agents of him who sent us. Peace to your dwelling, adieu!"

When they ceased, total darkness filled the lodge. No object could be seen. The inmates heard the door open and shut, but they never saw more of the two jeebi-ug.

The hunter found the success which they had promised. He became celebrated in the chase, and never wanted for anything. He had many children, all of whom grew up to manhood; and health, peace, and long life were the rewards of his hospitality.

Coyote Visits the Land of the Dead

Told by Barry Lopez

Coyote and his wife were staying in a nice village. One winter his wife became ill. She died. In time Coyote became very lonely. He did nothing but weep for his wife.

The death spirit came to him and asked if he was crying for his wife.

"Yes, my friend," answered Coyote. "I long for her. There is a great pain in my heart."

After a while the death spirit said, "I can take you to the place where your wife has gone, but if I do, you must do exactly what I say. You can't disregard a single word."

"What would you expect me to do? I will do whatever you say, everything, my friend."

"Well, then let's go."

After they had gone a ways the death spirit again cautioned Coyote to do exactly as he was told and Coyote said he would.

By this time Coyote was having trouble seeing the death spirit. He was like a shadow on an overcast day. They were going across the prairie to the east and the ghost said, "Oh, look at all these horses over there. It must be a roundup." Coyote could not see any horses but he said," Yes, yes."

They were getting nearer the place of the dead.

"Oh, look at all these service berries! Let's pick some to eat." Coyote could not see the berries, so the ghost said, "When you see me reach up and pull the limb down, you do the same."

The ghost pulled one of the limbs down and Coyote did the same thing. Although he could not see anything, he imitated the ghost, putting his hand to his mouth as though he were eating. He watched how the ghost did everything and imitated him.

"These are very good service berries," said the ghost.

"Yes, it's good we found them."

"Well, let's get going now."

They went on. "We are about to arrive," said the ghost. "Your wife is in a very long lodge, that one over there. Wait here. I will ask someone exactly where."

In a little while the ghost returned and said, "They have told me where your wife is." They walked a short distance. "We are coming to a door here. Do in every way exactly what I do. I will take hold of the door flap, raise it up, and bending low, will enter. Then you take hold of the door flap and do the same."

In this way they went in. Coyote's wife was right near the entrance. The ghost said, "Sit down here by your wife." They both sat down. "Your wife is now going to prepare some food for us."

Coyote could see nothing. He was sitting in an open prairie where there was nothing in sight. He could barely sense the presence of the shadow.

"Now, she has prepared our food. Let's eat."

The ghost reached down and brought his hand to his mouth. Coyote could see only grass and dust in front of him. They ate. Coyote imitated all of the actions of his companion. When they had finished and the woman had apparently put the food away, the ghost said to Coyote, "You stay here. I must go around and see some people. Here we have conditions different from those you have in the land of the living. When it gets dark here it is dawn where you live. When it's dawn for us, it is growing dark for you."

Now it was getting dark and Coyote thought he could hear voices, very faintly, talking all around him. Then darkness set in and Coyote could begin to see a little. There were many small fires in the long house. He began to see the people waking up. They had forms, very vague, like shadows, but he recognized some of them. He saw his wife sitting by his side and he was overjoyed. Coyote went around and greeted all his old friends who had died long ago. This made him very happy. He went among them visiting and talking with everyone. All night he did this. Toward morning he saw a little light around the place where he had entered the long house. The death spirit said to him, "Coyote, our night is falling and in a little while you will not see us. But you must stay here. Do not move. In the evening you will see all these people again."

"Where would I go, my friend? Sure, I will stay right here."

When dawn came Coyote found himself sitting alone in the middle of the prairie. He sat there all day in the heat. He could hear meadowlarks somewhere. It got hotter and he grew very thirsty. Finally evening came and he saw the lodge again. For a couple of days he went on like this, suffering through the daytime in the heat but visiting with his friends every night in the lodge. One night the death spirit came to him and said, "Coyote, tomorrow you will go home. You will take your wife with you."

"But I like it here very much my friend," Coyote protested. "I am having a good time

***Spirits Rising*, George Morrison (Ojibwa), 1990. Courtesy of the artist.**

and should like to remain."

"Yes, but you will go tomorrow. I will advise you about what you are to do. Listen. There are five mountains to the west. You will travel for five days. Your wife will be with you but you must not touch her. Do not yield to any notion you may have to do something foolish. When you have crossed and descended the fifth mountain you can do whatever you want."

"It will be this way, then," said Coyote.

When dawn came, Coyote and his wife set out. At first it seemed to Coyote as though he were alone, but he was aware of his wife's dim presence as she walked along behind. The first day they crossed the first mountain and camped. The next day they crossed the second mountain. They went on like this, camping each night. Each night when they sat across from each other at the fire Coyote could see his wife a little more clearly.

The death spirit had begun to count the days and to figure the distance Coyote had traveled. "I hope he does everything right," he thought, "and takes his wife on to the other world."

The time of their fourth camping was their last camp. On the next day Coyote's wife would become entirely like a living person again. Coyote could see her clearly across the fire now. He could see the light on her face and body but he did not dare to touch her. Suddenly a joyous impulse overtook him. He was so glad to have his wife back! He jumped up and ran around the fire to embrace her.

"Stop! Stop!" screamed his wife. "Coyote do not touch me!"

But her warning had no effect. Coyote rushed to her and just as he touched her she vanished. She disappeared and returned to the shadowland.

When the death spirit learned what Coyote had done he became furious.

"You are always doing things like this, Coyote," he yelled. "I told you not to do anything foolish. You were about to establish the practice of returning from death. Now it won't happen. You have made it this way."

Coyote wept and wept. His sorrow was very deep. He decided that he would go back, he would find the death lodge and find his wife again. He crossed the five mountains. He went out in the prairie and found the place where the ghost had seen the horses, and then he began to do the same things they had done when they were on their way to the shadowland the other time.

"Oh, look at all these horses. It must be a round-up!"

He went on to the place where the ghost had picked the service berries. "Oh, such choice service berries. Let's pick some and eat." He went through the motions of picking and eating the berries. He finally came to the place where the death lodge stood. He said to himself, "Now, when I take hold of the door flap and raise it up you must do the same." Coyote remembered all the things his friend had done and he did them. He saw the spot where he had sat before. He went to it and sat down. "Now your wife has brought us some food. Let's eat." He went through the motions of eating again.

Darkness fell and Coyote listened for the voices. He looked all around, but nothing happened. Coyote sat there in the middle of the prairie. He sat there all night but the lodge didn't appear again. In the morning he heard meadowlarks.

THE MEN WHO WENT TO THE SKY

❖ *Alabama* ❖

ADAPTED BY JOHN R. SWANTON

There were two men and a woman living in a certain place. The woman had a little child. By and by the child's mother died. Then the two men determined to try and get her back, and about March they started off to heaven. They traveled on and on until at last they came to where an old woman lived and stayed at her house all night. She gave each of them a boiled pumpkin to eat, and they thought that these would not be enough, but the minute one of them was consumed another appeared in its place, and they ate on until they were full. Going on farther, they came to some little people who were going to war on ducks and geese. Passing on, they came to where another old woman lived, and they spent the night with her. She said to them, "You are not to cross rivers on the way." She gave each a gourd with which they were to dip away the water of the streams they came to so that they could pass through them. Then they came to a third old woman and spent the night with her also. She said, "On the way are many great snakes," so she gave them bark of the bass tree [båksa] to tie about their legs. Having fastened this on, they continued their journey and came to masses of snakes piled together. They walked through these and the snakes bit them but did them no harm. By the time they had gotten through, however, their barks were worn out with the biting. Again they came to an old woman with whom they passed the night. She said, "There is a battle on the way. If you have tobacco, cut it up ready for smoking." They cut their tobacco up and she made cigarettes for them. She said, "When you see the battle, smoke cigarettes." They went on and by and by found the battle. Then they smoked cigarettes and the smoke covered everyone as with clouds, so that they passed safely through. Finally they came to the end of the land and found the sky, which was moving up and down. One of them said, "I am a panther," and jumped up upon it. The other said, "I am a wildcat," and did the same thing. Then they were carried far up and found some people living there. One day, as they traveled on, they came to a man and some dens. The man told them not to stop at the dens but to go by, which they did. Next night they came to another man and spent the night with him. He said, "The women's town is next. They will try to stop you, but do not stop." They found this town as he had said and the women tried to stop them, but they passed right on.

Dress (Seminole). Courtesy of W. E. Channing & Co., Santa Fe, NM.

Finally they came to where God (abå'ski djo'kole, "high living") dwelt. He said,

"Why did you come here?" and they told him that they had come for the mother of the child. Then he told them to stay there to the dance and he gave them a watermelon to eat. The men thought that the watermelon seed would be a good thing to save and plant at home, but he told them not to keep a single seed. He had it divided for them, and when they were through eating they put the seeds back, and God put the rind together and made it into a whole watermelon once more. He said, "You have come a long way," and they agreed that this must have been the case, for they had traveled an entire year. Then God took the cover off from something and let them look inside. They saw the house from which they had come just beneath. At the dance they saw the woman they were in search of but could not catch her. Then God gave them pieces of corncob and said, "When you see that woman again throw these at her." When they again saw her at the dance they threw the pieces of corncob at her. The last piece struck her, she fell down, and they seized her. Then God brought a big jug, put the woman into it, and screwed on the top. He said, "When you want to go back tell me." They said, "We will go tomorrow." Then they went to sleep, but when they woke up they found they were sleeping in their own house. The woman inside of the jar was groaning, saying, "You have brought me here and killed me." They were so sorry for her that they put the jar in the shade and unscrewed the top a little, whereupon she stopped groaning. Then they thought they would go to sleep, but when they woke up and opened the jar she was gone. She went back to heaven. If they had left the cover screwed on until she died she would have come back again. God gave the woman to them but they lost her again. If they had left this cover screwed down, people would still come back to earth; but since they did not, people do not come back any more.

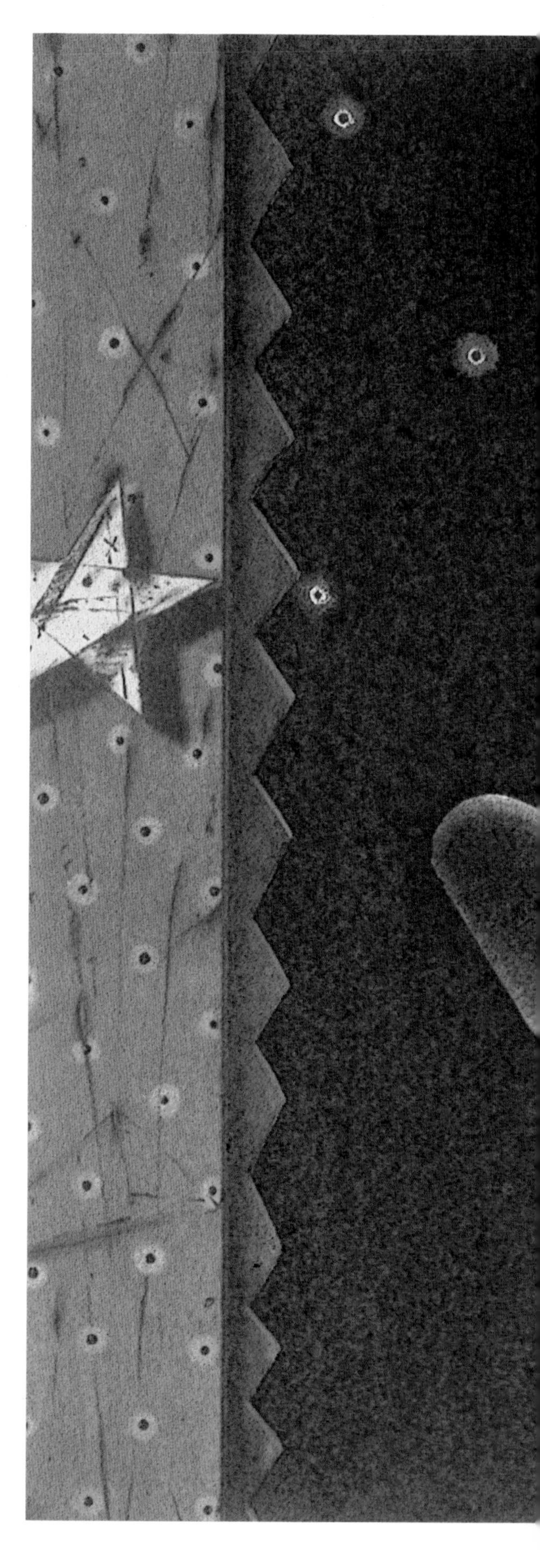

***Calvario Series #179*, Marty Avrett (Coushatta/Choctaw/Cherokee), 1994. Courtesy of the artist.**

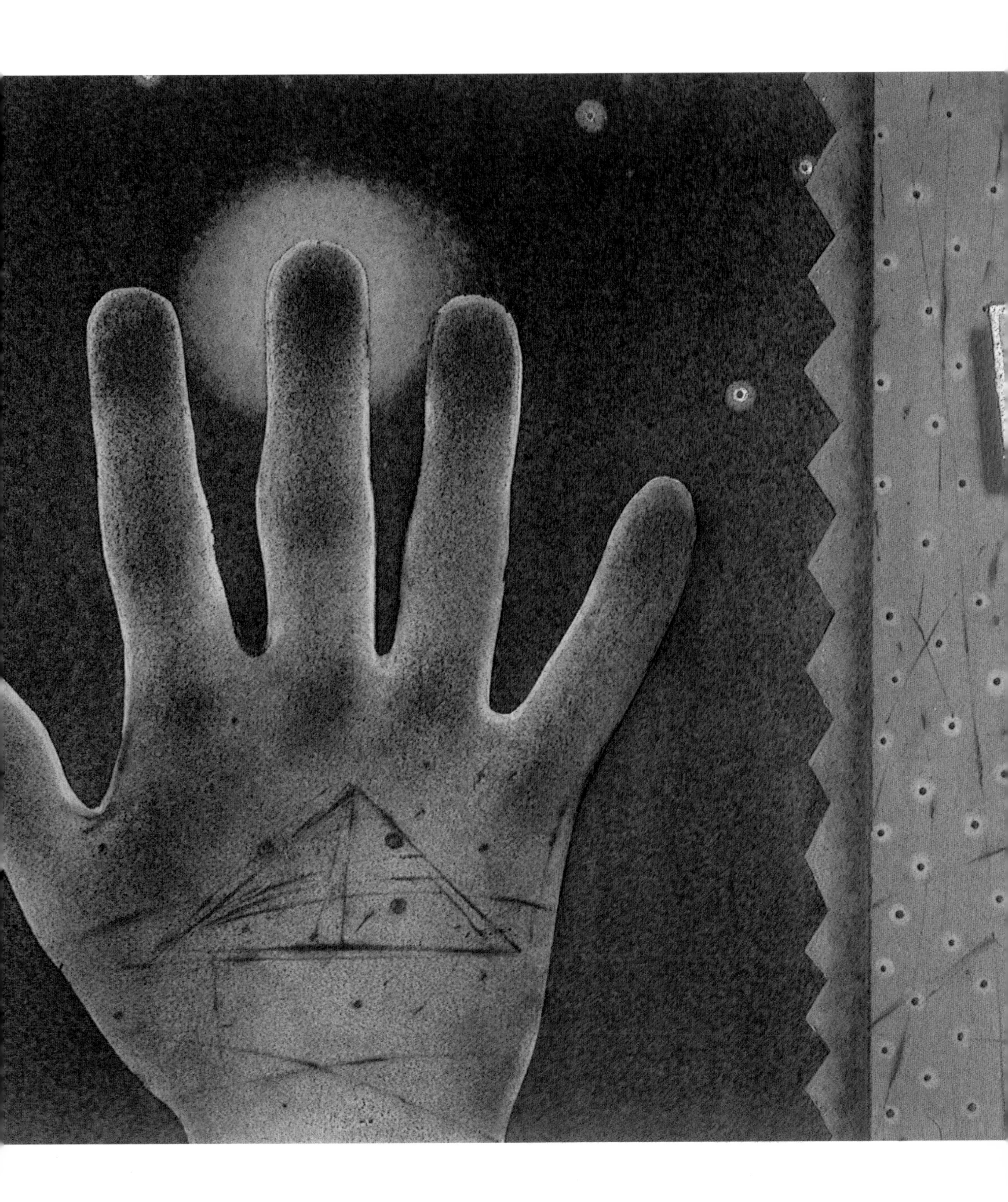

ALBERT HUMMINGBIRD MEETS DEATH

❖ *Nez Perce/Osage* ❖

TOLD BY W.S. PENN

One day, having overestimated his resistance to the sun and having stayed out too long, Albert Hummingbird was staggering home along the westbound road into the mission, hoping to hitch a ride on any cart or car that might pass. Along the sides of the road were Saguaro cacti, regularly spaced enough for the placards hung from them like Burma Shave signs. *Unwise and Unfortunate*, they read, *the man who tries to pass / Nahochass / Navaho-Hopi Crafts and Historical Assoc. / Genuine Artifacts / The Standard for 99 Years.*

Albert had almost reached the second set which read, *Cheer Up / Friend / You're nearly there,* when he noticed kangaroo mice hopping past, lizards and snakes slithering toward holes, birds abandoning the satin sky—a general movement of fauna as though something like an earthquake were coming. To the north was a stream of dust, rising from the earth like smoke. There was no road in that direction, so he assumed it had to be the smoke from a hogan drifting on the unfelt wind. He kept walking as a clanking, like rocks in a car's hubcaps, barely perceptible at first, grew louder.

When he turned again, there was a modified van bearing down on him, a row of air horns above the cab blasting. He dove behind a mound of earth as the van swerved, screeched, and a tire blew, flipping it onto the passenger's side with a sound as unnerving as the metallic boring of a dentist's drill as it plowed to a halt in the dry depression beside the road.

The van was customized with metallic paint, flames stencilled on the front fenders, bubble windows, and a cityscape complete with brown, smoggy air fused into the rear window. The driver, a little man with pale skin flecked with black dust like a coal miner, was still belted rigidly into his seat, both hands riveted to the steering wheel as if he expected the van at any moment to struggle to its feet like a horse and off they'd go.

"You okay?" Albert Hummingbird asked, climbing onto the van and pulling the driver's door open.

His dark punk glasses were askew on His nose and His face seemed to refuse to move. It didn't twitch, grimace, laugh, cry, or show anger or despair. It simply and completely waited for the van to end this siestal interlude and get under way again.

"Hey," Albert said, shaking His shoulder. It was then he heard a sound that he has since come to associate with Death as if He were made from scrap metal—a rattling clinking sound like surgical tools falling into a sterilization pan or the jangle of a girl gilded by vanity.

"Hey" Albert yelled, "are you okay?"

His beady bilious eyes, like a Gila's with cataracts, blinked once and His oversized head turned very slowly up toward him. "Ho," He said. "It's you."

Dragging Him from the van, Albert

The Gods Are Watching, **Susan Stewart (Crow/Blackfoot). Courtesy of the artist.**

stood Him on His feet and stepped back to take a look at Him. You could have strip-mined His person. He was encased in jewelry. Turquoise amulets hung from His neck; His arms, all the way up His loose plaid Sears and Roebuck flannel shirt, were mailed with tin and lapis lazuli; and on the heels of His Dingo boots were silver spurs. He staggered for a moment as the weight of the trinkets settled and His tiny feet took hold on the solid earth.

Extracting a screwdriver from one of the several pockets sewn to His khaki pants, He solemnly removed the winged figure of Mercury that ornamented the hood of His van. Albert watched Him, feeling as though he was watching a ritual the meaning of which had not existed until that moment and wondering why he neither feared nor hated Him—indeed, was almost glad for Him the way you're glad for an alarm clock even though you would rather be allowed to sleep. A small trickle of gasoline had begun to pool near His feet, and he was in the process of realizing the danger when He reached for the bulge of a cigarette pack in His breast pocket.

"Wait," Albert yelled.

He raised His other hand flat against his caution as though He were stopping an exaltation of larks. Carefully pacing off ten paces from the puddle of gasoline, He lit a cigarette and puffed on it, musing on what to do with a lame van. When He couched the stub of the cigarette between His thumb and middle finger in a position ready to flick it at the van, Albert began to run, diving over a rise in the earth just before the explosion. Peering over the hillock, he saw His dwarfish figure emerge from the black billowing smoke and clink-clank off west-southwest, angling away from the road that would take Him straight to Nahochass.

For one reason or another, Albert started to run after Him as though He were a person he wanted to help, to tell Him that if He followed the road . . . He stopped hurrying after Him when He turned, tossed the winged Mercury at his feet, and said, "Okay, already. I owe you one. You get to choose when and I'll pass over." Shaking His head, muttering, "You're going to be the end of me, yet," He resumed His slow, lugubrious clanking into the setting sun, sounding more like the movement of German tanks in a generic war film than Death on little cat's feet.

THE FAREWELL SONG

❖ *Havasupai* ❖

PERFORMED BY DAN HANNA AFTER A SONG BY HORNED HEART.

RECORDED AND TRANSCRIBED BY LEANNE HINTON

Spring Water Dripping,
land that I wandered,
that place.
Listen to me:
forget about me.
ha na.

I thought I'd live forever,
thought I'd travel forever;
that's how I was.
I thought I'd always be that way,
but now my strength is gone,
ha na.

I thought I'd always be that way.
That's how I was,
but now my strength is gone.
Land that I wandered,
that place.
Listen to me:
forget about me,
ha na

Horned animals,
I used to hunt them;
I thought I'd always be that way,
I'd be that way forever.
But now my strength is gone,
ha na.

That's how I was,
I was,
I was.
Thicket of bushes,
that place,
ha na.

I ran and ran
all around them;
listen to me.
Forget about me;
forget about me,
ha na.

Fallen logs
that I'd jump over,
that place
Listen to me:
forget about me,
ha na.

Sitting boulders
that I stumbled over,
that place.
Listen to me;
forget about me,
ha na.

OPPOSITE: ***Red Sky*, Jaune Quick-to-See Smith (Flathead/Shoshone/Cree), 1984. Courtesy of the artist.**

Trail lying there
that I once followed,
  once followed.
That place.
  Listen to me.
Forget about me;
  forget about me,
    ha na.

Arroyo,
arroyo,
  that I used to dash across.
That place.
  Listen to me.
Listen to me:
  forget about me,
    ha na.

Pointed Hill,
Pointed Hill,
  that place,
that I used to run up,
  that place.
Listen to me:
  forget about me.
To the very top
  I would come.
I'd stand there;
  I'd look into the distance.
That place
  Listen to me.
Forget about me;
  forget about me,
    ha na.

Faraway jackrabbit,
a young one,
  a brown one.
He leaped out of hiding,
  leaped out of hiding.
I went after him,
  went after him,
    ha na.

I caught right up;
I came up beside him;
  that's what I did.
The hunting cane
  that belonged to me:
I hooked him,
  caught him,
    ha na.

I roasted him,
roasted him
  and ate him.
I thought I'd live forever,
  thought I'd travel forever.
That's how it seemed to me,
  but now my strength is gone,
    ha na.

Faraway antelope
Faraway antelope
  a young one.
He leaped out of hiding;
  he came out suddenly.
He started off,
  and I went after him,
    ha na.

I caught right up,
I came up beside him;
  that's what I did.
The hunting cane
  that belonged to me:
I hooked him,
  caught him.
Roasted him,
  ate him,
    ha na.

I thought I'd live forever,
thought I'd travel forever,
  thought I'd always be that way;
that's how it seemed to me.

But now my strength is gone.
Land that I wandered,
that place.
Listen to me:
forget about me.
That's what I say;
that's what I say,
ha na

Land that I wandered,
that place,
listen to me.
I thought I'd always be that way;
that's how I was.
But it wasn't true.
I thought I'd be that way forever,
but it wasn't true.
I thought I'd be that way forever,
but now my strength is gone.
I thought I'd be that way forever,
ha na.

Deer hides
that belonged to me,
I hung them on a juniper.
I filled a tree with them;
I looked at them there.
I felt
so proud,
ha na.

Deer hides
that belonged to me,
I hung them on junipers.
I filled two trees;
I filled three trees.
I looked at them there.
I felt
so proud.
I thought I'd be that way forever,
ha na.

I thought I'd always be that way,
but now my strength is gone.
I thought I'd always be that way.
That's how I was,
how I was,
ha na.

I thought I'd live forever,
thought I'd travel forever;
that's how I was.
I'd be with the land,
it seemed.
That's how I was,
it seemed,
That's how I'd always be.
But now my strength is gone,
ha na.

The sky
spreading over me,
it seemed
I'd be with it forever,
it seemed.
I thought I'd always be that way,
but now my strength is gone,
ha na.

Listen to me:
forget about me,
Forget about me.
Now my strength is gone.
I thought I'd always be that way.
That's how I was,
how I was,
ha na.

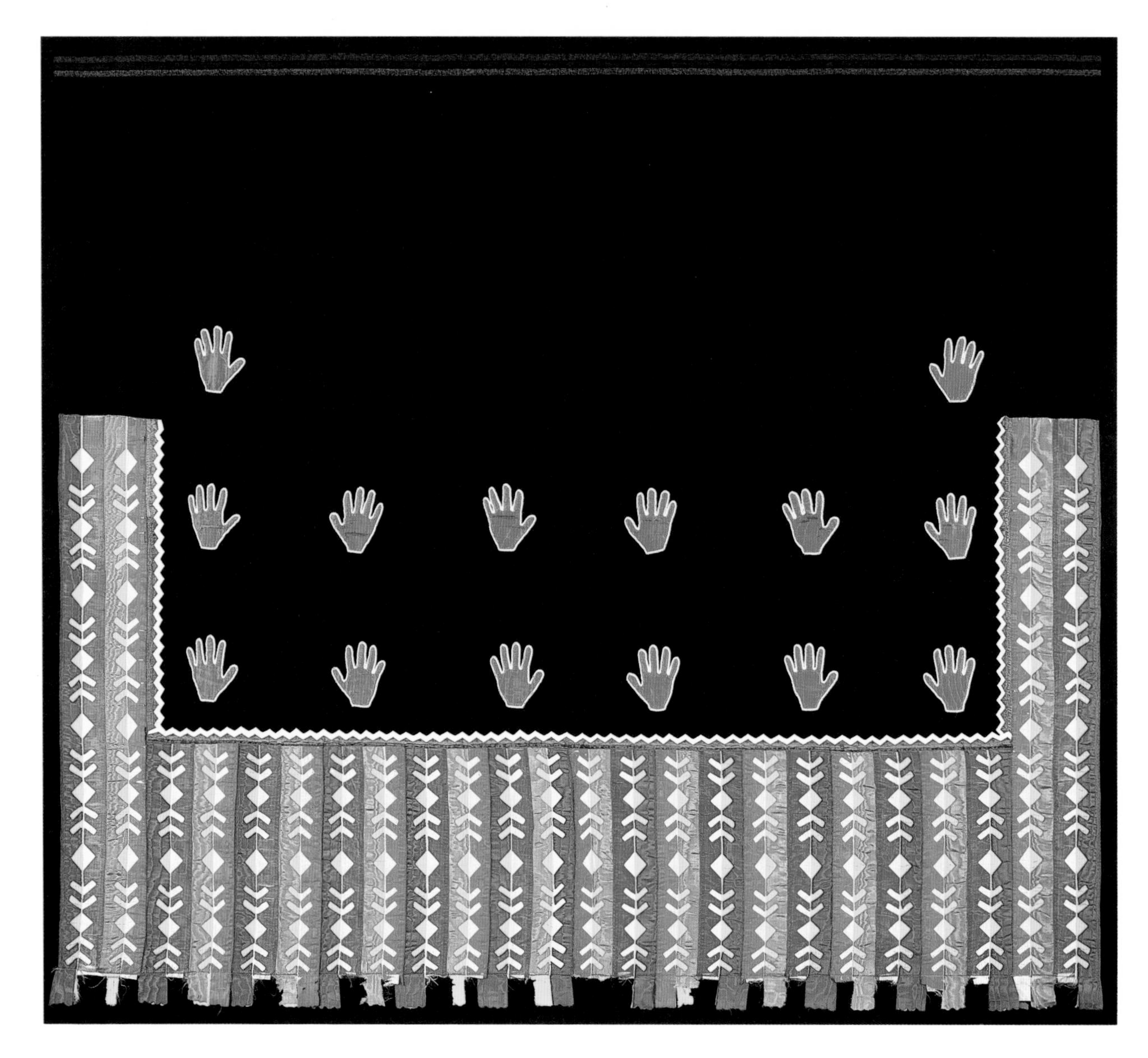

Blanket/Shawl **(Osage). Courtesy of America Hurrah Archive, New York, NY.**

Standing water,
I came there;
  I knelt down.
The drinking place
  where I always drank,
that place,
  listen to me.
Forget about me;
  forget about me,
          ha na.

Painted water hole
in the rock,
  I came there;
I knelt down.
  That place:
forget about me;
  forget about me,
          ha na.

The sun
over the hill,
  I saw it go down.
I started out running,
  started out running.
That's how I was;
  I didn't go slow,
          ha na.

That's not what I did;
I wasn't that way,
  that way.
I ran fast,
  ran fast.
I got home quickly,
  got home quickly,
          ha na.

I outran the sun;
I outran the sun.
That's what I used to do.
That's how I was,
how I was,
ha na.

I didn't sleep late,
didn't wait for the sun;
that's not what I did.
I wasn't that way,
that way,
ha na.

The dawn,
when it came,
I saw it.
I got up,
I got up.
The dawn,
I ran toward it,
ha na.

I thought I'd always be that way;
that's how I used to travel;
I thought I'd be that way forever,
but now my strength is gone.
I thought I'd be that way forever;
that's how I was.
Listen to me,
ha na.

Land that I wandered,
that place,
listen to me:
forget about me,
forget about me.
That's what I want,
what I want,
ha na.

My strength is gone.
I thought I'd always be that way,
that's how I was.
I thought I'd live forever,
I thought I'd live forever.
I'd always be with the land,
it seemed,
ha na.

I'd always be with the mountains,
it seemed;
that's how it was,
that's what I believed.
I felt
so proud.
I thought I'd be that way forever.
But now my strength is gone.
I thought I'd be that way forever.
That's how I was,
how I was,
ha na.

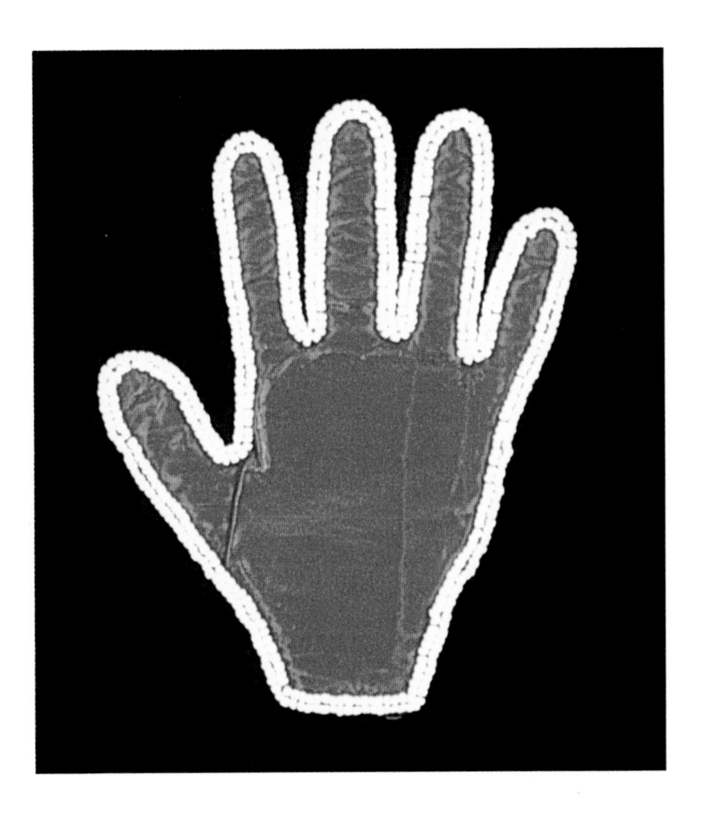

Detail of *Blanket/Shawl*

TELLING ABOUT COYOTE

❖ *Pueblo* ❖

TOLD BY SIMON ORTIZ

Old Coyote . . .
"If he hadn't looked back
everything would have been okay
. . . like he wasn't supposed to,
but he did,
and as soon as he did, he lost all his power,
his strength."

". . . you know, Coyote
is in the origin and all the way
through . . . he's the cause
of the trouble, the hard times
that things have . . ."

"Yet, he came so close
to having it easy.
But he said,
'Things are just too easy . . .'"
Of course he was mainly bragging,
shooting his mouth.
The existential Man,
Dostoevsky Coyote.

"He was on his way to Zuni
to get married on that Saturday,
and on the way there
he ran across a gambling party.
A number of other animals were there.
He sat in
for a while, you know, pretty sure
of himself, you know like he is,
sure that he would win something.
But he lost
everything. Everything.
And that included his skin, his fur
which was the subject of envy
of all the other animals around."

"Coyote had the prettiest,
the glossiest, the softest fur
that ever was. And he lost that.
So some mice
finding him shivering in the cold
beside a rock felt sorry for him.
'This poor thing, beloved,'
they said, and they got together
just some old scraps of fur
and glued them on Coyote with pinon
pitch."

"And he's had that motley fur ever since.
You know, the one that looks like
scraps of an old coat, that one."

Coyote, old man, wanderer,
where you going, man?
Look up and see the sun.
Scorned, an old raggy blanket
at the back of the closet nobody wants.

OPPOSITE: *Coyote 8*, Rick Bartow (Yurok), 1994. Courtesy of Froelick Adelhart Gallery, Portand, OR.

"At this one conference
of all the animals there was a bird
with the purest white feathers.
His feathers were like, ah . . .
like the sun was shining on it
all the time but you could look at it
and you wouldn't be hurt by the glare.
It was easy and gentle to look at.
And he was Crow.
He was sitting at one side of the fire.
And the fire was being fed large pine logs,
and Crow was sitting downwind
from the fire, and the wind was blowing
that way . . .
And Coyote was there.
He was envious of Crow because
all the other animals were saying,
'Wowee, look at that Crow, man,
just look at him,' admiring Crow.
Coyote began to scheme.
He kept on throwing pine logs into the fire,
ones with lots of pitch in them.
And the wind kept blowing,
all night long . . .
Let's see,
the conference was about deciding
the seasons—when they should take place—
and it took a long time to decide that . . .
And when it was over, Crow was covered
entirely with soot. The blackest soot
from the pine logs.
And he's been like that since then."

"Oh yes, that was the conference
when Winter was decided
that it should take place
when Dog's hair got long.
Dog said,
'I think Winter should take place
when my hair gets long.'
And it was agreed that it would. I guess
no one else offered a better reason."

Who?
Coyote?
O,
O yes, last time . . .
when was it,
I saw him somewhere
between Muskogee and Tulsa,
heading for Tulsy Town I guess,
just trucking along.
He was heading into some oakbrush thicket,
just over the hill was a creek.
Probably get to Tulsa in a couple days,
drink a little wine,
tease with the Pawnee babes,
sleep beside the Arkansas River,
listen to the river move,
. . . hope it don't rain,
hope the river don't rise.
He'll be back. Don't worry.
He'll be back.

OPPOSITE: ***Blanket and Bird*, Joe Feddersen (Colville), 1993. Courtesy of the artist.**

Remembering Grandfather's Stories, **Linda Lomahaftewa (Hopi/Choctaw), 1988. Courtesy of the artist.**

Coyote's Epilogue to the Telling

Told by Jarold Ramsey

(For Melville Jacobs and Mrs. Victoria Howard)

And now, let us leave this story-teller
and the disjointed story he has made of us;
let us leave the fireside, the lodge of drowsy people
who inherit this world once wholly ours:
let us separate, my friends, once more, becoming
birds of the great air
fish of the endless waters
lithe animals of the forest
nimble animals of the mountains—
and I, Coyote, last to go my way,
reality's handyman, look back and grin
like a dog to think these poor listening fools,
these people who were always "coming soon,"
the story-man himself,
all will rise, and go, and burrow
deep into the winter night, full of beginnings,
their world no more perfect than before
but such as it is
enabled, empowered with our names.

Index

❖ ❖ ❖ ❖ ❖

❖ Storytellers ❖

❖ Stories by Tribe ❖

❖ Artists ❖

❖ Art by Tribe ❖

Produced by Fair Street Productions and Welcome Enterprises, Inc.
Project Directors: Hiro Clark, Susan Wechsler
Editor: Deborah Bull
Art Director: Gregory Wakabayashi
Designer: Tsang Seymour
Art Coordinators: Sara Baysinger, Stephanie Lieblich
Photo Research: Photosearch, Inc.

Published in 1996 and distributed in the U.S. by Stewart, Tabori & Chang
a division of U.S. Media Holdings, Inc.
575 Broadway, New York, NY 10012

Distributed in Canada by:
GENERAL PUBLISHING COMPANY LTD.
30 Lesmill Road
Don Mills, Ontario, Canada, M3B 2T6

Distributed in all other territories by:
GRANTHAM BOOK SERVICES LTD.
Isaac Newton Way
Alma Park Industrial Estate
Grantham, Lincolnshire NG31 9SD, England

Sold in Australia and New Zealand:
PERIBO PTY LTD.
58 Beaumont Road
Mount Kuring-gai
NSW 2080, Australia

Library of Congress Cataloging-in-Publication Data
The telling of the world: Native American stories and art / edited by W. S. Penn.
p. cm.
"A Fair Street/Welcome book."
ISBN 1-55670-488-7
1. Indians of North America—Folklore.
2. Indian art—North America.
I. Penn, W. S., 1949-
E98.F6T245 1996
398.2'08997—dc20 96-9264
CIP

Printed in Singapore by
Toppan Printing Company

10 9 8 7 6 5 4 3 2 1

LITERARY CREDITS

From "Spearfish Sequence." Reprinted by permission of Dell Hymes.

"The Cry," by Peter Blue Cloud, from *Elderberry Flute Song: Contemporary Coyote Tales.* Copyright 1989 by White Pine Press. Reprinted by permission of White Pine Press, 10 Village Square, Fredonia NY 14063.

"The Beginning of the Skagit World," by Ella E. Clark, from *Indian Legends of the Pacific Northwest.* Copyright © 1953 The Regents of the University of California; © renewed 1981 Ella E. Clark. By permission of the University of California Press.

"How Coyote Made the World," by Jaime de Angulo, from "Indians in Overalls," *The Hudson Review*, vol. 3. 1950. Copyright © 1950, 1990 by Gui de Angulo. Reprinted by permission of City Light Books.

"Coyote and Swallowing Monster," from *Stories That Make the World: Oral Literatures of the Indian Peoples of the Inland Northwest As Told by Lawrence Aripa, Tom Yellowtail, and Other Elders*, edited by Rodney Frey. Copyright © 1995 by the University of Oklahoma Press, Norman.

"Creation of the Animal People," from *Indian Legends of the Pacific Northwest*, by Ella E. Clark. Copyright © 1953 by the Regents of the University of California; © renewed 1981 Ella E. Clark. By permission of the University of California Press.

"Remaking the World," from *American Myths and Legends*, by Richard Erdoes and Alfonso Ortiz, editors. Copyright © 1984 by Richard Erdoes and Alfonso Ortiz. Reprinted by permission of Pantheon Books, a division of Random House, Inc.

"Sweat Lodge," from *Journal of American Folklore 46*, 1933. Reproduced by permission of the American Folklore Society. Not for further reproduction.

"The Origin of Medicine," from *Voices of the Winds*, by Margot Edmonds and Ella Clark. Copyright © 1989 Margot Edmonds and Ella Clark. Reprinted with permission of Facts On File, Inc., New York.

"Second Beaver Story," from *Tanaina Tales from Alaska*, by Bill Vaudrin © 1969 by the University of Oklahoma Press, Norman.

"Buffalo and Eagle Wing," from *Voices of the Winds*, by Margot Edmonds and Ella Clark. Copyright © 1989 Margot Edmonds and Ella Clark. Reprinted with permission of Facts On File, Inc., New York.

"Frog and Brook." Reprinted from *All My Sins are Relatives*, by W. S. Penn, by permission of the University of Nebraska Press. Copyright © 1995 by the University of Nebraska Press.

"Coyote, Iktome, and the Rock," from *American Myths and Legends*, by Richard Erdoes and Alfonso Ortiz, editors. Copyright © 1984 by Richard Erdoes and Alfonso Ortiz. Reprinted by permission of Pantheon Books, a division of Random House, Inc.

"The Mouse Story (The Rich Man's Son)," from *Tanaina Tales from Alaska*, by Bill Vaudrin © 1969 by the University of Oklahoma Press, Norman.

"Home Boy," from *The North American Indians*, Vol. 4, by Edward Curtis, The University Press, Cambridge, MA, 1907-1930.

"Wolf Story." Reprinted from *All My Sins are Relatives*, by W. S. Penn, by permission of the University of Nebraska Press. Copyright © 1995 by the University of Nebraska Press.

"Coyote and the Mallard Ducks," from *Giving Birth to Thunder, Sleeping With His Daughter: Coyote Builds North America*, by Barry Holstun Lopez. © 1978 by Barry Holstun Lopez. Reprinted with the permission of Andrews & McMeel.

"A Youth's Double Abuses His Sister," from *Seneca Myths and Folk Tales*, by Arthur Parker, 1923. Courtesy Buffalo and Erie County Historical Society.

"The Legend of the Flute," from *American Myths and Legends*, by Richard Erdoes and Alfonso Ortiz, editors. Copyright © 1984 by Richard Erdoes and Alfonso Ortiz. Reprinted by permission of Pantheon Books, a division of Random House, Inc.

"Teeth in the Wrong Places," from *American Myths and Legends*, by Richard Erdoes and Alfonso Ortiz, editors. Copyright © 1984 by Richard Erdoes and Alfonso Ortiz. Reprinted by permission of Pantheon Books, a division of Random House, Inc.

"The Loyal Sweetheart," from *Voices of the Winds*, by Margot Edmonds and Ella Clark. Copyright © 1989 Margot Edmonds and Ella Clark. Reprinted with permission of Facts On File, Inc., New York.

"The Couple Befriended by the Moon," from *Nez Perce Texts (U. C. Pubs in Linguistics: Vol. 90)*, by Haruo Aoki. Copyright © 1979 The Regents of the University of California. By permission of the University of California Press.

"The Man Who Loved the Frog Songs," by Alanson Skinner and John V. Satterlee, from *Anthropological Papers of The American Museum of Natural History: Folklore of the Menomini Indians*, Vol. XIII, Part III, New York, 1915.

"The Man Who Looked at an Owl," by Alanson Skinner and John V. Satterlee, from *Anthropological Papers of The American Museum of Natural History: Folklore of the Menomini Indians*, Vol. XIII, Part III, New York, 1915.

"Montezuma and the Great Flood," from *American Myths and Legends*, by Richard Erdoes and Alfonso Ortiz, editors. Copyright © 1984 by Richard Erdoes and Alfonso Ortiz. Reprinted by permission of Pantheon Books, a division of Random House, Inc.

"The Sun's Myth." Reprinted by permission of Dell Hymes.

"Two Coyotes," from *Crow Texts*, by Robert H. Lowie; Luella Lowie. Copyright © 1960 The Regents of the University of California. By permission of the University of California Press.

"Rabbit and the Old Man," from *Myths and Tales of the Southeastern Indians*, by John R. Swanton, University of Oklahoma Press, 1995. First published in 1929 as *Bureau of American Ethnology Bulletin 88* by the Smithsonian Institution.

"Rabbit Deceives the Other Animals," from *Myths and Tales of the Southeastern Indians*, by John R. Swanton, University of Oklahoma Press, 1995. First published in 1929 as *Bureau of American Ethnology Bulletin 88* by the Smithsonian Institution.

"Coyote's Anthro," by Peter Blue Cloud, from *Elderberry Flute Song: Contemporary Coyote Tales.* Copyright 1989 by White Pine Press. Reprinted by permission of White Pine Press, 10 Village Square, Fredonia NY 14063.

"Nettie Reuben's Evening Star's Song." Reprinted by permission of William Bright.

"Bridal Veil Fall," from *Voices of the Winds*, by Margot Edmonds and Ella Clark. Copyright © 1989 Margot Edmonds and Ella Clark. Reprinted with permission of Facts On File, Inc., New York.

"Weaver Spider's Web," by Peter Blue Cloud, from *Elderberry Flute Song: Contemporary Coyote Tales.* Copyright 1989 by White Pine Press. Reprinted by permission of White Pine Press, 10 Village Square, Fredonia NY 14063.

"Coyote Marries a Man," from *Giving Birth to Thunder, Sleeping With His Daughter: Coyote Builds North America*, by Barry Holstun Lopez. © 1978 by Barry Holstun Lopez. Reprinted with the permission of Andrews & McMeel.

"Legend of the White Plume," from *Voices of the Winds*, by Margot Edmonds and Ella Clark. Copyright © 1989 Margot Edmonds and Ella Clark. Reprinted with permission of Facts On File, Inc., New York.

"Tolowim Woman and Butterfly Man," from *American Myths and Legends*, by Richard Erdoes and Alfonso Ortiz, editors. Copyright © 1984 by Richard Erdoes and Alfonso Ortiz. Reprinted by permission of Pantheon Books, a division of Random House, Inc.

"Coyote and the Woman," from *Stories That Make the World: Oral Literatures of the Indian Peoples of the Inland Northwest As Told by Lawrence Aripa, Tom Yellowtail, and Other Elders*, edited by Rodney Frey. Copyright © 1995 by the University of Oklahoma Press, Norman.

"Buffalo Woman, A Story of Magic," from Dee Brown's *Folk Tales of the American Indian* (formerly published as *Tepee Tales of the American Indian* by Dee Brown). Copyright © 1979 by Dee Brown. Reprinted by permission of Henry Holt and Co., Inc. Reprinted by permission of Sterling Lord Literistic, Inc.

"The Loon Story," from *Tanaina Tales from Alaska*, by Bill Vaudrin © 1969 by the University of Oklahoma Press, Norman.

"Men and Women Try Living Apart," from *American Myths and Legends*, by Richard Erdoes and Alfonso Ortiz, editors. Copyright © 1984 by Richard Erdoes and Alfonso Ortiz. Reprinted by permission of Pantheon Books, a division of Random House, Inc.

"Stone Boy," from *American Myths and Legends*, by Richard Erdoes and Alfonso Ortiz, editors. Copyright © 1984 by Richard Erdoes and Alfonso Ortiz. Reprinted by permission of Pantheon Books, a division of Random House, Inc.

"The Origin of the Long House," from *Seneca Myths and Folk Tales*, by Arthur Parker, 1923. Courtesy Buffalo and Erie County Historical Society.

"Cosechin," from *Stories That Make the World: Oral Literatures of the Indian Peoples of the Inland Northwest As Told by Lawrence Aripa, Tom Yellowtail, and Other Elders*, edited by Rodney Frey. Copyright © 1995 by the University of Oklahoma Press, Norman.

"Tongue." Reprinted by permission of Dell Hymes.

"The Legend of Godasiyo," by Jeremiah Curtin, from *Seneca Fiction, Legends, and Myths*, Washington, Government Printing Office, 1918.

"Coyote Goes Gambling," from "Coyote and Eagle's Daughter." Reprinted by permission of Dell Hymes.

"Swift-Runner and Trickster Tarantula," from Dee Brown's *Folk Tales of the American Indian* (formerly published as *Tepee Tales of the American Indian* by Dee Brown). Copyright © 1979 by Dee Brown. Reprinted by permission of Henry Holt and Co., Inc. Reprinted by permission of Sterling Lord Literistic, Inc.

"Child of the Sun." Reprinted by permission of Lee Francis (Laguna Pueblo).

"First Eagle Story," from *Tanaina Tales from Alaska*, by Bill Vaudrin © 1969 by the University of Oklahoma Press, Norman.

"The Black Bear Story," from *Tanaina Tales from Alaska*, by Bill Vaudrin © 1969 by the University of Oklahoma Press, Norman.

"Coyote and Crow," from *Indian Legends of the Pacific Northwest*, by Ella Clark. Copyright © 1953 The Regents of the University of California; © renewed 1981 Ella E. Clark. By permission of the University of California Press.

"The Tasks of Rabbit," from *Myths and Tales of the Southeastern Indians*, by John R. Swanton, University of Oklahoma Press, 1995. First published in 1929 as *Bureau of American Ethnology Bulletin 88* by the Smithsonian Institution.

"Coyote and Never Grows Bigger," from *Giving Birth to Thunder, Sleeping With His Daughter: Coyote Builds North America*, by Barry Holstun Lopez. © 1978 by Barry Holstun Lopez. Reprinted with the permission of Andrews & McMeel.

"The Wolves and the Dogs," from *Myths and Tales of the Southeastern Indians*, by John R. Swanton, University of Oklahoma Press, 1995. First published in 1929 as *Bureau of American Ethnology Bulletin 88* by the Smithsonian Institution.

"Speaks-in-Riddles and Wise Spirit," from *Coming to Light*, by Brian Swann. Copyright © 1995 by Brian Swann. Reprinted by permission of Random House, Inc.

"Coyote and Skunk," from *Coming to Light*, by Brian Swann. Copyright © 1995 by Brian Swann. Reprinted by permission of Random House, Inc.

"Enough Is Enough," from *Voices of the Winds*, by Margot Edmonds and Ella Clark. Copyright © 1989 Margot Edmonds and Ella Clark. Reprinted with permission of Facts On File, Inc., New York.

"Coyote and the White Man," from *Stories That Make the World: Oral Literatures of the Indian Peoples of the Inland Northwest As Told by Lawrence Aripa, Tom Yellowtail, and Other Elders*, edited by Rodney Frey. Copyright © 1995 by the University of Oklahoma Press, Norman.

"Dancing With Grief," from "Sex, Fingers, and Death." Reprinted by permission of William Bright.

"Woman Chooses Death," from *American Myths and Legends*, by Richard Erdoes and Alfonso Ortiz, editors. Copyright © 1984 by Richard Erdoes and Alfonso Ortiz. Reprinted by permission of Pantheon Books, a division of Random House, Inc.

"A Matter of Concentration." Reprinted by permission of W. S. Penn.

"A Mashpee Ghost Story," from *Voices of the Winds*, by Margot Edmonds and Ella Clark. Copyright © 1989 Margot Edmonds and Ella Clark. Reprinted with permission of Facts On File, Inc., New York.

"Coyote and Eagle Visit the Land of the Dead," from *Indian Legends of the Pacific Northwest*, by Ella E. Clark. Copyright © 1953 The Regents of the University of California; © renewed 1981 Ella E. Clark. By permission of the University of California Press.

"Memaloose Island, The Island of the Dead," from *Indian Legends of the Pacific Northwest*, by Ella E. Clark. Copyright © 1953 The Regents of the University of California; © renewed 1981 Ella E. Clark. By permission of the University of California Press.

"The Two Jeebi-ug," from *Schoolcraft's Indian Legends from Algic Researches*, Michigan State University Press, 1965 & 1991.

"Coyote Visits the Land of the Dead," from *Giving Birth to Thunder, Sleeping With His Daughter: Coyote Builds North America*, by Barry Holstun Lopez. © 1978 by Barry Holstun Lopez. Reprinted with the permission of Andrews & McMeel.

"The Men Who Went to the Sky," from *Myths and Tales of the Southeastern Indians*, by John R. Swanton, University of Oklahoma Press, 1995. First published in 1929 as *Bureau of American Ethnology Bulletin 88* by the Smithsonian Institution.

"Albert Hummingbird Meets Death." Reprinted by permission of W. S. Penn.

"The Farewell Song," from *Coming to Light*, by Brian Swann. Copyright © 1995 by Brian Swann. Reprinted by permission of Random House, Inc.

"Telling About Coyote." Permission granted by the author, Simon J. Ortiz. "Telling About Coyote" is from *Woven Stone*, University of Arizona Press, Tucson, 1992.

"Coyote's Epilogue to the Telling." Copyright © 1993 Jarold Ramsey.

PHOTOGRAPHY CREDITS

Page 1: Catalog No. P21-#14; Page 19: Photo by John Oldenkamp; Page 31 (*opposite*): Photo © Jerry Jacka; Page 35: Photo by Blair Clark, Catalog No. 24349; Page 37: Photo by Eduardo Calderon; Page 46: Photo by Damian Andrus; Page 48: Photo by Douglas Kahn, Catalog No. 25197; Page 50: Photo by Siegfried Halus; Page 52: Photo by Dr. Peter T. Furst; Page 58: Photo by Addison Doty; Page 72: Photo by John Oldenkamp; Page 80: Photo by Dr. Peter T. Furst; Page 96: Photo by Tom Patterson; Page 125: Photo by Paul Macapia and Ray Fowler; Page 128: Photo by John Oldenkamp; Page 130: Photo by John Bigelow Taylor; Page 131: Photo by Tom Patterson; Page 137: Photo by Blair Clark, Catalog No. 54004; Page 142: Photo by Addison Doty; Page 148 (*left*): Photo by Murrae Haynes; Page 150: Photo by John Bigelow Taylor; Page 155: Photo by Murrae Haynes; Page 157: Photo by Addison Doty; Page 158: Photo by John Oldenkamp; Page 161: Photo by Addison Doty; Page 171: Photo by John Oldenkamp; Page 175: Photo by Murrae Haynes; Page 178: Photo by John Oldenkamp; Page 179: Photo by Tom Patterson; Page 185: Photo by Ken Karp, Illustration for *Indian Stories from the Pueblos* by Frank G. Applegate, J. B. Lippincott Company, 1929; Page 204: Photo by Dr. Peter T. Furst; Page 219: Photo by Addison Doty

Acknowledgments

❖ ❖ ❖ ❖ ❖

For Rachel Antonia and William Anthony, Snowbird and Bear.

The work of many people has gone into this book and each of them should be thanked. First and foremost are the storytellers, ethnographers, and ethno-poets who told the stories, or preserved or revitalized the recordings, translations, and transmissions of essentially oral stories in the non-oral medium of print. In particular, I want to thank Dell Hymes, whose generosity and kindness began a relationship between us that I can only hope continues. Similarly, the people at Fair Street Productions must also be thanked: Deborah Bull, Stephanie Lieblich, Pam White all worked endless hours editing, checking, evaluating. Susan Wechsler, especially, kept in constant communication and made it seem as though my day had not begun without her call or her fax transmission; her ease and understanding and patience moved our relationship beyond business to friendship. I am also grateful to Welcome Enterprises—Hiro Clark, Gregory Wakabayashi, and Sara Baysinger—for the elegant design, and for keeping the production running smoothly, and to Stewart, Tabori & Chang for publishing the book. Thanks to all the writers, illustrators, and artists who have given permission to use their work in this collection. Finally, I want to thank those friends who helped, people like Lee Francis, who is the National Director of the Wordcraft Circle of Native American Writers and Storytellers, and my wife, Jennifer, for helping me make the time, and caring as much about my work as about her own.

The editors acknowledge the many institutions who provided us with information, illustrations, and support and especially thank the following individuals: Andy Ambrose; Joel and Kate Kopp/America Hurrah; Joanna Bigfeather/American Indian Community House Gallery; Marsha Kosteva/American Indian Contemporary Arts; James T. Bialac; Will Channing and Stephen Fadden/W.E. Channing & Co.; Kathy Shaw and Beth Regem/Jan Cicero Gallery; Kathleen Zurko/The College of Wooster Art Museum; Froelick Adelhart Gallery; Christy Hoffman and Tony Chavarria/School of American Research; Bernice Steinbaum/Steinbaum Krauss Gallery.

W. S. P.

***New World Flower*, Frank LaPena (Wintu/Nomtipom), 1990. Courtesy of the artist.**